MW01258131

THE CADILLAC

The Life Story of University of South Carolina Football Legend

Steve Wadiak

Mike Chibbaro

Stephen-
You are a true "Cadillac" and friend to me. Hope you enjoy the story of "The Cadillac."
Mike Chibbaro
08/14

THIRTY-SEVEN PUBLISHING

P.O. Box 3714
Greenville, SC 29609

www.thirtysevenpublishing.com

Copyright 2014 © by Mike Chibbaro
First Printing July 2014

All RIGHTS RESERVED
No part of this publication may be reproduced, stored in a retrieval system or transmitted, in any form or by any means—electronic, mechanical, photocopying, recording, or otherwise—without prior written permission from the author.

For information about special discounts for bulk purchases, please contact Thirty-Seven Publishing.

Cover design: Leigh Cohen
Graphic Design Coordinator: J.J. Puryear
Editorial Consultant: Ray Blackston
Page Layout: Michael Seymour
Editing: Amanda Capps
Printing: Bookmasters—Ashland, Ohio
Cover photo courtesy of University of South Carolina Archives
The Block C Gamecock logo on the back cover is used with permission from the University of South Carolina.
The name Cadillac was used with permission from General Motors Company.

ISBN - 978-1-4951-1439-7
Library of Congress Cataloging-in-Publication Data

Dedication

This book is gratefully dedicated to the man who introduced me to his hero and his friend—my father, Frank J. Chibbaro

and

to the woman who introduced me to her brother—whom she loved so deeply—Jeanette Wadiak Korlin.

Editor's Note:

Passages in this book that have been reprinted may have been edited for brevity and clarity. This includes—but is not limited to newspaper articles, book excerpts, transcripts, and letters. In all cases, these minor revisions were performed with great care to preserve the meaning intended by the original writers.

Contents

Preface
1 Burnside ... 1
2 Pinchy ... 11
3 Bronko ... 19
4 Destiny ... 25
5 High School ... 31
6 Navy ... 39
7 Discovered ... 47
8 Tryout ... 55
9 Fullback ... 63
10 Left Halfback ... 73
11 Debut ... 81
12 Fumble ... 91
13 Rex ... 103
14 Next Year ... 115
15 Friends ... 129
16 Prelude ... 139
17 The Game ... 151
18 MVP ... 161
19 Suspended ... 171
20 Pain ... 185
21 Visitors ... 197
22 Final Act ... 207
23 Saturday's Hero ... 215
24 The Future ... 225
25 Highway 215 ... 235
26 Grief ... 245
Epilogue ... 255
Appendix—
Leadership Lessons From "The Cadillac" ... 261
Acknowledgements ... 263
Sources ... 267

Preface

December 29, 1951
Montgomery, Alabama

At halftime of the 1951 Blue-Gray college football All-Star game, players on the Gray squad sat on benches in the cramped locker room of Montgomery, Alabama's Cramton Bowl and waited patiently for their coach's instruction.

The Blue-Gray game, first played in 1939, paired teams of college seniors—All-Stars, hoping to show off their skills and raise their stock with professional scouts. The teams were divided along geographic lines intended to mirror the allegiances of opposing sides in the American Civil War.

On the day of the 1951 game, Max Moseley from the "Montgomery Advertiser" pitched the game to his readers: "The greatest battle since Appomattox . . . the Blue-Gray football classic that takes place in Montgomery's Cramton Bowl. The kickoff is slated for 1:45 p.m. Upwards of 22,500 fans are expected to witness the clash between 48 outstanding senior gridders from north and south of the Mason-Dixon line."

The Gray team's head coach, Louisiana State's Gaynell Tinsley, had a problem—too many stars and not enough playing time for all of them to showcase their skills. Of the 48 players in the game, 28 would be selected the following January in the 1952 NFL draft.

Coach Tinsley was particularly overloaded with talent at running back. The team was blessed with eight gifted runners, including everybody's All-American, Fred Benners, from Southern Methodist University.

Among the eight Gray running backs was Steve Wadiak from the

University of South Carolina. Wadiak had earned a starting position in the Gray backfield, and he played well in the first half, rushing for 18 yards on three attempts and catching a pass for another 13 yards. Despite his efforts, the Gray team trailed 7-0.

In four seasons at the University of South Carolina, Wadiak rushed for 2,878 yards and eclipsed the Southern Conference rushing record of University of North Carolina star running back Charlie "Choo Choo" Justice. As a junior, Steve was named the 1950 Most Valuable Player in the Southern Conference despite playing for a team with a losing record.

Wadiak's natural gift was to run around, over, and past would-be tacklers. A rare combination of shifty moves, open field speed, and raw toughness distinguished him as one of the most respected running backs in all of college football. A local sports writer christened him with the nickname, "Th' Cadillac," forever associating Wadiak with the most well-engineered and classiest automobile of the day.

Wadiak became the "big man" on the USC campus and a matinee-type idol throughout the state of South Carolina. Dashing good looks and a chiseled physique made him a heartthrob among campus co-eds. Schoolboys mimicked his football moves on playgrounds, opportunistic business owners clamored for his friendship by never allowing him to pay at their establishments, and well-wishing boosters padded post-game handshakes with cash.

Uncomfortable in the limelight, the Chicago native was a quiet and unassuming hero. When praised, Wadiak deflected attention toward his teammates. His humble upbringing often left him to feel as though he didn't deserve the attention. That same unassuming nature also made him approachable. Students, teachers, and locals felt like they knew their hero.

The culture of college all-star games was about individualism versus a team mentality. Players worked hard during a week of pre-game practices in hopes that coaches would notice and award them highly coveted playing time. It was this blatant "me-first" environment that made what happened at halftime in the Gray team's locker room all the more unbelievable.

During halftime, Steve overheard his coaches discussing their predicament of trying to juggle playing time for eight different running backs, while also dealing with a short supply of defensive backs.

One assistant coach for the Gray team was Rex Enright, head coach of the University of South Carolina Gamecocks and a mentor and father figure to Wadiak during his four years at USC. In the locker room, Wadiak caught the attention of his coach and offered a suggestion.

"Put me on defense," Wadiak said.

Enright smiled at Wadiak's request. Steve's unsolicited willingness to play defense was exactly the kind of unselfish behavior that had so endeared him to Enright during his time as a Gamecock.

The request to play defense was all the more remarkable because the Blue-Gray game afforded Steve his first real opportunity to run behind a wall of talented blockers. Throughout college, he had struggled to perform behind the blocking of an undersized offensive line. His South Carolina teams also struggled to develop a balanced offensive attack that could relieve some of the attention Wadiak consistently drew from opposing defenses. Steve had performed well in practices—and now, in the first half, his stock was on the rise.

Enright informed Coach Tinsley of Wadiak's insistence on playing defensive back in the second half. Tinsley was perplexed. Who in his right mind would willingly give up offensive playing time in an all-star contest? Also, Tinsley knew Wadiak as one of the nation's top running backs. That didn't necessarily translate to an ability to play defense.

Enright assured Tinsley of Wadiak's sincerity, explaining that Wadiak had played on a high school team that consisted of only 11 players and that he was confident in his ability to play defensive back. Tinsley agreed to Wadiak's offer, and in the second half, he inserted Steve into the Gray team's secondary.

"We had seven of the finest running backs in the country assembled there—but none as great a runner as Wadiak—and not a single one was a defensive back," Enright said after the game. "But Steve offered to play defense. It was indicative of the kind of man he is. He readily agreed to play defense and played one of the finest ball games from a defensive standpoint ever played on any field."

The Gray team overcame a 7-0 halftime deficit and went on to win the game 20-14. Less than a month later, the Pittsburgh Steelers made Wadiak the 30th overall selection in the 1952 NFL draft.

Steve was closing in on the fulfillment of his lifelong dream—to play football in the National Football League. His was a dream forged on the sandlots of Chicago's South Side, a dream that survived a tour of duty in the U.S. Navy during World War II, and a dream fine-tuned and propelled toward fruition during his record-breaking four-year career at the University of South Carolina.

In 1952, Steve Wadiak was so close to fulfilling that dream. So very close.

1
Burnside

A cold, steady rain pelted the streets of Chicago's South Side on Friday morning, January 8, 1926. Pedestrian activity was limited to those braving the elements to get to work. The residents of the two-story wooden home at 9322 University Ave., in the Burnside neighborhood, had been awake for several hours. The home was a flurry of activity as the family anxiously awaited the arrival of a new life.

Anna Wadiak, age 30, lay in her bed on the first floor of the home, and the frequency of her labor pains compelled her husband, Nick, to summon the doctor. Anna had already given birth to four children, delivering a child roughly every other year for the past eight years. She knew what the next few hours would involve.

Her first two, Walter and Joe, now nine and seven years old, respectively, scurried about the house oblivious to the happenings. Following the boys were two girls, Olga and Jeanette, ages five and three. They sat quietly around the wooden kitchen table as their father spoke with a neighbor who had volunteered to retrieve the doctor.

The Burnside neighborhood was a relatively small triangular plot of land, framed by railroad tracks at 89th Street to the north, 94th Street to the south, Kimbark Avenue to the east, and Drexel Avenue to the west. It was named in honor of Civil War General Ambrose Burnside, an unheralded military leader, who eventually became a well-liked politician and railroad executive. Burnside was noted for his unique facial hair: Strips of hair trailed down and around his face to join his mustache, yet his chin was clean-shaven. This style of hair was referred to as "burnsides." Subsequently, the syllables were inverted to form the modern term, "sideburns."

Burnside was a neighborhood comprised of hardworking, family-oriented first generation immigrants and their children. It was home for the Wadiaks, the Gabors, the Demkowiczs, the O'Rourkes, the Garritanos, and dozens of other families whose roots were scattered across Europe.

As word of the impending birth spread up and down University Avenue, the residents began to organize. Ladies planned meals. The men made sure the Wadiaks had plenty of coal to heat their home. In the Burnside neighborhood, births were community events. They provided opportunities to do what the residents did best—help one another.

Nick and Anna Wadiak considered themselves blessed. They lived in America. Both were employed. Their children were healthy. They owned a home in a neighborhood full of people who genuinely cared about one another. There was much cause for optimism.

Americans were enjoying the prosperity and frivolity of the Roaring '20s. Technological advances such as the radio and the phonograph opened new avenues of entertainment to the working class. The proliferation of the automobile and the opening of cross-country highways like the 2,451-mile Route 66 helped to mobilize a nation.

The country's 30th President, Calvin Coolidge, inspired confidence in the American people and resolved to restore dignity and honor to the office of the President. He reigned over an economic era that became known as "Coolidge Prosperity"—an ironic foreshadowing to the Great Depression that was just a few short years away.

Popular singer Al Jolson recorded a hit song later in 1926, "I'm Sitting on Top of the World." The song's lyrics epitomized the carefree, lighthearted era of the '20s.

I'm sitting on top of the world,
Just rolling along.
Just rolling along.
I'm quitting the blues of the world.
Just singing along.
Just singing along.
Glory Hallelujah.

Babe Ruth and the New York Yankees ruled the baseball world. Jack Dempsey was the heavyweight champion of the world. Red Grange, a running back for the Chicago Bears, was single-handedly legitimizing the National Football League. The Chicago Blackhawks were in their first year of existence in the National Hockey League.

Italian-born silent film star Rudolph Valentino was the iconic star of the era. His death later in 1926, at the age of 31, would cause mass hysteria among adoring female fans. Nearly 100,000 people lined the streets of New York for his funeral. There were even reports of suicides by heartbroken fans.

Aviator Charles Lindbergh was a little over a year away from flying his single-engine Spirit of St. Louis across the Atlantic Ocean.

The Wadiaks' new baby entered the world in an era that had no shortage of American heroes.

"The Chicago Tribune" and the "Chicago Daily News" kept Chicagoans up to speed on the events of the world. "The Daily Calumet Index," affectionately known as "The Cal," served Chicago's South Side. On the morning of January 8, 1926, the "Daily Calumet" featured two contrasting stories. Anthony Kozloyski of 8243 Burley Ave. was heralded for giving a quart of blood to save the life of his sister, Anna Postuszny. Adjacent to this story was the sad report that Stephen Peer, of 9238

Brandon Ave., shot and killed himself in his home the night before.

There were plenty of reasons to be excited about bringing a baby into the world during this time. Perspective evoked gratitude. Both Nick and Anna knew the pain that life could bring, and they often reflected on the journey that had brought them to University Avenue.

Nick and Anna were immigrants from Ukraine. They came to America from a region of Central Europe known as Galicia, a rural area that borders Ukraine and Poland.

In the late 1800s, poverty in Galicia was widespread. Starvation and disease were the norm throughout the rural regions of Ukraine, Poland, and Germany. Several hundred thousand people from Central Europe took part in what became known as the Great Emigration, which preceded World War I. Impoverished Ukrainians emigrated to the United States, Brazil, and Canada. The first wave of Ukrainian immigrants to the United States was generally composed of uneducated peasants who took jobs in the mines and factories of Pennsylvania, New York, and New Jersey. Between 1870 and 1914, it is estimated that over 500,000 Ukrainians came to the United States in search of opportunity and hope for a better life. In the midst of political and economic turmoil, two young Ukrainians found their way to the Midwest of America.

Nicholas Wadiak was 23 years old in 1911 when family arranged for his steerage to the United States. Initially, he settled with some relatives in New Jersey. Drawn by the economic opportunity of the Midwest and hoping to escape harsh mining work in the East, Nick made his way to Chicago. He found work as a carpenter on the Illinois Central Railroad, eventually landing in the Burnside neighborhood, which provided easy access to railroad repair shops.

Nick was quiet, reserved, and steady. *Docile* was a word often used to describe him. Like so many men of his generation, he kept his feelings to himself. He worked hard. He enjoyed the company of men his age but had little time for much else. He lived his life in the shadows, never wanting to draw attention to himself.

Anna Kupczak was born on April 13, 1896. Her childhood was not easy. Anna's mother passed away when Anna was a child. Her father remarried, and Anna had difficulty adjusting to the changes associated with her new family. Children were expected to perform a difficult regimen of chores on the farm. At age 15, she left Ukraine and spent two years laboring on a potato farm in Germany before an uncle living in Wisconsin sponsored her steerage to the United States.

In 1913, 17-year-old Anna boarded a crowded boat that would bring her to America. She carried a small bag with all of her belongings and had the equivalent of two American dollars to her name. As she boarded the boat, she walked down a series of narrow staircases that would take her three levels down to the "steerage" section of the boat, where she would share cramped quarters with hundreds of other immigrants. The living conditions were inhumane.

In 1911, the United States Immigration Commission provided a report to President William H. Taft, which candidly described the typical plight of a steerage passenger:

> *The open deck space reserved for steerage passengers is usually very limited, and situated in the worst part of the ship, subject to the most violent motion, to the dirt from the stacks and the odors from the hold and galleys . . . the only provisions for eating are frequently shelves or benches along the sides or in the passages of sleeping compartments. Dining rooms are rare and, if found, are often shared with berths installed along the walls. Toilets and washrooms are completely inadequate; saltwater only is available.*

> *The ventilation is almost always inadequate, and the air soon becomes foul. The unattended vomit of the seasick, the odors of not too clean bodies, the reek of food and the awful stench of the nearby toilet rooms make the atmosphere of the steerage such that it is a marvel that human flesh can endure it. Most immigrants lie in their berths for most of the voyage, in a stupor caused by the foul air. The food often repels them. It is almost impossible to keep personally clean. All of these conditions are naturally aggravated by the crowding.*

As the ship made its way across the sea, Anna passed time by getting to know the people around her and listening to their unique stories and experiences. Finally, her ship entered the New York Harbor Upper Bay near Ellis Island, and Anna got her first glimpse of Manhattan. For most passengers, one of the first images of America would be the sight of the majestic Statue of Liberty. A Polish immigrant during this era described seeing Lady Liberty in this manner: "The bigness of Mrs. Liberty overcame us. No one spoke a word for she was like a goddess, and we know she represented the big, powerful country which was to be our future home."

After enduring all the indecencies of inspection and evaluation at Ellis Island, Anna finally arrived at her uncle's Wisconsin farming community. She joined her sister Mary on this farm, but, once again, tragedy struck Anna's young life as her sister died giving birth to a baby shortly after Anna's arrival.

Working on the Wisconsin farm, Anna became a hired hand and nursemaid. She often cried herself to sleep, horrified by the idea that she had exchanged one meaningless existence for another.

Devoutly religious, Anna pleaded with God to show her a way to a better life—a life that would have more meaning and purpose than her daily regimen of chores and the task of caring for children that were not her own. Hope became her sustenance. She truly believed she would have a chance to raise her own children in a land of opportunity.

Friends told her about Chicago. The very name of the city had a ring to it. During her darkest days, she would simply let the rhythmic sound of the name *Chicago* roll around in her head. Sometimes, she found herself repeating it—as if saying the name might transport her to this dream city. She longed to find her way to Chicago.

Anna eventually scrounged up enough courage and money to make her way by train to the city of her dreams. When she stepped onto the bustling streets of Chicago, she felt alive. This was the America she longed for.

She quickly found work at the Hotel Florence, a thriving establishment founded by railroad inventor and entrepreneur George Pullman. She rented a room in a small boarding house. Her life was changing. A new world was opening up to her.

Anna's English was weak. Her understanding of "American ways" was limited. Like so many immigrants, she struggled with the most basic of tasks. Finally, an older American woman at the hotel took notice of Anna. She admired her work ethic and began to tutor Anna in English and teach her how to survive in her new homeland. She was the angel Anna so desperately needed.

Anna was outgoing, resourceful, and tough. She was a survivor. She enjoyed working in the hotels and restaurants of Chicago and was energized by her contact with new people. After leaving her job at the Hotel Florence, she found work as a dishwasher at Fables restaurant near the intersection of 79th and Stony Island Avenues. Anna would be a faithful kitchen worker at Fables over the next several decades.

Anna, like most of her fellow Ukrainian immigrants, relied heavily on her religious faith to sustain her through the challenges of life in America. Many of the early Ukrainian immigrants attended various churches in search of one that would appeal to their strong sense of orthodoxy and tradition. Finally, the Ukrainians rallied and established Chicago's first Ukrainian Orthodox Church in 1909: St. Peter and Paul Ukrainian Orthodox Church. The Reverend Volodymyr Petrovsky served as the first priest and oversaw the construction of the church's sanctuary, which opened in 1911 in the heart of the Burnside neighborhood, at 9211 Chauncey Ave. (later named Avalon Avenue).

The new church building became a rally point for devout Ukrainians. A fire destroyed the church within two years of its construction, but the spirited Ukrainians quickly rebuilt. In a strange land, St. Peter and Paul served as the thread that connected the Ukrainians to the traditions and faith of their homeland. Here, the paths of Nick Wadiak and Anna Kupczak crossed.

They were born in the same geographic area of Central Europe, yet their treks to the U.S. were markedly different. They did not arrive at the same time—and, upon arrival—they migrated from Ellis Island in different directions. Their common faith eventually united them. Nick and Anna were married at St. Peter and Paul in 1916. Nick was 28, and Anna was 20. Their first child, Walter, was born within a year.

Hard work and persistence allowed them to purchase an attractive two-story home on University Avenue. Its value in the 1930s was approximately $5,100. Initially, it was more than they could afford, so they rented the top floor of the house to another family for $27 per month.

Their home was warm and comfortable. An icebox and a pantry were stocked with food. The neighborhood was full of caring friends. A local church kept them in touch with their ethnic, religious, and social

9322 University Avenue in Chicago, Illinois:
the childhood home of Steve Wadiak

traditions, and healthy children brought life to their home. It was into this setting that Stephan Wadiak arrived on the morning of January 8, 1926.

"It's another boy!" Word spread rapidly among the residents of University Avenue. "The Wadiaks have a new baby boy."

The Italians brought sauce and fresh baked bread, Polish friends brought kielbasa, and fellow Ukrainians brought borscht and pastries. The Wadiaks would have enough food for weeks. Neighbors offered to take the other Wadiak siblings away for a few days so Anna could rest and recover.

Stephan was a healthy baby boy born to the Wadiaks the day after they celebrated their traditional orthodox Christmas (Followers of the Ukrainian Orthodox religion celebrate Christmas on January 7.). Anna had no time to recover from preparing a traditional 12-course Ukrainian Christmas dinner before giving birth to her son.

In the quietness of the evening hours on January 8, Anna nursed her newborn son. Stephan stared up at her through sparking hazel eyes. While savoring those eyes, Anna questioned her ability to be an adequate mother. *What kind of boy will he be? Will he be outgoing and fun-loving like me or quiet and reserved like his father? Will he become famous like Rudolph Valentino? What will he become?*

Holding him to her chest, she closed her eyes and prayed: "Dear God, please keep my little Stephan safe. Protect him in this world. Give him a very full and wonderful life."

2
Pinchy

During the early 1930s, 91 children lived and played on University Avenue. None was more popular than young Steve Wadiak.

He entered the world with a zest for life. He loved his family and his neighbors and seemed to have a passion for everything. The streets of his Burnside neighborhood were avenues of adventure.

At age nine, Steve secured a part-time delivery job at a grocery store owned by the Demkowicz family—who, like the Wadiaks, had emigrated from Ukraine. The store provided one-stop shopping for its customers and served as a hub for the Burnside community. Men gathered at the store corner. If a local family had a need, they sent word to the store, and their neighbors quickly mobilized.

Thanks in part to his grocery delivery job, Steve had become the most popular nine-year-old in the neighborhood. His helpful attitude, boundless energy, and boyish smile were endearing. When he wasn't making deliveries, Steve took initiative: He unloaded delivery trucks, straightened the items on the shelves, and swept the aisles.

Steve embraced the neighborhood's culture of selflessness. At a young age, he was already demonstrating a strong work ethic and a genuine love for other people.

Steve saved money from each of his paychecks, and his saving had a specific purpose. One of the older boys in the neighborhood had allowed Steve to hold his leather football, and Steve savored the experience of clutching the worn leather and laces in his fingers. Footballs were scarce on University Avenue. Steve knew if he were ever to own one, it would never leave his sight.

One of Steve's favorite childhood activities was going to the movies. Anna Wadiak, through her job at Fables restaurant, often obtained free passes to the majestic Avalon Theater, located at 1641 E. 79th St. Built in 1927, the 2400-seat Avalon was a Broadway-caliber venue. It originally opened as a home for live stage acts, but in the '30s, it operated exclusively as a motion picture venue.

On Saturdays at the Avalon, Steve was captivated by the exploits of cowboy film stars such as Tom Mix, Gene Autry, and John Wayne. After a double feature of Westerns, Steve used sticks to take imaginary aim at fire hydrants on his 14-block walk home. At night, sandwiched in the same bed with his two older brothers in their upstairs bedroom, Steve often struggled to fall asleep. When he finally dozed off, Steve's family chuckled about his talking in his sleep as he relived the actions of his cinematic heroes.

Sports became young Steve's ultimate passion. He saw school as a necessity—a means of connecting with friends. The playground at Oliver Perry Elementary School became Steve's first opportunity to express his love for physical activities and competitive games.

Although he was a bright kid, Steve lacked a desire to learn about subjects that had little to do with what really interested him. On days when he knew the weather would keep him from his favorite outdoor activities, Steve would sometimes fake an illness to avoid attending school. This pattern continued until the day a neighbor made a suggestion to Steve's mother on how to cure her young son's recurring illnesses.

The Wadiaks' neighbor suggested that the next time Steve complained, Anna should give him a tablespoon of cod liver oil—a foul-tasting liquid that was generally regarded as a cure for just about anything that ailed you. The cod liver oil worked. Steve's mysterious illnesses ended, and his school attendance improved dramatically.

If Steve were missing, he could usually be found on an expansive field one block north of the Wadiaks' home. This field was known by all as "the prairie." It was a large, open expanse of flatland that served as a makeshift multi-sport ball field for dozens of neighborhood kids. On their own initiative, young boys cut the grass and weeds of the prairie and marked out ball fields. Intense games of sandlot football, baseball, or field hockey broke out at different times of the year. Only a heavy blanket of snow could curtail the endless sporting activities that took place on the prairie.

At a very young age, Steve followed his older brothers to the prairie and stood on the sidelines, longing for the day when he too would be old enough to participate. His animated personality made him a favorite with the older boys, and they soon assigned him duties that, while not yet elevating him to the level of teammate, at least granted him a degree of inclusion. Steve served as bat boy, water boy, or ball boy, anything to keep him close to his neighborhood heroes and their daily competitions.

One hot summer day, in the middle of an intense baseball game, Steve sat on a bench in the middle of a group of older boys. He observed the boys as they took powered tobacco from a small circular tin can and put it in their mouths. Wanting to be just like the older boys, Steve asked one of them if he could have a "pinch." The older boys laughed him off, but Steve was persistent. Day after day, he asked to partake.

Finally, one of the older boys came up with a solution for their hero-worshiping bat boy. The older kid filled one of the empty tin cans with a mixture of coffee grounds and sugar. He gave it to Steve and instructed him to have a pinch.

Steve's heart raced, unsure of what he was really getting into but knowing he was willing to do whatever it took to gain acceptance into this fraternity of older neighborhood athletes. Steve reached into the can and pinched a small amount of the mixture between his thumb and forefinger. Then, he tilted his head back and pressed the mixture between his cheek and gum, mimicking the exact movements of the older boys, who burst into laughter.

Nearly everyone in the neighborhood had a nickname, and on this day, Steve earned his. Watching Steve partake of this faux tobacco mixture, one of the older boys blurted out, "Way to go, 'Pinchy.'" The name stuck. From that day forward, Steve Wadiak was known throughout the Burnside neighborhood as "Pinchy."

The eighth grade boys at Oliver Perry had a graduation day tradition—they constructed a human pyramid: big guys on bottom; little guys on top. Once constructed, on the count of three, the students collapsed into a pile of uncontrollable adolescent laughter.

Pinchy Wadiak had observed this tradition many times. In the spring of 1940, he sat in class and daydreamed about the June afternoon when he and his buddies would carefully construct the pyramid and collapse with a roar. It was a tradition that was made for the fun-loving Pinchy. It was physical, it was funny, and it involved his buddies.

Mrs. Romberg, the principal at Oliver Perry decided, however, that it was time for a change. Generally regarded as an "old maid," she had little or no interest in things of a physical nature, or, for that matter, anything that involved her male students' having fun. She detested the pyramid, and soon she put word out that the tradition would come to an end with the Class of 1940. Even worse than her curtailment of the treasured ritual was what she had in mind to take its place.

Mrs. Romberg informed all of the eighth graders that they were to take part in a ceremonial dance to mark the end of their tenure at Oliver Perry. She envisioned well-dressed boys and girls dancing rhythmically together on stage in front of an auditorium full of doting parents and friends.

Although Pinchy was never openly defiant against authority figures in his life, this ceremonial dance business pushed him to his limit. There was no way he was going to embarrass himself by dancing around on stage in front of all his friends and family.

Despite outcries from her male graduates, the stern Mrs. Romberg refused to budge. She made her intentions plain and simple: No dance, no diploma. Those choosing not to dance would receive their diplomas privately in her office at the conclusion of the commencement ceremony. Steve didn't care if he had to spend the rest of his life in the eighth grade. He would not do it.

Many of the boys went home and petitioned their parents to excuse them from this nightmare of a ceremony. Steve pleaded his case to his mother, and Anna Wadiak listened patiently to her son. She witnessed his steadfast determination and knew he would never budge on the issue. So, she went to see Mrs. Romberg.

"I have a question," Anna said to the principal. "Is the diploma Steve will receive in your office any different from the one that the other students will receive in the auditorium?"

"No, it will be the same diploma," Mrs. Romberg replied.

"Okay, then, Steve will just receive his diploma in your office after the ceremony," Anna responded. Mrs. Romberg was taken aback by the support of a mother for her son's defiance.

When graduation day arrived, anxious parents and extended family members filled the auditorium. Conspicuously absent from the packed auditorium was the infectious persona of Pinchy Wadiak.

"Where's Pinchy?" several students asked.

Word finally leaked out that he was in the principal's office, where he would receive his diploma in private because of his refusal to dance. As the graduation ceremony drew to a close, the majority of the 150 spectators vacated the auditorium and made their way down the long corridor leading to Principal Romberg's office. They crowded their way into the office where Pinchy sat all alone waiting to receive his graduation certificate.

When word of the supportive crowd reached Mrs. Romberg, she grew livid as she realized her obligatory ceremony had been upstaged by the ever-popular Pinchy Wadiak. Mrs. Romberg had underestimated the impact of a young boy who had spent the first 13 years of his life endearing himself to an entire community of people.

Pinchy received his diploma surrounded by a neighborhood of adoring fans gathered in the close quarters of Mrs. Romberg's office. He enjoyed his own personal graduation ceremony—and he didn't have to dance.

Anna Wadiak worked every day except Thursdays from 4 p.m. to nearly 1 a.m., and Nick toiled at the railroad. Their work ethic and family unity allowed the Wadiaks to survive the worst of times in America—the Great Depression. Not only did the family not go hungry, but also, even in those tough times, their meals were hearty: Chickens were bought at a discount from an enterprising neighbor, fresh vegetables sprouted from a local garden, and the butcher shop at Demkowicz's store provided fresh cuts of beef and veal when the Wadiaks could afford it.

Holidays were full of family traditions, and homemade gifts abounded—mittens, gloves, scarves . . . a store-bought toy was a rarity.

The Wadiak children pitched in around the house with chores and responsibilities. Saturdays were for cleaning. Anna prided herself on keeping her home spotless. Steve's weekly assignment was to take all the cushions off the furniture and beat the dust out of them on the front porch.

As soon as the chores were completed, the Wadiak children often joined several other neighborhood friends in their favorite Saturday activity—"junking." This scavenger-based activity consisted of rummaging through neighborhood trash to locate empty tin cans from the Rosemary Company. Labels from Rosemary cans could be accumulated and redeemed for toys, which were displayed in the window at the redemption store.

Steve's sister Jeanette accumulated 99 Rosemary labels, bound them with a rubber band, and presented them, along with 99 cents she'd saved, to obtain her first store-bought doll. Sister Olga and brother Joe used their labels for roller skates. Pinchy too scrounged and saved Rosemary labels for the first store-bought possession of his young life. When he had enough labels, he made his way to the redemption store and pushed his cluster of paper labels across the counter. In exchange, the storeowner handed Steve his most treasured childhood possession.

Steve secured his new acquisition against his body, holding it tightly with all of his strength. He walked proudly through the streets of the South Side, feeling as though he had just been handed his passport to fun and fame.

That night at bedtime, the three Wadiak boys piled into their already crowded bed. Shoulder to shoulder, Walter, Joe, and Steve welcomed a new leather bedfellow—Steve's first football.

3
Bronko

By the early 1930s, nearly one-third of American households owned radios, providing the people not only with a source of inexpensive entertainment, but also a window to a larger world.

The Wadiaks' family radio was situated in the living room of their home. Daily, it squawked forth disheartening economic news of the lingering impact of the Stock Market crash of 1929. By 1931, unemployment had risen in the U.S. to 16.8 percent with an estimated eight million Americans out of work. Twenty-five hundred banks failed, and several car manufacturers shut down as Americans could not afford the luxury of the automobile.

The Wadiaks and their fellow Chicagoans heard updates on the gangster wars that bloodied Chicago's downtown streets on a regular basis. Later in 1931, public enemy number one, Al Capone, was captured and convicted of tax evasion. In April, the Chicago Board of Education announced that it lacked the funds to pay its teachers. The Great Depression, along with an unaccountable period of government graft and corruption, left the city of Chicago and Cook County financially insolvent.

However, the same radio that delivered the dire news of the day provided an entertaining diversion for families seeking an escape: Music, comedy, and adventure were piped into American homes via the airways.

In 1931, a popular show was broadcast on NBC's Blue network. The first radio show to cater directly to children, it succeeded in capturing the attention of young people across America, and the Wadiak children were no exception.

"The Adventures of Little Orphan Annie" featured an 11-year-old redheaded curly-haired orphan girl, who wandered from adventure to adventure with her beloved dog, Sandy. The show began with a catchy theme song that summoned children to sit in front of their radios:

Who's that little chatter box?
The one with pretty auburn locks?
Whom do you see?
It's Little Orphan Annie.
She and Sandy make a pair,
They never seem to have a care!
Cute little she,
It's Little Orphan Annie.

Steve found the adventure stories intriguing, but ultimately, his loyalty to the show stemmed from a promotional offer made by the show's sponsor, Ovaltine. Ovaltine is a granulated powder that can turn an ordinary glass of milk into a chocolate delight. Sales of Ovaltine depended on the appetites of young children like Steve. The company boosted its buyer loyalty by offering an alluring promotion: Young listeners were encouraged to save the labels from Ovaltine containers and send them to the manufacturer in exchange for a secret decoder ring.

The ring arrived in the mail with a handbook that walked the user through a series of steps to uncover a secret message. Audience members were instructed to listen for hidden clues during the broadcasts. The advertisements hooked Steve's imagination, as well as his competitive spirit. He became obsessed with obtaining the decoder rings and deciphering the clues.

Steve was determined not only to solve the secret codes, but also to figure them out faster than any of his neighborhood friends. Steve drank Ovaltine flavored milk constantly. He trimmed the labels from the empty cans and readily volunteered to replenish his family's supply by making trips to Demkowicz's corner store.

Steve collected and saved every prize the Ovaltine company had to offer. He secured those treasures next to his favorite collectibles. Placed carefully in a dresser drawer was a shoebox containing Steve's most valued possessions, including an assortment of sports trading cards. Most of the cards were purchased along with an accompanying stick of bubble gum at the corner grocery store, while others were acquired through trades with neighborhood friends.

The cards were carefully organized and arranged within the box. Local favorites and personal heroes were given special treatment. Treasured most were the hometown heroes. In baseball, it was the Chicago White Sox whose cards held the place of honor. In football, it was the Chicago Bears.

Steve often studied the names and faces on his collection of sports cards, as well as the trivial information about the players printed on the back of each card. Steve found this information far more interesting than anything he had ever studied at Oliver Perry Elementary School.

Radio brought to life the heroes of Steve's sports card collection: baseball in spring and summer; football in fall and winter.

In the early 1930s, the White Sox signed Luke Appling, a young shortstop from High Point, N.C. By 1933, Appling had become a fixture in the White Sox starting lineup, and as their lead-off hitter, he hit over .300 in nine consecutive seasons. In 1936, Appling hit a league-leading .388, yet his contributions were never enough to lead his teammates to a World Series. Like so many South Side youth, Steve followed the daily box scores and radio accounts of Appling. Naturally, the shortstop's baseball card held a very high market value in the Burnside neighborhood.

On Sunday afternoons in the fall and winter, the Wadiak boys gathered in the den to listen to the exploits of the Chicago Bears, or as they became better known, "The Monsters of the Midway."

The Bears' backfield in the early '30s was comprised of two superstars: veteran tailback, Red Grange, and Red's partner, a bruising mammoth of a man named Bronko Nagurski.

At 6'2" and 225 lbs., Nagurski was a punishing runner who also was a bone-crushing tackler on defense. With Nagurski and Grange leading the way, Halas's Bears captured back-to-back league championships in 1932 and '33, victories that shaped Steve Wadiak's earliest memories of 1930s football.

WGN radio announcer Bob Elson was the familiar voice of the Bears. His smooth Midwestern delivery inspired such iconic announcers as Chicago's Harry Carey and Jack Brickhouse. His descriptions of the Bears games hooked the imagination of the Wadiak youngsters, as they listened with keen interest whenever Nagurski had the ball, and Elson dramatically described his running style.

The Wadiaks' interest in Nagurski ran deeper than the football field. They shared a common heritage. Both families were Ukrainian immigrants. Bronko's parents initially made their way from Ukraine into Canada around the turn of the century. Immigrants without United States relatives were forced to locate in Canada. Thus, Bronko was born in 1908 in Rainy River, Ontario. He was christened Bronislau, a name that was shortened by his first grade teacher to Bronko.

The Nagurski family eventually crossed the U.S. border in 1912 and settled in frigid International Falls, Minn. Bronko's father, Mike, was also a large Ukrainian man who was a born entrepreneur. He owned a grocery store, a farm, and a sawmill—and he built houses on the side. These businesses and the duties required to run them provided physical outlets for young Bronko. He chiseled his muscles chopping wood, clearing fields, and running through the woods of frigid northern Minnesota. In high school, Bronko's physical skills made him successful in both football and basketball. Nagurski took his athletic abilities to the University of Minnesota, where he quickly became a national college football hero.

At the beginning of Nagurski's senior season, the Gophers were the favorites to win the Big Ten championship. Behind Nagurski, Minnesota ripped through its first five opponents by a combined score of 153-27. Midway through the season, the Gophers played a road game in Evanston, Ill., against Northwestern, on a day when Bears Coach George Halas was in attendance. Jim Dent, in "Monster of the Midway," describes what Halas witnessed in Evanston on this day:

> *Against Northwestern the Bronk scored a late touchdown for the 26-14 win. He stumbled over the end line and rammed his shoulder into several hundred-pound bags of cement stacked at the retaining wall behind the end zone. Each one fell.*
>
> *Sitting in the stands that day was none other than George Halas, who had made the short trek up from Chicago. He sneaked onto campus wearing a hat pulled down over his forehead and an overcoat with the collar turned up . . .*
>
> *What Halas saw that day was the toughest man in college football. After the game, Halas sneaked into the Gophers' dressing room. He stood in the corner, hat brim down, collar up, and watched Nagurski undress and then walk around the locker room in his underwear. Halas*

could never have imagined the sculpting of his body—the slabbing of leg muscles, the upper body powerfully developed from the plowing. He took note of the big man's grace and fluidity and the feet that seemed to glide across the floor.

In the prairie, alone with his dreams, Steve pretended he was Bronko Nagurski. He tucked his football under his arm and ran through, over, and around imaginary tacklers. One by one, he ran over the New York Giants, the Philadelphia Eagles, and the Green Bay Packers, on his imaginary way to becoming the next great running back of the National Football League.

With each run Nagurski made, with each victory he helped the Bears achieve, and with each award he garnered, the Bronk gave hope to a star-struck young boy in South Chicago—hope that he, too, could rise from a humble Ukrainian ancestry to become one of America's great football heroes.

4
Destiny

Gathered in their living room and listening to news of the Nazi air raids on London, the Wadiak family was startled by a violent thud that shook the structure of their home. Pieces of plaster fell from the ceiling and shattered on the hardwood floor. To the family, it felt as if German Luftwaffe had bypassed London and conducted an air raid on Chicago instead.

The Wadiaks were by then accustomed to unannounced earth-shattering interruptions; the noises began about the time Steve hit adolescence. Fueled by a testosterone-driven obsession with physical fitness, Steve established a life of never-ending exercise. His upstairs bedroom hosted his intense daily fitness regimen, and any unexpected thud came most likely from an accidental drop of his heavy leather medicine ball.

"That's it. We have got to do something with that boy," Nick Wadiak said emphatically, referencing the intrusive upstairs movements of his youngest son. Normally indifferent to the extracurricular activities of his children, Nick considered Steve's workouts an unacceptable disruption of their otherwise peaceful home. When the docile head of the Wadiak home reached his limit of tolerance, Steve's older brothers, Walter and Joe, offered an idea to help their exercise-crazed younger brother.

Behind the Wadiaks' home sat a detached empty wooden garage. Walter and Joe suggested to Steve that he convert the garage into a gymnasium. Steve enthusiastically embraced the idea, and soon, he and his friends went to work furnishing their private gym. They scavenged for any piece of used exercise equipment they could find. A broken treadmill was patched together and made operational. A leather punching bag hung in one corner, and a pull-up bar was anchored in the opposing corner. A set of free-weights and a medicine ball completed the furnishings of "Steve's Gym."

The converted garage became a gathering place for athletically-minded boys of the neighborhood. Joining Steve most frequently in his personal house of pain was his close friend Louis Guida. They competed in fitness challenges to determine who could perform the most push-ups, sit-ups, or pull-ups before collapsing. Steve's gym was open year-round, although sweltering summer temperatures turned it into a combination sauna/gymnasium. In winter, Steve overcame the frigid cold via intense workouts designed to raise body temperatures quickly.

Steve coupled his gymnasium workouts with long, early morning runs in the prairie near the Wadiak home. Only a Chicago blizzard kept Steve from his runs, and when the weather warmed, Steve and his friends ran barefoot along the sandy shores of Lake Michigan, completing their "Great Lake workout" with a rejuvenating swim in the lake's cool waters.

Tuley Park was located at 91st and St. Lawrence, about a mile from the Wadiak home. It featured a popular swimming pool that served as a summer-time gathering spot for neighborhood youth. Most kids enjoyed frolicking in the pool and having fun with their friends as a diversion from the summer heat. Steve swam laps, using the water to strengthen and stretch his muscles while building up his cardiovascular system. Through those laps, he perfected a smooth and powerful swimming stroke, a stroke that served him well when he swam against strong tides in Lake Michigan.

Steve's dedication to physical training to enhance his athletic ability was ahead of his time, as athletes had yet to fully discover the performance-enhancing benefits of physical conditioning and weight training. In the early 1940s, even professional athletes typically didn't train in the offseason; they worked second jobs in order to make ends meet and provide for their families.

The prairie continued to serve as a multi-field sports complex for games of football, baseball, and field hockey, although Steve was no longer the pesky little kid who hung around the fields hoping the older boys would give him a chance to participate. Everyone still called him Pinchy, but he was one of the big boys, taking part in every form of highly competitive games. When teams were selected, Steve's natural speed and burgeoning strength made him a top pick, and it was there upon the playing fields of the prairie that his athletic gifts were unleashed and discovered.

Football became Steve's greatest passion, offering him the perfect opportunity to combine his enjoyment of physical contact with his love for team-centered camaraderie. On the prairie, football was a full contact game played with makeshift equipment and limited padding.

The physical exertion of the game became the perfect outlet for neighborhood teenagers' limitless energy. Games were intense, and occasionally, a fight broke out, or somebody got hurt. However, when darkness fell and competition ceased, a sense of neighborhood sportsmanship prevailed: Everyone made sure there were no serious injuries; the winners were congratulated, and the losers were consoled. Daily, the boys left the prairie exhausted and bruised yet looking forward to the next day's battle. A warm bath and a hot meal regenerated their bodies, and their competitive spirits were renewed as they went to bed dreaming of tomorrow's game.

The neighborhood took notice of Steve's athletic abilities. The buzz around supper tables in the homes along University Avenue often involved Pinchy's exploits on the prairie that day; his long touchdown runs became prairie legends. Everybody wanted to be on Pinchy's team because they knew such inclusion greatly improved their chances of winning.

Parents too noticed something different about the youngest Wadiak boy. On their morning commute to work, men observed his familiar silhouette sprinting across the prairie, the boy's sunrise runs as consistent as the milkman's early morning deliveries. To all who gave witness, Steve's ambition and desire seemed fueled by something beyond the reach of the typical teenager.

Consistent with his health-conscious nature, Steve was careful about what he ate—preferring fresh vegetables and home-cooked meals to popular, less nutritional foods. Fortunately for him, his mother liked to cook. Prior to going to work each day, Anna Wadiak baked fresh bread, a skill she learned growing up in Ukraine, which was known as the "wheat field of Europe." It was from a steady helping of Anna's breads—often slathered with butter—that Steve got his needed carbohydrates.

On Thursdays, Anna used her day off to expand her baking to include pastries, her specialty being tasty crullers, or, as they were sometimes called, "angel wings." These were bow tie-shaped fried pastries dusted with powdered sugar and honey, treats that soon became too much of a temptation for health-conscious Steve to resist. Anna baked the crullers and left them unattended while they cooled in her kitchen. More than once, Steve and his gym-mates were lured inside by the scent of the fresh pastries, and they finished them off before other family members had a chance to partake. The sugar rush the boys received simply ignited another round of exercises in Steve's gym.

In contrast to the stability of home and the camaraderie of team sport, the corner of 93rd Street and University Avenue stood out to Steve as an unappealing gathering spot for men he neither related to nor understood. On that corner, the men passed around bottles, made crude comments to unsuspecting females, and usually ended up fighting with one another. From his early days of working at Demkowicz's grocery store, Steve had taken note of these men. Many of them had gathered on the corner for years. Steve sensed a meaningless existence for these street-corner icons, as they filled most of their free time standing around on the corner, involving themselves in trivial conversations before stumbling their way home after another evening spent drinking. Night after night, they repeated the same behavior, and Steve saw nothing attractive in their lives.

Driven by an intense desire to "make something of himself," Steve swore he would never become a street-corner bum. He equated much of their purposeless lives and behaviors to their daily dependency on alcohol. Thus, at a young age, Steve promised himself that he'd never take a drink of alcohol. Life was too good sober! Spending hard-earned money on something that would impair physical capabilities made no sense to him. There were games to win and muscles to grow, and if Steve Wadiak were to be addicted to anything, it would be Anna's breads and pastries.

Abraham Lincoln once stated that he believed it was his duty to prepare for his ultimate destiny. Such resolute belief inspired Lincoln's passion for learning, as he borrowed and read every book he could find within a 50-mile radius. He once walked six miles before his 12th birthday to obtain a copy of a book on English grammar, this in order to improve his writing and speaking abilities. Through his lifelong commitment to learning, Lincoln became knowledgeable in a vast array of subjects, and that knowledge later helped him fulfill his ultimate destiny. Lincoln truly believed that "destiny prepared was destiny served."

Steve Wadiak may never have walked any great distance to read a book, but he ran and swam hundreds of miles, cranked out thousands of push-ups, sit-ups, and pull-ups, and trained his body relentlessly in pursuit of his goals. Driven to take the gifts bestowed upon him and to become the very best athlete he could possibly become, Steve trusted that in his own life, destiny prepared would also be destiny served.

5
High School

Steve began his high school years excited about the opportunity to play organized football. Up to that point, football had been a game played with neighborhood friends on a remote prairie. High school would bring uniforms, coaches, referees, stadiums, cheerleaders, and fans.

A single roadblock stood between Steve and his dream of playing organized football: his mother. Anna Wadiak strictly forbade her sons to participate in a sport she considered violent and a waste of time. Fear drove her prohibition.

While working one day at Fables restaurant, Anna was summoned to the hospital. She was told only that her teenage son Joe had been involved in an accident. Upon arriving at the hospital, she found Joe writhing in pain from a badly broken leg. Anna looked at the mangled condition of her son's limb and experienced what all loving parents experience as they witness their child suffering—the intensity of Joe's physical pain transferred to her own heart.

Joe's leg was set and a cast applied. He spent the night in the hospital, and it wasn't long before Anna gained understanding of the nature of Joe's accident. When he sustained his injury, Joe was playing football on the prairie—tackle football without any pads.

Football! Anna thought as she discovered the culprit behind her son's anguish. While staying with her son in the hospital, she vowed that no Wadiak boy would ever again play that awful game.

Steve Wadiak's bliss was a football tucked under his arm and an open field in front of him. Everything about him—from his competitive spirit to his stocky athletic body—was made for the gridiron. He could never abandon his calling, and his insistence on continuing to play was one of the rare times when Steve acted against his mother's wishes. He not only kept playing football on the prairie, but also went out for football when he enrolled as a freshman at Chicago's Fenger High in the fall of 1939. The only thing that tempered his excitement was the fact that he had to hide his involvement from his mother.

Routinely, Steve would enter his home through the back door and quickly stuff his dirty football gear into a small cubby-hole underneath a spiral staircase. His mother's daily work schedule gave him the freedom to wash his clothes without her knowledge. In time, Anna uncovered her youngest son's deception. She discovered the dirty football clothes in their secret hiding place, and immediately, her mind went to the hospital. She relived the painful vision of Joe's contorted leg. A righteous anger welled up inside her. Unable to bear thinking about her youngest child suffering such an injury, she intended to put a stop, once and for all, to Steve's football playing days.

Fortunately for Steve, his older brother intervened on his behalf. "Ma, you can't take football away from Steve," Joe pleaded. "He's gifted, and football is what he loves. You can try to take it away, but he will always find a way to do what he loves to do."

Anna stared at Joe, bewildered by his pleading the case of his little brother when that meant playing a game that had caused such a horrible injury to his own leg.

Anna could not find the words to challenge her son's appeal, so she walked away and decided to give the matter more thought.

Anna knew Joe was right. She had heard the men at the Demkowicz's corner grocery store talking about Steve and his athletic abilities. Although she could not fully comprehend the reasoning behind their admiration for her son, there was something in the way they spoke about him that appealed to a sense of motherly pride. Steve was a good son. He was respectful, helpful, and obedient. While unable to understand the purpose of the football games Steve played, she was willing to accept that he found happiness in playing them.

Anna stuffed Steve's dirty football gear back into his secret hiding place. She would not speak a word to Steve about finding them. The following Sunday, she arrived early at St. Peter and Paul Ukrainian Orthodox Church where she lit a candle and offered a prayer on behalf of her son and his extracurricular activities. She prayed a mother's prayer for the safety and protection of her youngest son. She prayed that she would never be called to the hospital to find him in pain.

With the intercessory prayers of his mother, an endless passion for the sport of football, and the shadow of a world war looming over him, Steve embarked on what would become, at best, a mysterious high school career. The poorly documented nature of the three and a half years he would spend at two different Chicago high schools would leave future admirers with many more questions than answers. However, the reality is that Steve's high school playing days became collectively a victim of circumstances that kept him out of the limelight of Chicago high school athletics.

As a freshman at Fenger High in 1939, Steve found the athletic field crowded. Fenger was an established high school with a proven athletic history. From 1938-1954, Fenger would claim four Chicago Prep Bowl championships—an annual event held at Soldier Field that pitted the Chicago Public League champion against the Catholic League champion. As a lightweight freshman who stood barely over five and a half feet tall, Steve got lost in the crowd. He saw a number of talented athletes ahead of him and doubted he'd ever get a chance to showcase his talents at Fenger. After some coaxing from close friends, Steve decided to transfer to the newly constructed Chicago Vocational School (CVS) in the fall of 1941.

The construction of CVS was financed by $3.5 million in funding from the Works Progress Administration. It is located at 2100 E. 87th St. and first opened its doors to 850 male students in the fall of 1940. CVS was built primarily to equip students with skills that would help them land vocational trade jobs at the larger Chicago industrial companies. School officials lauded the success of their mission by boasting about early graduates who were getting jobs as railroad mechanics and being paid an impressive wage of 95 cents per hour. Basic high school classes were also taught, but clearly, the emphasis at the all-male institution was on learning a trade.

With the pending outbreak of World War II, the school was turned over to the United States Navy in June of 1941; it became a training school for aviation mechanics. Vocational classes for CVS students continued to be taught at the 87th Avenue school, and non-vocational classes were moved to an empty building at the old Calumet High School on Normal Avenue. The original CVS buildings would be returned to the Chicago School System in 1946, at which time, females were first allowed to enter the school. Today, CVS is an active high school with an enrollment of approximately 2,500 Chicago area students.

In its early years, CVS fielded athletic teams in football, basketball, and wrestling, with baseball added in 1943. Steve spent his sophomore year at CVS as a member of the school's junior varsity team, coached by longtime mentor and friend Chip Garritano. Steve's close friend, Louis Guida, joined him in the backfield of the JV squad. Guida later became a highly successful football and wrestling coach at Chicago's

Mendel High School. In 1941, both the varsity and junior varsity squads played a series of unofficial scrimmages, as the school had not yet become an official part of the Chicago High School League.

Steve joined the varsity squad in 1942, and the team continued to experience growing pains in its early years of formation. The 1942 squad lacked equipment and depth—an old team photo shows only 11 boys wearing a collection of mismatched uniforms. The team owned but a single football and had to ration among its players a limited number of shoulder pads and cleats. The school did not have its own football field, so practices were held at Avalon Park, located approximately three miles from the school. Many of the players would run that three-mile distance as part of their daily conditioning regimen.

Steve Wadiak, Number 7, (top row, far right) is pictured with the 1942 Chicago Vocational High School football team.

(Photo courtesy of Jerry Kalwasinski)

No official record of the 1942 season exists, other than unsubstantiated folklore that purports that the 1942 team won all five of its scheduled games. Their opponents included games against Morgan Park,

Bowen, South Shore, Hirsch, and Parker High Schools. In 1943, CVS played an expanded schedule against tougher competition, and they struggled against the more established and larger schools in the area.

Heralded as the team's best runner, passer, kicker, and defensive player, Steve Wadiak was clearly the star of the 1942 and '43 teams. In later years, Wadiak's high school coach, Beryl McNabb, made a bold but unsubstantiated claim to a Chicago newspaper that in the three years Wadiak played at CVS, he remarkably scored a touchdown in all 27 games in which he participated. He would become the first athletic star of CVS, a school that later produced several highly recognized athletes, including Chicago Bears Hall of Fame linebacker Dick Butkus, four-time Super Bowl winner with the San Francisco 49ers, Keena Turner, three-time Notre Dame All-American Chris Zorich, and University of Michigan and NBA basketball star, Juwan Howard.

Given the unofficial nature of the CVS schedule, local media outlets rarely documented the results of CVS football games. Only a couple of articles in the "Chicago Tribune" database reference the early football accomplishments of CVS. In 1943, as CVS began to play some of the more competitive and larger public high schools, the following two clips appeared:

> *October 1, 1943—Leo swamped Chicago Vocational 41 to 6 last night at Shewbridge Field in a practice game. Scoring in every quarter Leo, All-City champs, built up a 20-0 lead at the half. However, Steve Wadiak, who replaced Ed O'Neil at left halfback, contributed the longest run, a 73-yarder off right tackle in the fourth period that went for Vocational's only score.*

October 9, 1943—Senn High of the north section of the City League defeated Chicago Vocational, 33-13, yesterday in a nonleague game in Winnemac Park. Vocational, a new addition to the City League, will play only exhibition games this season. Steve Wadiak of Vocational made the longest run of the game in the third quarter when he sped around end for 80 yards and a touchdown.

Steve was also a member of the CVS wrestling squad. In the first two years of the CVS wrestling program, the team lost only a single match. Their loss was attributed to an injury by a key wrestler. Due to the lack of depth on the team, they were unable to substitute another wrestler and had to forfeit his match.

CVS in its early years attracted a number of Chicago's best athletes. Its early success would be a prelude to the school's storied athletic history: CVS won the prestigious Chicago Prep Bowl in 1955 and 1975, along with nine Chicago Public League football championships from 1955-1976. CVS would capture four city championships in basketball and wrestling as well.

After the attack on Pearl Harbor by the Japanese on Dec. 7, 1941, it became increasingly difficult to find an 18-year-old boy walking the halls of CVS. Likewise, the homes on University Avenue were void of single males in the 18-30-year-old age group. They had either been drafted, or they had enlisted in the Armed Forces. On Jan. 8, 1944, in the middle of his senior year of high school, Steve Wadiak celebrated his 18th birthday.

Steve's brothers, Walter and Joe, were serving in the military. Walter was part of the Army's 7th Division, and Joe was with a shore patrol unit in the Navy. Both Anna and Nick Wadiak dreaded the thought of having all three of their sons fighting in the war. They had witnessed military service vehicles turning down their street, and they had heard the screams of mothers who were informed that their sons had been lost on the battlefield. They listened daily to radio reports about the advancing German and Japanese forces. Like all Americans, the Wadiaks lived with the uncertainty and fear of a nation at war.

From his early days on the prairie serving as a mascot, water boy, or bat boy, Steve longed to emulate the behaviors of the neighborhood boys he admired. Most of his heroes and mentors from the neighborhood were away serving their country in the military. He knew some of them would never return home.

Steve took note of the path of Bill Mitchell, a fellow CVS football and wrestling teammate. Mitchell had been the backbone of the undefeated 1942 CVS wresting team. The 1943 wrestlers began with a strong showing as well, until midseason when Mitchell answered Uncle Sam's call.

Steve knew what he had to do. His competitive and courageous spirit, forged on the athletic fields of Chicago, was now being called to a higher purpose. Shortly after his 18th birthday, without asking permission from his parents, Steve walked into a Navy recruitment office and offered his services to defend the country that had provided his family with such freedom and opportunity. When Anna Wadiak got the news that her baby had enlisted, she broke down and cried.

6
Navy

In early February of 1944, Steve Wadiak reported for service at Great Lakes Naval Training Center, a 172-acre training facility located on the southwest shore of Lake Michigan, only 50 miles from Steve's childhood home on University Avenue.

Shortly after the conclusion of the Spanish-American War in 1902, United States military leaders noted that some of their best sailors were from the Midwestern region of the U.S. This prompted President Theodore Roosevelt to commission the construction of Great Lakes Naval Training Center, located nearly 1,000 miles from the nearest ocean. Great Lakes would become and remains the Navy's largest training center. From the time of the attack on Pearl Harbor on December 7, 1941, to the surrender of the Japanese on August 14, 1945, over four million Americans served in the United States Navy. One million of those were trained at Great Lakes Naval Training Center.

At military training facilities across the U.S., it was generally held that athletics helped future soldiers develop the character and toughness needed for the battlefield. Great Lakes, with an abundance of athletic talent, became known for its outstanding sports teams. No sport was more conducive to creating the military's desired character traits than football. Frank Knox, Secretary of the Navy during World War II, was one of the strongest proponents of football, and he expressed his affinity for the sport in an interview that was published in the Great Lakes base newspaper. Knox stated:

This is a war where you kill or get killed! And I don't know anything that better prepares a man for bodily contact, including war, than the kind of training we get on the football field. There is a definite relationship between the spirit which makes great football players and the spirit that makes great soldiers or sailors.

During the war years, the draft depleted college and professional football ranks of their best talent. As a result, military football teams were considered the nation's very best. Military gridiron squads were stocked full of household names from the most prominent college and professional teams. The training base teams not only competed against other training facilities, but also played a full schedule of games against the nation's top college teams. The Associated Press even developed a combined ranking system that resulted in the publishing of a weekly college/service football poll.

When Steve Wadiak arrived at Great Lakes in 1944, the Great Lakes football team was coming off an impressive 10-2 season and an overall ranking of sixth in the final AP college/service poll. Great Lakes' most impressive victory of the season came against an undefeated and number one-ranked Notre Dame team. They hosted the Fighting Irish in front of a partisan crowd of 22,000 at Ross Stadium on the campus of Great Lakes. Future Heisman Trophy winner Johnny Lujack led a Notre Dame team in pursuit of its first undefeated season since 1930. The Great Lakes team trailed most of the game but scored on a dramatic 50-yard touchdown pass late in the game to secure a hard fought 19-14 upset win.

One of the stars of the 1943 Great Lakes team was Ken Roskie, a talented 220-lb. fullback who played for Coach Rex Enright at the University of South Carolina. Roskie, a native of Rockford, Ill., started for the Gamecocks in 1941 and '42, before enlisting in the Navy. He was drafted by the Green Bay Packers after the 1943 season at Great Lakes and played two seasons in the NFL for three different teams.

Steve Wadiak's unheralded high school athletic career would not likely have qualified him for consideration by the powerful Great Lakes football team. Instead, Steve began eight weeks of basic training in the same manner as thousands of other recruits. He was assigned a number and given "dog tags" to be worn at all times. Sadly, it was these tags that were so often relied upon for the identification of casualties on the battlefield.

Steve Wadiak's U.S. Navy dog tags

(Photo courtesy of Jeanette Wadiak Korlin)

Steve embraced the physical demands of basic training at Great Lakes. He thrived on endless calisthenics, long runs in the bitter cold weather, and many other endurance tests that pushed a man to his physical limits. His time in his makeshift gymnasium on University Avenue had prepared his 18-year-old body for just about anything the Navy threw his way.

During his 28-month stint in the Navy, Steve was stationed at three different training facilities. After basic training at Great Lakes, he was transferred to Norfolk, Va., before finally moving to Corpus Christi, Texas, where he was trained as an aerial gunner.

The Navy opened a new world of experiences to a young boy who had rarely ventured outside the boundaries of the Windy City. Steve experienced new cultures and made friends from different parts of the country. While on his way to Corpus Christi, Steve was allowed a short stopover in New Orleans. There, he purchased an oversized postcard that featured a black and white photograph of a packed Sugar Bowl stadium. Steve scribbled a message on the back of the card and sent it to his buddies back home in the Burnside neighborhood:

Hi Guys,

I'm in New Orleans now on my way to Texas and having a hell of a time. We can spend nine hours here and then catch the train. What a town. I'm in heaven. I'll write later.

Love,

Pinchy

While in Corpus Christi, Steve was part of the largest naval aviation training facility in the world. The base was spread across 20,000 acres and included nearly 1,000 airplane hangars. By the end of the war, more than 35,000 naval aviators had received their wings at Corpus Christi. Among its distinguished graduates is former President George H.W. Bush, who, in 1943, became the youngest graduate of Corpus Christi's pilot training school. Bush was three days shy of his 19th birthday when he completed the 10-month training program at Corpus Christi. He was then sent to fly Navy bomber planes off the deck of the USS San Jacinto. By the time the war ended, Bush had completed 58 combat missions.

At Corpus Christi, Steve underwent corrective surgery for a lingering nasal ailment. Shortly before he enlisted, he was whacked across the nose with a hockey stick while playing field hockey with the Burnside neighborhood youth. The blow resulted in a deviated septum, and the Wadiak family could not afford corrective surgery. Eighty-five percent of Steve's right nostril was obstructed, and he relied on daily use of inhalers to help open his nasal passageways.

After living with the problem for almost two years, Steve was finally able to have it surgically repaired during his stay at Corpus Christi. While recovering from the surgery in the base hospital, Steve received a surprise visit from his sisters, Jeanette and Olga. The trip was sanctioned by Steve's worried mother, Anna. Steve's sisters brought food and gifts from home, but most importantly, they brought a visible reminder of a family's love for its youngest member.

Steve Wadiak with his sisters
Jeanette (left) and Olga

(Photo courtesy of Jeanette Wadiak Korlin)

Steve's training as an aerial gunner at Corpus Christi was the most intense of his military career. Aerial gunners were often required to fly long missions while sitting in cramped quarters at very high altitudes. They had to fully grasp the complexities of firing weapons from a moving target at another moving target. Such training was not for the physically or mentally weak. Steve found himself spending most of his early training days in the classroom. Gunner candidates were bombarded with a massive amount of information about the inner workings of machine guns, ammunition, the physics of air-to-air gunnery, and techniques for split-second recognition of enemy aircraft.

Initially, trainees were required to achieve a high level of proficiency at disassembling and reassembling their weapons. This process was known as "stripping," and as a final test of proficiency, trainees had to perform it flawlessly while blindfolded and wearing gloves.

After mastering the basics of their weaponry, trainees were schooled in how to sight their guns in order to hit their intended targets. Candidates were introduced to complex concepts such as deflection—the distance they needed to aim from the attacking fighter's current position to compensate for its movement and the movement of their own planes. This was a time prior to the invention of the electronic computing gun sight, therefore gunners had to be able to compute deflection rates in their heads in order to accurately aim their weapons. With the introduction of such mind-blowing mathematical and physical elements, students with fantasies of heroically shooting down Japanese fighter pilots were quickly grounded in reality.

Once the intensive classroom work was completed, gunner candidates were given the opportunity to learn to fire their weapons. Training began with gunners firing stationery guns at moving targets and progressed to their firing weapons from moving platforms at moving targets. Also, the regular use of flight simulators began during the training of World War II pilots and gunners. After proficiency was reached in these ground tactics and in simulators, trainees were allowed to use their skills in an actual aircraft.

To be an aerial gunner, a man had to successfully cope with the extreme physical pressures associated with high-altitude flying. To test potential flight candidates, the military employed altitude chambers, which simulated high-altitude conditions, including hypoxia—the loss of oxygen. Each candidate was pushed to his physical limits in order to gauge his abilities to withstand the worst possible flying conditions.

Steve never had to put his training into practice in an actual battle. Like so many Navy men, his call to combat duty was cut short by the Manhattan Project and the dropping of atomic bombs on Hiroshima and Nagasaki in August of 1945. Still, the intensity of the training would mark Steve's life. Imagining himself 20,000 or 30,000 feet in the air—cramped behind a gun turret and tasked with the responsibility to protect his pilot against approaching enemy aircraft—matured Steve in ways that even the most brutal game of football could not.

Prior to the attacks on Hiroshima and Nagasaki, many military personnel, including Steve, lived with the inevitable fear that they might eventually lose their lives fighting in the Pacific Theater against the ruthless and relentless Japanese military. While use of the atomic bomb represented the most violent acts in the history of mankind, it also resulted in the eventual surrender of the Japanese Empire and the saving of countless numbers of American soldiers who would have lost their lives had the battle waged on.

Steve's time in the Navy would prove to be a season of physical and mental growth. Naval medical records dated Jan. 27, 1944, reveal that Steve entered the Navy at 5'6 ½" and 160 lbs. His resting heart rate was

88, and he had a 33-inch waist. Upon his discharge on June 1, 1946, his body had undergone a transformation as a result of the disciplined Navy lifestyle. His discharge medical records indicated that he had grown an inch and a half to 5'8" and had added 18 pounds to his stocky frame, bringing his weight up to 178 pounds. Steve's resting heart rate had slowed to 74 beats per minute, and his waist size had not changed.

On June 1, 1946, Steve was honorably discharged from the Navy at the same location where he began his military career, Great Lakes Naval Station. He enlisted in the Navy as a boy who had just reached his 18th birthday. Twenty-eight months later, he was discharged as a man.

Petty Officer 3rd Class Steve Wadiak

(Photo courtesy of Jeanette Wadiak Korlin)

7
Discovered

They called themselves "birddogs." They were a loose collection of knowledgeable men across the United States who searched for talented athletes and recommended them to their coaching friends. Most college football programs in the 1940s had few assistant coaches and limited recruiting budgets, so they relied heavily on their "birddog" networks to help them scout, recruit, and sign talented players.

In 1947, Bill Milner was a Chicago-based birddog. His loyalty was attached to the University of South Carolina and its head football coach, Rex Enright. After a successful high school career in Waynesville, N.C., Milner was signed by Enright to a football grant-in-aid at South Carolina in 1940. Milner quickly became a starting guard for the Gamecocks, but participation in an ROTC training program led him to Duke University where he joined a talented Duke football team, and in 1943, became a First Team All-American. After a stint in the military, Milner returned to Duke to complete his college education and was once again named All-American in 1946. Milner would receive a diploma from Duke, but his heart remained with South Carolina and the man who had given him his first opportunity.

After college, Milner signed with the Chicago Bears who had selected him in the 15th round of the 1944 NFL Draft. As a rookie in 1947, Milner often spent free time visiting the sandlots of Chicago in search of athletes who might help his former coach and mentor, Enright. Milner had little to gain from his bird-dogging efforts, other than repayment of a debt of gratitude to Enright.

In the fall of 1947, Milner's nose for talent got wind of an unstoppable running back who was playing for the Roseland Mustangs, a local semi-pro team. He decided to check out the Mustang star and provide Enright with a full report on the young man who was known throughout Chicago as Pinchy Wadiak.

After two and half years away from his family and the familiar surroundings of his Burnside neighborhood, Steve returned home in June of 1946. Nick and Anna Wadiak were thankful for the safe return of their youngest son, as Steve's older siblings were one-by-one launching their adult lives and vacating the family home.

The neighborhood felt different to Steve after the war. Some of the neighborhood youth had not returned home, and others returned encumbered by the physical and emotional scars of war. Across the United States, veterans attempted to return to life as normal, but for many, finding "normal" proved an elusive task.

Steve's class work in Corpus Christi had earned him credit hours toward his high school diploma, and shortly after his discharge from the Navy, Steve graduated from Chicago Vocational High School. Just like in eighth grade, Steve would miss out on participation in a formal graduation ceremony and instead would be handed his diploma by his high school principal.

Steve joined returning veterans in discovering a post-war economy greatly influenced by an over dependence on wartime production. Jobs were scarce, so Steve found work where he could, mostly part-time, low-wage assignments around the railroads and various construction sites.

At 21 and in the top physical condition of his life, Steve had not given up on his athletic dreams. The Roseland Mustangs Athletic Club recruited the former Chicago Vocational standout to play for their football team and most likely offered to pay him a small sum for each game he played. Steve would have played for free. Playing football connected Steve to the once innocent life he left behind when he enlisted in the Navy. Wearing cleats, shoulder pads, and a leather helmet brought clarity to a sometimes confusing post-war world.

Semi-professional football teams were gaining popularity across the country and were comprised mostly of men who hadn't gotten a chance to go to college and were unwilling to let go of their gridiron dreams. The rosters of the teams consisted of former high school heroes who had returned from the war, as well as grizzled older men who were looking for a diversion from the daily grind of their jobs.

Technically, cash payments received by semi-pro players would have rendered them ineligible to ever compete in the sport at the amateur level. The National Collegiate Athletic Association, however, was still a few years away from being formally established as the authoritative body governing collegiate athletics, so the enforcement of standards governing amateur athletes remained inconsistent during this era.

Wadiak joined a 1946 Roseland Mustang team that became one of the most successful in the Midwest semi-pro circuit. Over a seven-year period from 1946 to 1953, the Mustangs posted a record of 90-26-9. Wadiak's physical toughness and explosive running skills immediately earned him the respect of his Mustang coaches and teammates. He quickly became the star of the Mustangs, and word of his exploits spread throughout Roseland and surrounding communities.

Roseland's games were played in Chicago's public parks and were well attended by neighborhood residents. They came to watch men they knew—men who had played at their local high schools and now worked at nearby railroads and factories and lived in their communities. Fans relished the fact that they could watch players on Saturday and sit next to them at church on Sunday.

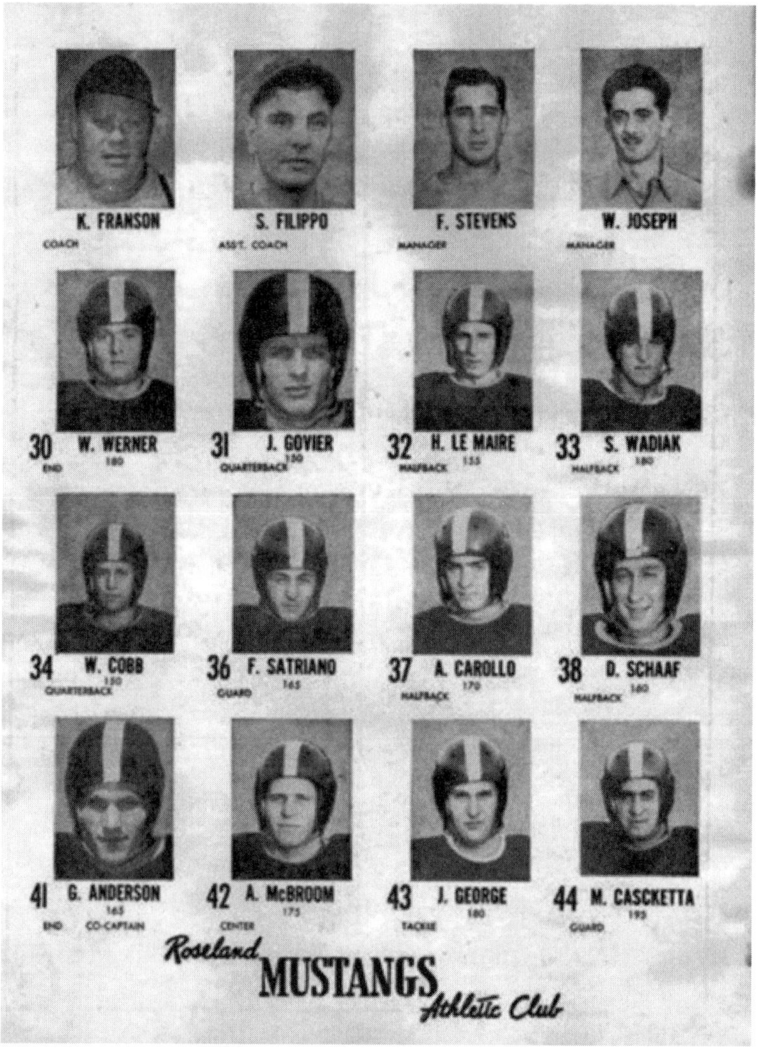

The 1947 Roseland Mustangs

(Photo courtesy of the Roseland Historical Society)

On a cool, sunny fall Saturday afternoon, the Bears' Bill Milner set out on a bird-dogging mission. He attended a Mustang game at Avalon Park on East 83rd Street in order to make an honest appraisal of the phenom who was creating such a buzz on the sandlots of Chicago. He watched "Number 33" play fearless football on both offense and defense and lead his team to a convincing victory. He took note of the intensity of Wadiak's effort and determination on the field.

When he carried the ball, Wadiak refused to be tackled—churning and fighting for extra yardage. He was a natural leader on the field, with his teammates looking to him every time they needed a boost.

After the game, Milner found Wadiak sitting on a wooden bench resting his exhausted body. Wadiak had played every down of the game and was completely drained from his efforts. Milner sat down next to Wadiak and introduced himself. An avid Chicago Bears fan, Steve heard Milner's name and immediately recognized it as the former college All-American who was in his rookie season with the Bears.

Steve couldn't imagine what one of George Halas's boys was doing in Avalon Park watching a rag-tag semi-pro team. Little did Steve know that this meeting would be the catalyst that would forever change the trajectory of his life.

After the two exchanged pleasantries, Milner posed a question to the star of the Mustangs: "Hey, kid, you ever think about going to college to play football?"

College? Steve didn't really know how to respond. No one in the Wadiak family had ever gone to college. Steve thought it was quite the accomplishment that he was able to earn a high school diploma. Most Burnsiders did well to finish high school. Then, they typically moved on to working in the local factories, railroads, or stockyards. College was something that was meant for the more affluent, not the sons and daughters of European immigrants living on Chicago's South Side.

Milner's question, however, included a phrase that got Steve's attention: "to play football."

Steve had listened and read of the feats of his heroes, and he knew that the road to football stardom ran through the college campus. His childhood hero, Bronko Nagurski, had gone from the frozen backwoods near the Canadian border to the campus of the University of Minnesota. Could he follow in the footsteps of the Bronk?

Milner went on to describe Rex Enright as a father figure to him, a former Notre Dame football player who also had experience in the National Football League. Milner told Wadiak that Enright was a man who could be trusted. He assured Steve that Enright would teach him the finer points of the game, and that he would look out for his best interest. Milner disclosed that he would not be a Chicago Bear if it were not for the influence of Coach Enright.

With each word Milner spoke, he delivered hope to a young man looking to find himself—to discover his destiny. Steve felt good to be back home among his family and friends, but restlessness stirred inside him. Perhaps a venture to the South held the answer.

Wadiak told Milner he was interested, and that it would be okay for him to contact Coach Enright on his behalf. With the politeness he had been taught as a young boy, Steve extended his hand to Milner and thanked him for coming to watch him play. He wished Milner the best of luck with the remainder of the Bears' season. That night, Milner made a phone call to Coach Enright in Columbia, S.C. He described what he had seen—a powerfully built, fast, tough kid who had the manners of a gentleman.

Enright trusted his birddog. He had trained him to know what it took to be a college football player and what kind of character he expected in the men who suited up as members of his team.

In January of 1948, Rex Enright sent Wadiak a one-way train ticket to Columbia. Enright explained to Wadiak that when he arrived, his skills would be assessed in order to determine whether or not he could play for the Gamecocks.

Enright made no promise of a scholarship, playing time, or a future at the Southern school. Enright's only assurance was that he would give him a chance to make his team.

While he was contemplating Enright's offer, Wadiak concluded his 1947 season with the Mustangs with a memorable performance in the league championship game. Playing left halfback, Steve broke loose on touchdown runs of 87, 40, and 35 yards to lead the Mustangs to a 21-0 upset victory. His impressive performance added to his iconic status among neighborhood sports fans.

Steve explained to his parents the opportunity that was before him. They did not fully understand why a college would pay for a young man to get an education in return for playing football. Ultimately, it was Steve's decision.

Accustomed to traveling light from his Navy days, Steve packed only a handful of clothes in a small gym bag and began his journey to South Carolina. He did not expect his stay in South Carolina would be very long. As he packed his bag, he had more questions than answers. *What would this place called South Carolina be like? Would they accept an immigrant's son from Chicago? Could I possibly pull my weight in a college classroom? Was Coach Enright truly the kind of man Milner had described? If Enright didn't like what he saw, would he give me a train ticket back home?*

Anna Wadiak hugged her son as he left to catch the train to South Carolina. As she stood in the cold on the front porch of her home and watched her son walk down University Avenue to catch the trolley that would carry him to the train station, she recalled her own decision in 1913 to leave her uncle's farm in Wisconsin in search of a new life and adventure in the city of Chicago. Anna recalled boarding a train as a 17-year-old—she had a one-way ticket to a new and better life. While she hated to see her son leave, she unselfishly hoped that Steve's train ride to South Carolina would be the beginning of her son's own great adventure.

8
Tryout

Steve Wadiak began his journey to Columbia, S.C., aboard a train Southern travelers affectionately referred to as "The Carolina Creeper." The train earned its nickname because it stopped in every town, big and small, along the 1,000-mile path from Chicago to Charleston, S.C.

After spending nearly two days aboard the slow-moving locomotive, Wadiak stepped onto the platform of Columbia's Gervais Street train station in early February of 1948. He had left Chicago in the middle of winter wearing his heavy overcoat. He arrived in South Carolina's capital city on a mild afternoon and quickly realized he was significantly overdressed.

In the athletic office on the campus of the University of South Carolina, Head Coach Rex Enright enlisted the services of Pat Vella, one of his most dependable players, to pick up Steve at the train station.

Vella had come to USC from Enright's hometown of Rockford, Ill. He was an undersized quarterback with a big heart and a deep sense of appreciation for the opportunity that had been given to him by Coach Enright. Vella was a poster boy for the university. When Enright needed someone to make a good impression on a recruit, he counted on the likeable Vella to serve as host. Conveniently, Vella was one of the few ballplayers on Enright's squad who owned a car—a rickety Hudson Terraplane he had purchased for $300 after his discharge from the Navy.

Vella spotted Wadiak standing on the train platform holding a small gym bag. He approached Steve, introduced himself, and offered a welcoming handshake. Nearly 65 years later, Vella recalled that handshake and his initial impression of Steve with exacting detail.

"He looked me square in the eye and shook my hand firmly," Vella said. "He had a look about him. I knew I was going to like this guy."

Vella and Wadiak had much in common: They were from the same area of the country, their parents were of European ancestry, and both men had served in the U.S. Navy. Vella spent the better part of World War II aboard the USS North Carolina, seeing significant action in the Pacific Theater. Their meeting on the train platform that day would mark the beginning of a close friendship.

As they turned onto Sumter Street, Steve stared out the window at the capitol building—an impressive granite structure capped by a recognizable copper dome.

Vella pulled his car over on Sumter Street, in front of the centerpiece of the university's campus—The Horseshoe—a U-shaped brick pathway lined on either side and throughout by mature oak and elm trees. Eleven buildings, mostly classrooms and dormitories, were stationed around the pathway's perimeter. The university was founded in 1801, and most of the structures on The Horseshoe were constructed prior to the Civil War.

A handful of students carrying books on their hips walked across the brick paths that crisscrossed throughout The Horseshoe. It was Wadiak's first glimpse of college life, and that life looked peaceful to him.

Vella delivered Steve to the Carolina Field House on the corner of Sumter and Greene Street. He took Wadiak into a room known as the "blue room"—a cramped 10-by-12 room adjacent to the Field House's athletic locker rooms. The room served as a meeting space for coaches, its meager furnishings consisting of a couple of tables, some folding chairs, and a chalkboard. Coach Enright stood waiting in the room along with his line coach, Hank Bartos.

"So, my good friend Bill Milner says the boys in the Chicago sandlots can't stop you," Enright said as he welcomed his potential recruit. His compliment brought a smile to Steve's face.

"What do you say we let you put on some cleats and take you over to the field and let you stretch your legs a little," Enright continued.

After his marathon train ride, Wadiak was ready for some outdoor physical activity. Vella escorted Steve down the hallway into the football locker room on the ground floor of the Field House. Steve noticed lockers filled with equipment—shoulder pads, jerseys, cleats, and helmets. He had never seen so much athletic equipment in one place. The teams Steve had played for in the past struggled to find enough useable equipment to outfit 11 players. Steve noticed an equipment room containing a bin full of leather footballs. He realized he was a long way from the prairie behind his University Avenue home, where a lone football was shared among dozens of neighborhood kids.

Steve was given a pair of gym shorts, football cleats, and a sweatshirt with embroidered lettering—*Property of USC Athletics.* As Vella and Wadiak dressed, Red Wilson, a veteran end from Macon, Ga., joined them. Once dressed, the three men walked across the street and onto Davis Field, the school's baseball field, where a handful of baseball players were playing catch in the outfield grass. Vella, who seemingly knew everyone on campus, stopped for a moment to chat. Then, the three men continued walking across Davis Field and through a gate onto Melton Field—the Gamecocks' practice football field.

Melton Field served as the home stadium for Gamecock football teams until 1934, when WPA funds were utilized to construct Carolina Stadium adjacent to the State Fairgrounds, approximately two miles south of USC's campus. Melton Field was lined with 15 rows of wooden bleachers on either side. A brick gate entranceway honoring William

Davis Melton, a former president of the university, stood on the Greene Street side of the field. Wooden light poles stood in front of the bleachers, allowing for nighttime activities.

Melton Field had a long history of multi-use. Shortly after the Civil War, the field was used by federal troops for drills and parades. Around 1880, the field was part of a 20-acre farm owned by the university. ROTC candidates frequently used the field for marches and drills. The South Carolina football team shared it with intramural athletic teams, as well as local high schools that frequently used the field on Friday nights. Its dormant Bermuda grass bore the marks of frequent, multipurpose use.

The Gamecock football team was coming off a respectable 6-2-1 1947 season in which they defeated their archrival, Clemson, surprised the University of Miami on the road, and upset a strong Wake Forest team 6-0 on Thanksgiving Day in Charlotte. The "Garnet and Black" yearbook referred to the 1947 campaign as the greatest season in Carolina's history.

Enright's team was returning a talented offensive backfield led by junior quarterback Bo Hagan and sophomore running sensation Bishop Strickland. Standout fullback Bobby Giles had graduated from the 1947 squad, a void that sent Enright in search of a capable replacement.

Coach Enright and Coach Bartos sat a few rows up in the wooden stands and observed as Vella and Wilson put Wadiak through a series of light drills in order to gauge his instincts and physical attributes. Vella gave Steve a few handoffs and instructed him to pretend he was exploding through an open hole in the line. Wilson feigned an effort to tackle Wadiak in order to disrupt his running surge. Vella then tossed Wadiak a few passes to test his hands' receptivity to the pigskin.

Wadiak moved through the drills gracefully; he showed no signs of rustiness as a result of sitting aboard the cramped Carolina Creeper for the past couple of days. Vella, a former sprinter in high school, raced Wadiak in 40-yard sprints. When Vella accelerated, he found the stockier Wadiak close by his side, keeping step all the way. Vella knew his coach was looking for a new fullback. A single glimpse of Wadiak's hefty build would lead one to think that fullback was his natural position, but Wadiak's speed reminded Vella more of a breakaway runner than a short-yardage guy.

After about 45 minutes, Enright blew a whistle and told Vella, Wilson, and Wadiak he had seen enough and instructed them to head back to the Field House and shower. As the men were walking across Davis Field, Enright pulled Vella aside and questioned him about the tryout.

"Do you think he can help us out?" Enright asked as Wadiak and Wilson walked on ahead.

"I do," Vella said with assurance. "I think he's a good, tough kid who can play here."

Vella liked the guy. He thought Steve would fit in well with the rest of his teammates. Fitting in with the rest of the guys, many of whom hailed from various regions of the Deep South, would require Chicago-born Wadiak to be confident in his abilities yet humble in disposition. Loudmouth prima donnas were not welcome among veteran Gamecock players. Vella sized up Wadiak as a guy who would not disrupt the team's chemistry.

Back in the locker room, the three men showered and dressed, and it was there that Vella caught his first glimpse of a shirtless Steve Wadiak. Vella was impressed by the physique of the 22-year-old Wadiak—it was a physique chiseled from several years in the gymnasium behind Steve's Chicago home and one refined even further through the disciplined physical training of the Navy.

"I thought I was looking at Charles Atlas," Vella recalled. "He had this muscular barrel chest and a massive neck. Not an ounce of fat on him. Just pure muscle."

After Wadiak showered and dressed, Vella escorted him across the street to the back of the physical education building and into Coach Enright's office, where Wadiak would learn of his fate. Enright wasted no time in telling Steve that he planned to offer him a chance to play for the Gamecocks. The coach then explained how the athletic scholarship program worked.

"We'll pay for your education, your housing, and your meals—and give you a little spending money every month," Enright explained. "What we ask in return is that you go to class, stay out of trouble, and give us everything you got out there on the football field."

Enright also shared that he had a stable of excellent running backs returning to the team and that he couldn't promise Steve any more than a fair shake at cracking the lineup. Enright was offering Steve the greatest opportunity of his life—a free education, free meals, and a chance to join a group of guys who loved playing football. Steve thanked Coach Enright for the offer and told him he should probably square it with his parents, but he fully intended to accept the opportunity put before him.

Enright rose from his chair and moved around his desk to shake the hand of his newest Gamecock. Their handshake marked the beginning of what would become a unique player-coach relationship. As Wadiak started to walk out the door, he turned and appeared slightly embarrassed as he asked Coach Enright a question: "Coach, I wasn't sure how long I would be here, so I didn't pack very many clothes . . . "

Before he could get any further, Enright smiled and cut him off. "Don't worry, my boy. We may be a little short on big All-American lineman around here, but we got plenty of clothes. We can cover you until you get your things shipped down here."

9
Fullback

By the time Steve Wadiak joined the Gamecock football team, the 1948 spring semester at USC was already three weeks in session. Steve was sent to the admissions office with a note from the athletic office, instructing the registrar to enroll Steve in classes. Wadiak was advised to declare his major as physical education, the department chaired by Coach Enright.

Wadiak completed a series of forms at the registrar's office and initiated a request to Chicago Vocational High School for his high school records. His application for admission contained only one question that stumped him. *Religion?* His choices were Baptist, Methodist, Presbyterian, Lutheran, Episcopal, Catholic, and Jewish. The religion of Steve's upbringing, Ukrainian Orthodox, appeared nowhere on the list. Wadiak chose Catholic, the one most familiar to him.

Several of Steve's closest friends from the Burnside neighborhood were Catholic, and Steve and his sister, Jeanette, had attended Mass on many occasions at Our Lady of Hungary Church. Anna Wadiak never objected to Steve and Jeanette's attending Mass with their friends. Her only objection would have been to their electing not to attend church at all.

After putting "Catholic" on his admission form, Steve was assured he would be contacted by the school's priest, Father Frederick H. Suggs, who presided over the Newman Club at the St. Thomas More Center for Catholic Students. The 1948 "Garnet and Black" yearbook explained the purpose of the Newman Club:

The objectives of the Newman Club are the preservation of Catholic culture and providing fellowship for members of the local organization. Meetings are held in Legare College every first and third Tuesday of the month. Socials follow every other meeting, and the hour glass turns many times while eating, dancing, gaming or just playing in general is enjoyed.

The Newman Club became a non-football outlet for Steve to integrate his life with those of fellow campus students. Generally, the Catholic population at this Southern school was comprised of people more like Steve than the rest of the student body. Many of them claimed ethnic backgrounds, and several came from Midwestern or Northeastern hometowns.

Steve regularly attended Mass at St. Peter's Church on Assembly Street. Because the Mass was performed in Latin, Steve could not understand much of what was going on, although the reverent environment of St. Peter's provided a connection to a lifelong commitment to his faith.

Steve signed up for 16 hours of class work. His course load included Grammar and Composition, Introduction to Education, and Art Appreciation, with his remaining classes comprised of offerings from the Physical Education Department. It had been nearly four years since Steve had sat in a traditional classroom. He realized that class work would likely be the biggest adjustment to college life, and he struggled to catch up with the content he'd missed during the first three weeks of classes.

Sitting in his Grammar and Composition class, Steve felt as though the professor were speaking a foreign language as he talked about the conjugation of verbs, prepositional phrases, and dangling participles.

The lessons of his English classes at Chicago Vocational High School were a distant memory, and he was drowning in academia. He confided in a veteran teammate about his struggles, and he was quickly advised to drop the class rather than risk the potential of receiving a failing grade—a consequence that might have an impact on Steve's eligibility to participate in athletics. Steve dropped the class and felt a deep sense of relief.

Spring football practice began within a few days of Wadiak's arrival at USC. The Gamecock squad held six weeks of spring football drills, practicing most weekday afternoons on Melton Field. Initially, Steve was thrown in with a group of younger players, including a handful of fellow freshmen, who, like Steve, had arrived a semester early to take advantage of the repetitions provided in spring drills. One of the early arrivals was Vince Gargano, an offensive lineman from Brooklyn, N.Y.

Enright had used his birddog contacts in the Northeast to locate Gargano, who had completed an outstanding high school career at Brooklyn's Lafayette High School, the same school that produced Major League Baseball Hall of Famer Sandy Koufax. Gargano and another outstanding New York prepster, Walt Shea, were invited to meet Coach Enright and Assistant Coach Bartos at the New Yorker Hotel prior to a football awards banquet in December of 1947.

"Coach Enright offered us a scholarship right there on the spot in the hotel," Gargano recalled. "He also talked us into skipping our high school graduation and coming on down to the university in January and starting our college careers."

Gargano and Shea joined a list of several other Gamecock football players whom Enright had extracted from the Northeast to join the

Gamecocks in prior years—players such as Al Grygo, Dominic Fusci, and Phil Cantore.

Like many of Enright's Northern transplants, Gargano remembers a bit of culture shock the day he arrived in Columbia.

"I remember getting off the train and noticing that there were separate restrooms for whites and blacks. We learned that whites and blacks weren't supposed to walk on the same side of the street. I had never seen anything like that," he recalled.

It was expected that Wadiak would spend a year on the freshman team, but at age 22, his physical maturity made it clear to the coaches that he would be significantly out of place with a group of 18-year-olds fresh out of high school. The coaches quickly determined that, due to Steve's military service, he could forego participation on the freshman squad during his first year, and he was promoted to the varsity squad shortly after spring drills were underway.

The varsity squad returned a significant number of experienced players, and Steve cautiously tried to find his place among the veterans. Players recall that he had a quiet and unassuming nature about him. He was simply trying to fit in. Bill Rutledge, a football fullback and a heavyweight on the Gamecock boxing team, recalled Steve during his earliest days on the football field: "I remember seeing him the first afternoon we were in spring practice. None of us had heard anything about him, and we weren't even sure who he was. He was dressed in uniform, standing all by himself watching everybody else. He was the new guy on the block."

The depth of the USC backfield made it difficult for an unknown Wadiak to get noticed. Midway through spring practice, Coach Enright discussed his backfield with Jake Penland of "The State" newspaper.

I'm pretty well satisfied with the backfield . . . Jack Couch, Harry DeLoach, Ernie Lawhorn and Billy Kincaid are fighting it out for left half and any of the four could be the No. 1 man there. Bishop Strickland will be our right halfback, but Freddie Bargiacchi is right behind him. Red Harrison is a fixture at fullback, and back of him are Bill Rutledge, Dick Frantz and Ashley Phillips, who has been switched from quarterback. Barring injuries, we should be in good shape in the backfield.

There was no mention of Wadiak in the early spring Gamecock depth chart. Steve was quickly positioned as a fullback by the Gamecock coaches. Given his stocky frame and the team's current personnel needs, fullback seemed like the best fit. At fullback, his responsibilities were mostly blocking and carrying the ball on plays designed for short yardage. There were no highlight films available for the Gamecock coaches to see Wadiak's explosive breakaway speed, so in the spring of 1948, his greatest talents remained undiscovered by his coaches. Steve humbly accepted his assignment at fullback and gave everything he had to learning the new position.

Much of the preseason hype centered around Bishop Strickland, a 5'10" 195-lb. rising sophomore. Strickland was an area high school sensation from Mullins, S.C., and one of Enright's most highly touted in-state recruits. Strickland made an immediate impact on the Gamecock squad, leading the team in rushing in 1947 as a freshman with 510 yards and an average of 5.4 yards per carry. Coming off his impressive 1947 season, Strickland had sewn up the starting position at right halfback.

Spring practice concluded with an intra-squad scrimmage at Melton Field at 8 p.m. on Wednesday, March 24, 1948. Admission was 50 cents with proceeds going to fund the activities of the Block C Club, a campus association that consisted only of varsity Gamecock athletes.

Approximately 5,000 spectators showed up for the contest to get an early glimpse of the 1948 Gamecock squad.

When Steve stepped onto Melton Field, he could not believe the number of people who had shown up on a weeknight to watch a scrimmage. Wearing white pants, a garnet jersey, and a leather helmet, he stared wide-eyed at the largest football audience of his life, and he felt a rush of adrenaline as he joined his teammates for warm-up calisthenics.

Earlier in the semester, Steve read in the local newspaper that the South Carolina General Assembly had appropriated $175,000 to increase the seating capacity of Carolina Stadium to 30,000. He could only imagine what it might be like to run out onto a football field with 30,000 fans cheering. The sheer numbers, coupled with the chatter around campus and the city of Columbia, furthered his understanding that he resided in a football-loving community.

Fifty-three varsity football players divided into Red and Black teams for the contest. The Red team backfield featured Wadiak at fullback and his friend Pat Vella at quarterback. Bo Hagan was the starting signal caller for the Black squad. Standout running back Bishop Strickland did not dress for the contest, as he was nursing a bruised knee. Coach Enright did not want to risk further injury to his up-and-coming superstar.

Coach Enright himself had been confined to his home while recovering from an eye infection; he had missed a number of spring workouts and looked forward to returning to the field to assess the progress of his team.

Hagan, a junior from Savannah, Ga., led the Black squad to a 13-0 victory in a game atypical of a spring intra-squad scrimmage—fumbles, penalties, and missed assignments were common. The versatile Hagan was a bright spot for the Gamecocks, connecting on several passing plays while handling the kicking, punting, and punt return chores for his team. The Red team's quarterback, Pat Vella, was knocked out of the game early with a broken nose—a common injury in the 1940s when face masks on helmets were nonexistent.

Wadiak handled the ball only twice in the game. His first run was for 12 yards around right end. His second attempt gained five yards up the middle, thus he spent much of the game on the sidelines watching his teammates perform.

Coming out of spring training, Van Newman, sports editor of "The Gamecock," summarized the outlook for the Gamecocks' crowded backfield, and his comments evidenced the hype around Strickland. Wadiak, however, had made enough of an impression to earn a mention as a possible backup fullback:

> *Melton Field is swarmed with halfbacks in spring practice. Leading the glory-boys is Bishop Strickland, last year's offensive star. If the Bishop proves the type star his teammates up front will play their hearts out for, he could be one of Carolina's greatest backs, rivaling such standouts as Grygo, Stascia, and Clary. Co-captain Jack Crouch is probably the other starter at the other half, but Harry DeLoach who at the end of last season was coming along like a whirl away will play lots of offensive ball.*
>
> *Freddie Bargiacchi is still a fast and elusive runner and will be heard from. Ernie Lawhorn is small but fast and a good passer and will see action, although he may be used primarily on defense. Billy Kincaid is also back.*

Fullback will be Enright's strongest position. Red Harrison, the Jacobs Blocking Trophy winner in S.C., the best linebacker seen in these parts for many a moon and a plunging driving runner will be the top man in this spot. The heavyweight boxing star Billy Rutledge is a good runner at times looking better in this department than Harrison and will be a hard man to keep on the bench. Dependable Dick Frantz is a fine blocker and a hard-running Steve Wadiak will also be around for relief.

As Steve read these words in the campus newspaper, he felt a tinge of disappointment. He knew he could show his coaches and teammates more than they had seen in the spring workouts. He felt out of position at fullback, and he longed for an opportunity to run the football in the open field. A sweep, a reverse, or even a short pass in the flat were the plays he hoped to have called for him. These were the plays that led to his legendary runs in the Chicago sandlots. Instead, he was relegated to off-tackle left, off-tackle right, or the fullback dive. He was accustomed to being the "go-to guy," therefore the spring of 1948 was the first time in years that Steve found himself in the shadows on a football field.

At the end of spring football practice, Enright suggested that Wadiak join the Gamecock track team. He told Steve it would be a good way to meet people and stay in shape, plus he'd get one hour of academic credit for his participation on the team. Wadiak joined Coach Weems Baskin's track team, and his speed quickly earned him a spot in the 100-yard dash.

Wadiak had never been trained as a sprinter, and his 195-lb. frame was not typical for the sport—yet he carded some impressive 100-yard dash times running with the Gamecock cindermen. In an early meet against Davidson College, he posted a time of 10.2, which earned him a third-place finish. He went on to carve a tenth of a second off this time against Clemson for a second-place finish behind teammate Rupert Drews, a speedster from Charleston who was recognizable around campus by his signature thick "Coke-bottle" glasses.

Wadiak recorded his fastest time of the season, a 10.0, against Presbyterian College, which garnered him third place, once again finishing behind his teammate Drews. To put Wadiak's speed in perspective, his 100-yard dash time was only seven-tenths of a second shy of the world record set in 1948 by U.S. Olympic gold medalist Mel Patton.

Having completed his first semester of college, Wadiak returned to Chicago for the summer. Academically, he had struggled, posting three D's, a B, and a withdrawal from his English class. His effort on the football field had drawn the attention, but not the affection, of his coaches. He struggled to distinguish himself in a crowded Gamecock backfield, which limited his chances to handle the football. Knowing he was out of position at fullback, Steve vowed to return to Columbia stronger, faster, and more determined. His workouts became more intense, his personal resolve more focused. All he needed was a chance, and when it came, he would be ready.

Back in Chicago, Wadiak described his time in Columbia to his buddies, telling them of warm weather, attractive co-eds, and the football-crazy people about town. His friends were envious, and as summer stretched across the Midwest, he could not wait to return to his newfound home.

10
Left Halfback

In late August of 1948, 60 varsity football candidates began preseason workouts in the sweltering heat and humidity in Columbia, S.C. Each day, the players met for a hearty breakfast at the athletic training table in Stewart Hall. The first of two lengthy daily workouts on Melton Field began shortly after breakfast.

The initial week of practice consisted of lots of calisthenics and conditioning designed to help coaches determine who had kept in shape over the summer. The combination of intense physical exertion and the suffocating heat left many players on the sideline heaving their breakfasts before the end of the morning workout.

Coach Rex Enright had four weeks to get his boys ready for their opening game against the Newberry Indians. The Gamecocks' eight-game 1948 schedule was highly competitive and included road contests against Furman, Tulane, West Virginia, and Tulsa. In addition to their home opener against Newberry, Carolina would host archrival Clemson, as well as Maryland and Wake Forest. Despite the schedule, optimism remained high in the Gamecock camp as 37 lettermen returned from the previous year's 6-2-1 team.

A week after the 60 veterans began workouts, another 40 freshmen football players joined their upperclassmen teammates. The first order of business for the freshmen was a longstanding Gamecock football ritual that would involve the new recruits parting with their hair. The unsuspecting freshmen were met on the first day of practice by upperclassmen armed with scissors, razors, and a vicious gleam in their eyes.

The football players were not experienced barbers, so they left the freshmen with butchered haircuts—and that made the event all the more enjoyable. The upperclassmen razzed and chided the freshmen throughout the initiation ritual—not surprising since they'd all experienced it during freshman year. Head shaving was a rite of passage for admission to the Gamecock football fraternity.

Steve Wadiak had already been on campus for a semester, yet he was still technically a freshman and not exempt from the head-shaving requirement. As the scalping began, Steve stood to the side and observed as locks of various lengths and colors began to litter the floor of the Gamecock locker room at Carolina Field House. Steve had a head full of thick, neatly combed, wavy brown hair with which he had no intention of parting.

One of the scissor-carrying veterans caught Steve's attention and grinned as he made a move toward him, indicating that Steve was next up in the barber's chair. Steve did not return the smile but simply stared back through his piercing hazel eyes at the approaching teammate.

In the short time Wadiak had been at Carolina, he had earned a reputation as a no-nonsense guy. He never goofed off in practice and ran every drill and every play with an intensity that quickly earned the respect of teammates and coaches. He was living with the other USC athletes in the Preston dormitory across from Melton and Davis Field. Regarded as a quiet guy who didn't bother anybody and likewise didn't want to be bothered by others, Steve garnered only one complaint against him from his roommates—that he would sometimes come in at night and disturb their sleep by turning on a light and doing a few sets of push-ups before retiring.

As the armed teammate stepped closer, Wadiak simply shook his head from side to side, indicating that he had no intention of voluntarily parting with his locks. Wadiak was a 22-year-old Navy veteran, not an 18-year-old kid who had spent the summer cruising around town with his high school sweetheart and bragging about his football scholarship to USC. When it was apparent that Wadiak was not going to submit to this humiliating ritual, the would-be barber turned away and set his sights on another freshman. Nothing was ever said by anyone about Wadiak exempting the head-shaving requirement. It was clear to his teammates that Wadiak was not the typical freshman.

Jake Penland of "The State" newspaper predicted that the 1948 Gamecocks would likely win six or seven games. Head Coach Rex Enright was more guarded in his optimism, stating, "We are not predicting anything great for our squad, but we do believe that our personnel has those necessary possibilities to develop into a winning combination that would be difficult to stop or run over."

As the Gamecocks began contact drills, injuries began to mount, and trainer Jess Alderman kept busy trying to help a number of players with pulled muscles, bruises, and strains that were typical of the early days of practice. Injuries, along with a decision by sophomore running back Freddie Bargiacchi to forgo his college football career for an opportunity to play professional baseball with the Memphis Chicks, opened a door for Wadiak. His impressive times in the 100-yard dash the previous spring did not go unnoticed by the coaching staff, and he began to get some looks for the left halfback position.

On September 17, only six days before the Gamecocks' opening game, Enright scheduled an unpublicized scrimmage against the University of North Carolina in Chapel Hill. Enright was close friends with UNC Head Coach Carl Snavely, and this was the second year in a row the two had decided to schedule a clandestine preseason scrimmage that was closed to media and fans. The two teams would not face each other in the regular season, although both belonged to the 17-member Southern Conference.

The scrimmage was supposed to be a secret, but with the Gamecocks conspicuously absent from their daily routine at Melton Field, word spread quickly around town that the team had traveled to Chapel Hill for the practice game. Fans were eager to hear how they fared against "the other Carolina," yet few informative details flowed from the event.

The USC-UNC encounter gave the coaches a chance to gauge the true progress of their teams. Players looked forward to having physical contact with someone other than their own teammates. The Gamecocks were not full strength going into the scrimmage, as two of their key offensive weapons, halfback Bishop Strickland and end Red Wilson, did not dress because of nagging injuries.

The Tar Heels were loaded with talent and expected to be one of 1948's premier college football teams. They would fulfill their preseason expectations, winning nine of their 10 regular season contests in 1948, including wins over football powerhouses Texas, Georgia, LSU, and Tennessee.

UNC was led by Charlie "Choo Choo" Justice, one of the most prodigious running backs in the college game. Justice was a high school star from Asheville, N.C., where he played for Lee Edwards High School and averaged an amazing 25 yards per carry in 1942, his senior season. His performance made him one of the most sought after high school recruits in the country. On Christmas Day in 1942, however, Justice received his draft notice. He was allowed to defer his enlistment until his high school graduation in June of 1943, at which time he joined the United States Navy and was assigned to Bainbridge Naval Base in Maryland. Shortly before leaving for Bainbridge, Justice married his high school sweetheart, Sarah Hunter.

At Bainbridge, Justice quickly distinguished himself as an athlete playing for the base football team. He was the only high school boy on a team that was mostly comprised of college and pro players. While Justice was playing at Bainbridge, a Baltimore sports reporter noted that he ran the football like "a runaway train" and tagged him with the nickname "Choo Choo"—a fitting name for Justice, whose father had spent his life working as a railroad engineer.

At the end of World War II, college coaches scrambled to sign the plentiful supply of talented football players being discharged from the service. Justice attracted attention from all the major schools, including Notre Dame and Southern Cal. He received written scholarship offers from 22 schools and a host of oral offers from others.

As Justice pondered his options, two factors drove his final decision—he wanted to play football in the South, and he wanted his wife, Sarah, to have the opportunity to attend college with him. Both North Carolina and South Carolina were actively recruiting Justice, and he was initially leaning toward the Gamecocks.

Reportedly, Justice wrote a letter to both North and South Carolina offering to attend their school using funds from the GI Bill, if they would pay for his wife's education. UNC's Coach Snavely was skeptical about signing the war veteran, and Justice recalled the recruiting process and his decision to attend UNC:

> *I don't think he (Snavely) liked the looks of me. I only weighed 155. The first time I ever met him, my wife, Sarah, and I got in the car with him in High Point. Coach Snavely asked my wife to sit in the back . . . he wanted to talk to me. The only thing he ever said, though, was "How much do you weigh, Charlie?"*
>
> *We went to Winston-Salem for lunch, then on to Chapel Hill. He*

> *didn't even talk to me about a scholarship then. He left me in Chapel Hill and went somewhere else, but some alumni kept pushing the thing.*
>
> *I was going to South Carolina, but my brother Jack talked to me and told me that since North Carolina was where I was going to live, I should go there.*
>
> ("Unforgettable Days in Southern Football" by Clyde Bolton, Strode Publishers, 1974)

Despite Snavely's low-key recruiting approach, Justice and his wife enrolled at UNC, and he began a college football career that would lead him to iconic status among the Tar Heel faithful. During his four-year career at UNC, Justice racked up 4,883 yards of total offense—a record that stood until 1994—and he finished second in the Heisman Trophy balloting in 1948 and 1949.

In October of 1950, Dr. Samuel Tilden Habel used Justice as a sermon illustration from the pulpit of the First Baptist Church in Chapel Hill: "When we call on Charlie Justice to go all the way, we are placing on him a great responsibility—asking him to give everything, all his mind and all his body in going all the way," he preached. "Likewise, you should go all the way in your work or profession, and above all else, go all the way in Christian living."

Among the congregation that day was Charlie Justice.

Prior to Justice's arrival at UNC, the Tar Heels had never appeared in a bowl game, but in three of Justice's four years at UNC, they went to postseason bowl games. Today, an eight-and-a-half-foot statue stands outside the entrance to UNC's Kenan Stadium commemorating the athletic accomplishments and heroic status of Charlie "Choo Choo" Justice.

The Gamecocks were outmanned in the scrimmage against the vastly more talented Tar Heels. Throughout the day, Enright was frustrated by his team's inability to move the football against their opponent who consistently controlled the line of scrimmage. With Strickland sidelined, Enright was looking for an answer.

Late in the scrimmage, backup quarterback Pat Vella made a recommendation to his coach.

"I suggested that he give Wadiak a try at halfback," Vella recalled. Running quarterback for the reserves, Vella had seen firsthand the explosiveness of Wadiak. He knew Steve just needed a chance to showcase his talent.

"Does he know the plays?" Enright questioned.

"Yeah, he knows the plays," Vella replied.

Enright consented, for he had nothing to lose, and he was somewhat embarrassed that his team was not more competitive against Coach Snavely's Tar Heels.

Near the end of the long afternoon, Wadiak was summoned onto the field to join a Gamecock offense directed by Vella. The quarterback stared straight at Wadiak and called the play: "Left quickie on two." It was Vella's way of saying to his friend, "Now is your time to show them what you got."

Left quickie was a play designed as a direct handoff to Wadiak, the left halfback, who was to follow his blocking through a hole in the left side of the line. It was designed to pick up a few yards and build offensive momentum. Wadiak took the handoff from Vella, exploded through a small seam in the line, and quickly darted outside. He turned on his sprinter's speed and left a bevy of unsuspecting Tar Heel defenders in his wake as he raced 60 yards for a surprising Gamecock score.

As Wadiak raced toward the goal line, several of the Gamecock players on the sideline took notice and began to cheer. It was a rare bright spot in an otherwise disappointing scrimmage. Al Grygo, a former Gamecock and NFL player with the Chicago Bears, was serving as backfield coach and standing next to Enright when Wadiak took off on his open-field jaunt. Enright turned to Grygo and asked, "Where have we been hiding him?"

After an exchange of the football, the Gamecock offensive unit stepped back on the field. Enright wanted to see if Wadiak's run was a fluke, so he told Vella to run him again. Vella once again called "left quickie," and Wadiak repeated his feat, breaking a couple of tackles at the line of scrimmage and dashing 70 yards in the open field for his second touchdown.

As his Gamecock squad celebrated Wadiak's second consecutive scoring run, Enright looked across the field and caught a glance from a surprised Coach Snavely on UNC's sideline. For a moment, Snavely must have thought his superstar Justice had slipped on a Gamecock jersey. The back-to-back breakaway runs by Wadiak were characteristic of the kind of runs that propelled Justice to All-American status in 1948 and 1949.

On the bus ride back to Columbia, Enright sat in his customary front seat and took out a pencil and began to mark on his depth chart. He erased Wadiak's name from the fullback slot and penciled him in as a backup at left halfback, behind the team's co-captain, Jack Crouch.

Enright's mind began to wander as he replayed Wadiak's memorable showing in Chapel Hill. He felt a sense of excitement as he pondered the potential of a Gamecock backfield featuring Strickland at right halfback and Wadiak at left halfback. The coach also made a note to send a message to his trusted birddog, Bill Milner, and let him know about the progress of his discovery from the sandlots of Chicago.

11
Debut

Rex Enright's 1948 USC football team opened its season against the Newberry College Indians—a small liberal arts college founded by the Lutheran Church and located about 30 miles northwest of Columbia. The Gamecocks had historically dominated Newberry on the football field, winning 10 of the 11 previous encounters. The coach of the Indians was Billy Laval, who had previous successful stints as the head coach of South Carolina (1928-34) and Furman (1921-27). Newberry was expected to be an easy opening night "tune-up" for Carolina.

Game time was 8:15 p.m., but many of the Gamecock players began to wander into their locker room at Carolina Field House in the early afternoon, eager to get their season underway. Wadiak stepped in front of his locker and admired his neatly pressed, garnet Gamecock jersey bearing the number 37. A clean pair of white football pants lay alongside his helmet. A pair of white athletic socks was stuffed inside Steve's black football cleats. He looked around at a locker room lined with uniforms for all 60 players. The scene was a stark contrast to his high school and sandlot playing days.

Anticipation and excitement filled the city of Columbia and the USC campus in the weeks prior to the start of the football season. Sports pages chronicled the details of every Gamecock preseason workout. Marching band and cheerleader practice, pep rallies, and the general chatter among students combined to build enthusiasm for the opening of the Gamecocks' season.

Once the team was dressed in its game uniforms, Coach Enright gathered the players for a brief word. Never one for "rah rah" speeches, the low-key Enright simply told his squad to execute the things they had worked on in practice, and the score would take care of itself. The team huddled in a circle and recited the Lord's Prayer before boarding a bus that carried them the short two-mile distance to the State Fairgrounds, home of Carolina Stadium.

Carolina Stadium had a seating capacity of roughly 17,000, but rarely were its wooden bleachers filled for any game other than its annual contest against archrival Clemson. Over the summer, lights were installed, and the game against Newberry would be the first night game played at Carolina Stadium. An adult ticket to the game cost $2.60, while grammar school students could enter the game for 50 cents as part of a program called the "knot-hole" gang. An estimated 14,000 fans were expected for the 1948 season opener. It was a comfortable but warm evening in Columbia as the sun began to set over the stadium's west stands, and the two teams went through pregame workouts.

Shortly before kickoff, Gamecock Co-captains Al Faress and Jack Couch met the Newberry captains at midfield for the coin toss, won by the Gamecocks, who elected to receive. On the game's opening offensive play, Bishop Strickland fumbled the ball away on the Gamecocks' 38-yard line. Newberry, however, couldn't generate any offense and was forced to punt. Carolina took over on its 15-yard line.

Backfield Coach Al Grygo grabbed Wadiak by the arm and told him to be ready for action on the Gamecocks' next series. After two consecutive 30-yard runs through the middle of the Newberry line by fullback Red Harrison, Grygo sent Steve into the game to replace senior Co-captain Crouch at left halfback.

On Wadiak's first play of his collegiate football career, he took a quick pitch from quarterback Bo Hagan and ran around left end for a gain of 12 yards. He felt a rush of adrenaline with his initial physical contact. As he pulled himself up from the ground, he was warmed by the applause and cheers of the partisan Gamecock fans. Trotting back to the huddle, Steve heard the public address announcer call his name: "Wadiak on the carry for the Gamecocks."

It was a simple 12-yard pick-up on a routine run around end. Steve had made many more spectacular and dazzling runs in his high school and sandlot days; however, none of those had been witnessed by more than a handful of neighborhood well-wishers. Steve's modest gain against Newberry marked the beginning of an entirely new and much larger stage for him to showcase his athletic abilities.

On the next play, quarterback Hagan connected with Red Wilson for a touchdown pass, and the Gamecocks jumped on top of the Indians 6-0. After a stalled Newberry possession, the Gamecocks took over and quickly scored again, propelling them to a 13-0 early first-quarter lead.

On the ensuing Carolina offensive series, Wadiak re-entered the game. Strickland brought the crowd to its feet with a dazzling 79-yard touchdown run that was subsequently nullified by a Gamecock clipping penalty. On the next play, Wadiak burst through the line for 30 yards, running over a couple of defenders in the process. It was a run that sent a buzz through the stands. Who is this Wadiak fellow? Where did he come from? Gamecock fans began to search their programs to find out what little information was available about Number 37. The program contained only Wadiak's vital information:

- Height—5'9"
- Weight—193 lbs.
- Hometown—Chicago, Ill.

In the fourth quarter, Steve broke into the end zone on a two-yard run for his first score as a Gamecock and finished the game with 60 yards on five rushing attempts. By the end of the game, the Gamecocks had dismantled the outmanned Indians and captured a lopsided 46-0 victory.

In 1948, colleges were just beginning to abandon the one-platoon system, in which the majority of players played both offense and defense. At South Carolina, lack of depth forced the team to retain a hybrid version of the one-platoon system, with its best athletes playing both ways. Wadiak's hard-hitting style had the Gamecock defensive coaches begging for more of his time. Against Newberry, Wadiak saw action as a defensive back and also was a member of the Gamecock special teams.

Steve loved the physical nature of the game; in modern football terminology, he'd likely be referred to as a "headhunter." He confided to a sports writer that he liked playing defense as much as offense. Enright knew, however, that Wadiak's offensive skills were far too valuable for him to risk injury trying to make tackles. There were other, more expendable players to perform that duty, so Wadiak was used sparingly on defense.

During the week following the opening game, local media representatives scrambled to find out all they could about the relatively unknown Wadiak. It was the beginning of a history of "misinformation" about the Chicago native that would continue throughout his college career. Local media incorrectly referred to him as a sophomore transfer from a junior college. His age was reported as 20 when in fact he was 22. His mysterious high school career remained a source of speculation and erroneous reporting.

Despite the fact that they knew very little about his background, local sports pundits quickly began to tout Steve as the next up-and-coming star of the Gamecocks. Van Newman, sports editor of "The Gamecock," referred to him as the "Chicago rocket." Others called him Rex Enright's secret weapon.

Wadiak quickly became a fan favorite with the Gamecock faithful. Students began to recognize him around campus, especially female students, who were drawn to his rugged good looks and cagey background. Surprised by the attention, Steve felt as though he had done little or nothing to earn his growing stardom.

One devout Gamecock fan would quickly become Steve's greatest admirer. As an adolescent, Cliff Turner began showing up day after day at the Gamecock football practices at Melton Field in the early 1940s. His loud shouts and antics were noticeable to all the coaches and players. It was obvious from his nonstop and sometimes incoherent speech that Cliff was developmentally disabled.

After practice, Cliff would follow the players to the Gamecock locker room, running up to many of them and punching them in the shoulder while repeating the phrase, "I know you. I know you." It was his way of connecting with the players and letting them know he was on their side.

The kind-hearted Rex Enright was drawn to Cliff and figured if he was going to keep showing up every day, he should probably put his support to good use. Enright unofficially adopted Cliff as a part of the Gamecock football team, extending to him nearly unrestricted access to coaches and players. The example that Enright set in his treatment of Cliff communicated to the players that Cliff was to be treated with respect, no matter how obnoxious or annoying his behavior might become. Secretly, Enright hoped that seeing Cliff and his struggles might be a motivational lift for his boys that would help them keep the game of football in perspective.

Cliff's outgoing personality made him known throughout the

downtown area of Columbia. Everybody knew Cliff, and most everyone loved Cliff. Downtown merchants were kind to him and rarely allowed him to pay for anything. It was common for Cliff to bypass a long line at a movie ticket counter and walk directly into the theater smiling broadly as he passed by ushers and other patrons.

On the Carolina campus, Cliff became a fixture at all sporting events. At football practice, he would join the team for calisthenics as the Gamecock squad warmed up at Melton Field. At halftime of basketball games, he provided entertainment with a lay-up routine that brought laughter to the Gamecock fans. Springtime meant that Cliff would heckle umpires and opponents at baseball games on Davis Field.

Cliff's constant wanderings around Columbia knew no boundaries. Coach Enright and his family lived at 2500 Heyward St., a little over a mile from campus, and routinely, Cliff would show up at their home uninvited. Coach Enright's daughter Alice recalled one of Cliff's unexpected visits: "I had just come out of the shower, and I was still in my slip when I saw Cliff standing in the middle of our house," she said. "He just looked at me and poked me on the shoulder and said, 'You Enright's daughter.'"

Coach Enright knew that Cliff helped keep his team loose. Former Gamecock sports publicist and longtime South Carolina football historian Don Barton remembers a day in which Cliff broke up the intensity of a long afternoon practice.

"One day, the team wasn't practicing very well, and Coach Enright had about all he could take," Barton recalled. "In a move of desperation, Coach Enright took off his whistle and gave it to Cliff, and in front of his team pronounced Cliff as the new head coach."

Barton explained that Cliff was stunned by the recognition, and that he turned to Enright and said, "Me, Coach?" Enright confirmed his decision.

Cliff looked squarely at Assistant Coach Frank "Punchy" Johnson. A former standout athlete at the University of Georgia, Johnson earned his nickname through a history of absent-minded behavior. He was the head basketball coach at USC, and a legendary story asserts that Johnson once drove his team to the wrong school for a game. He was known to yell at players who weren't even on the field at the time, often frustrating his pupils.

The 1948 Carolina Gamecocks: On the second row is Steve Wadiak (No. 33) with his arm around Cliff Turner.

(Photo courtesy of USC Archives)

Cliff saw the opportunity to do something that he had heard the players talking about many times. As he looked at Coach Johnson, he announced to the team with a big smile on his face, "Me coach. I fire him," and he pointed directly at Coach Johnson.

The entire team and coaching staff, including the likeable and good-natured Coach Johnson, burst into laughter.

Cliff suffered with every Gamecock loss and celebrated each victory. He constantly badgered any player he thought wasn't hustling or giving his all. He also had an eye for talent, and Wadiak's skill and passion for the game quickly caught Cliff's attention.

Each day as the Gamecocks exited their locker room at the Field House, Cliff would wait for Steve, and when he saw him, he would immediately run up to him, give Steve his customary punch in the arm, and offer to carry Wadiak's helmet while they crossed Davis Field toward Melton Field. While some of the guys grew weary of Cliff, Steve remained patient with him at all times, treating Cliff with the same level of respect he extended to teammates and coaches.

Next up on the Gamecocks' schedule was a 100-mile trip to Greenville, S.C., to take on their first Southern Conference opponent, the Furman Purple Hurricanes. The game turned out to be a hard-fought defensive battle in front of 15,000 fans at Furman's Sirrine Stadium.

Despite the defensive struggle, the game did not lack excitement. Gamecock standout end Red Wilson was hit in the face on the opening kickoff and suffered a badly broken nose. He recalled that he stayed in the game, even though he was bleeding like a "stuck hog." Later in the game, Wilson was blocking downfield when a Furman halfback attempted to put a knee in Wilson's bloody face. Wilson took off after the culprit and chased him nearly 80 yards into the opposite end zone where he proceeded to pummel the Furman player with a flurry of wild punches. The two players were finally separated, and Wilson was ejected from the game.

The Gamecocks managed to score a winning touchdown in the final three minutes to secure a 7-0 win. The defense continued to play well, as it had not been scored upon in eight quarters of competition.

Following the win over Furman, the Gamecocks traveled to New Orleans to take on a talented Tulane squad. After battling to a scoreless tie at halftime, the Carolina team was defeated 14-0. Coach Enright was not overly disappointed by his team's performance against a powerful Tulane team that went on to win nine of its 10 games, including a 46-0 thrashing of in-state rival LSU. Next up for the Gamecocks would be their annual contest against archrival Clemson.

No game meant as much to the entire Gamecock faithful as their battle against Clemson. As the Gamecocks returned on their charter flight from New Orleans, the attention of coaches and players turned immediately to the biggest game of the year.

On their first day of practice in preparation for Clemson, the Gamecocks' number one fan and unofficial assistant coach, Cliff Turner, made sure each and every player understood the importance of the contest. As the Gamecocks filed out of their Field House locker room and strode toward practice, Cliff badgered them with his normal shoulder punches. Instead of his familiar chant of, "I know you. I know you," this time of year called for a special message from Cliff: "Beat Clemson. Beat Clemson. Beat Clemson!"

12
Fumble

The South Carolina-Clemson football rivalry began on a rainy Thursday morning in November of 1896. What started as a "sideshow," or a minor attraction at the South Carolina State Fair, grew over the next 100 years to become arguably the most significant annual event in the Palmetto State.

The 2,000 spectators who attended the first Carolina-Clemson game paid 25 cents admission. Today, the rivalry game is played before 80,000 fans, and the face value of a ticket has soared to $75. When it was rumored in 1952 that the two teams might not play each other, the South Carolina General Assembly stepped in and passed a resolution ordering the game to be played. This has helped establish the Carolina-Clemson rivalry as the third longest uninterrupted NCAA Division I football series in the country.

The University of South Carolina was founded in 1801 and for nearly 80 years enjoyed its status as the state's largest and most notable public college. In the mid-1880s, Benjamin "Pitchfork" Tillman emerged as the leader of the agrarian movement in South Carolina and quickly asserted that the people of the state were underserved in the area of agricultural education. Tillman led an effort to establish a separate institution that would better serve the state's farming needs. In presenting his case for the new agricultural institution, Tillman stated that the existing school in Columbia was for "the sons of lawyers and of the well-to-do, who sneered at the agriculture students as if they were hayseeds." This would be one of the first in a century full of barbs tossed back and forth between supporters of the two schools.

Thomas Green Clemson came to the Upstate of South Carolina in 1838 when he married Anna Maria Calhoun, daughter of famous South Carolina statesman John C. Calhoun. Upon Clemson's death in 1888, he left his sizeable plantation and a significant portion of his assets to establish an educational institution that would focus on teaching scientific agriculture and mechanical arts to students in South Carolina. Pursuant to Clemson's wishes, the Clemson Agricultural College opened in 1893 as an all-male military school. The school remained all-male until 1955, when it was changed to a civilian co-ed institution.

With Clemson College taking over the responsibility for agricultural education, the University of South Carolina lost students, as well as much-needed federal funding. Its declining enrollment led to the university's being downgraded in name from the University of South Carolina to South Carolina College. While running for governor in 1890, Tillman boldly called for South Carolina College to close its doors permanently, throwing additional fuel on an already simmering fire between the two schools. Travis Haney and Larry Williams, in "Classic Clashes of the Carolina-Clemson Football Rivalry," aptly summarized the environment at the beginning of this infamous rivalry:

> *So, there was plenty of bad blood already present when the two schools took up this new, violent sport. The gridiron became an instant battleground for all the hostilities and grudges of people with clashing ideas and passions.*

Over the years, the rivalry grew in popularity and intensity. On both campuses, the days leading up to the big game were marked by spirited ceremonies that typically involved some type of public desecration of a replica of the opposing school's mascot. Until 1960, the game was played in Columbia on a Thursday during State Fair week, which was officially established as a state holiday. Despite the expanding capacity of Carolina Stadium, it would never be large enough to hold all who wished to attend the game.

Clemson dominated the early years of the football rivalry, winning 27 of the first 44 contests leading up to the 1948 game. With Coach Rex Enright's arrival at USC in 1938, the Gamecocks became more competitive. On the day he accepted the head-coaching job at Carolina, Enright was given clear instruction about the importance of defeating Clemson. The new coach learned very quickly that while every game mattered, wins over Clemson would have the greatest direct impact on his job security.

Enright's preparation for the rivalry game was meticulous. Annually, he assigned trusted assistant, Ted Petoskey to scout the Tigers in each of their games leading up to Big Thursday. Enright and his staff spent late hours after practice going over game films looking for any tendencies or weaknesses they might exploit in the Clemson team.

Clemson employed the single-wing offense—a complex scheme that was originated by legendary college football coach Glenn "Pop" Warner. The single wing included an unbalanced line and featured a quartet of backs—a quarterback, a fullback, a tailback, and a wingback. The success of the single wing relied on a center who was adept at snapping the football to any one of the backs who might be in motion as the play started. The offense then consisted of a series of deceptive motions designed to confuse defenders, and it oftentimes would leave fans and referees confused as to which player was carrying the football.

Clemson was 3-0 coming into the 1948 game, with wins over Presbyterian College, North Carolina State, and an impressive 21-7 road victory over Mississippi State. The Tigers were led by All-American back Bobby Gage, who, during the previous season, finished third in the nation in total offense. Gage was a versatile athlete who was skilled at running, passing, and kicking the football, in addition to being one of the Tigers' top defenders.

Clemson's colorful Head Coach Frank Howard was in attendance at South Carolina's victory over Furman on the first Friday night in October. Howard was keenly aware of the need not to give the Gamecocks any further motivation for their upcoming rival game, so he was glowing in his praises of the Gamecocks after watching them narrowly defeat Furman 7-0.

Howard told Jake Penland of "The State," "Carolina looks much better than last year. The team is better organized. I wouldn't be surprised to see them in a big bowl. I don't see anybody on their schedule that they'll lose to."

When Penland pressed Howard about whether or not his bold prediction would mean his Clemson team would lose to the Gamecocks, Coach Howard validated his claim. "Aw, we can't beat those Gamecocks," he answered. "They're too strong, and they've got too many reserves." Penland noted that despite the fact that Howard thought his team didn't have a chance in the State Fair classic, he still planned to go through with the game.

Howard concluded, "We've got hotel reservations in Columbia, and it wouldn't make much sense to pay for all those rooms and not use them."

Coach Enright also took part in downplaying his team's chances, noting that his squad was severely hampered by injuries to a number of key players. Running back Bishop Strickland was admitted to the campus infirmary with a severe sinus infection, key defender Len Ekimoff and fullback Red Harrison were injured in the Tulane game, and quarterback

Bo Hagan was battling the lingering effects of a charley horse. Enright said, "It'll be a long road in getting ready for Clemson."

Despite the injuries, Enright put his team through a series of spirited workouts leading up to the game. A portion of their practices were held in the outfield of Columbia's City Park, home of the Columbia Reds minor league baseball team. The location allowed Enright and his staff more privacy than their normal practice site located in the heart of the Carolina campus.

The 1948 game was Wadiak's first against the Tigers. Twenty-six of his teammates were natives of South Carolina, and they made certain that Steve and the other non-South Carolina natives understood the importance of the rivalry game. It wasn't until Steve stepped onto the playing field of Carolina Stadium on game day, however, that he fully grasped the significance of the contest.

The stadium had seats for roughly 17,000 fans, yet on this beautiful and clear fall day, nearly 25,000 fans were jammed into the facility. Portable bleachers were added to the end zones, and a significant number of standing-room-only tickets were sold. A few thousand fans were turned away at the gates. The atmosphere was electric, and Steve felt his adrenaline level reaching an all-time high. He believed he had been preparing all his life for a game like this.

Four minutes into the game, with the ball on the Gamecock 39-yard line, USC quarterback Bo Hagan lateralled the ball to Wadiak who started to run wide around right end. As he turned upfield, five Tiger defenders closed in on him. Fullback Red Harrison threw a block that occupied two of the pursuers. Wadiak burst back to his left, leaving the other three Tigers grasping for a piece of him. As a Tiger defender closed in around mid-field, Wadiak came to a momentary stop, causing the would-be tackler to flail unsuccessfully at the spot where he thought Wadiak would be. Steve then cut sharply to his left and sprinted downfield. By the time the Tiger defense caught up with him, Wadiak had raced 43 yards to the Clemson 25-yard line.

The crowd erupted. It was the biggest run of Steve's young Gamecock career. Two plays later, quarterback Hagan fired a pass over the middle to his favorite target, Red Wilson, who collected it at the 12-yard line. Wilson spun to his right and dashed into the end zone. Bayard Pickett's extra point gave South Carolina a 7-0 lead.

Clemson struggled to get its single-wing offense in sync in the first half. Despite the deceptive nature of the offense with all of its fakes, reverses, and trickery, South Carolina's defense consistently showed up at just the right spot to slow down the powerful Clemson backfield. The Gamecock defense held Clemson scoreless in the first half and enjoyed a 7-0-halftime lead.

With the final seconds of the third quarter ticking away, the Tigers got a much- needed break. Clemson's Dick Hendley launched a 47-yard punt that was fielded by Bishop Strickland around the Gamecock 10-yard line. Strickland started to cut across the field but was hit squarely in the midsection by Clemson's Phil Prince, jarring the ball loose and sending Strickland somersaulting through the air. The fumble was recovered by the Tigers, deep in Gamecock territory.

Three plays later, fullback Fred Cone attempted to score from the two-yard line on a dive play. When he appeared to be stopped at the line of scrimmage, he spun to his left and shuffled the ball to teammate Carol Cox, who jogged untouched into the Gamecock end zone. After a missed extra point, USC held a slim 7-6 lead with a quarter left to play.

The Gamecocks started their next drive on their own 28-yard line. After two runs by Strickland, Carolina faced a third-and-one situation. USC lined up in its typical straight T-formation with Wadiak at left halfback. Eight Clemson defensemen crowded the line of scrimmage as quarterback Hagan turned and handed the ball off to Wadiak. A Clemson defender broke through the line and closed in to make the tackle, but the quick-footed Wadiak darted sharply to his left and turned on his speed, sprinting 46 yards before he was forced out of bounds on the Clemson 17-yard line.

A nervous Coach Enright stood on the sideline and puffed on one of several cigarettes he had lit during the game. He knew that if his boys could push across another score, the game would likely be secure, given the stellar play of his defense.

The Gamecocks' ground attack with Wadiak and Strickland advanced the ball to the three-yard line. Earlier in the game, Strickland had fumbled, and Enright knew they could not afford to lose this scoring opportunity. He sent in a play that had worked earlier in the game—a quick pitch to Wadiak, who would run around right end led by the blocking of his two backfield mates, Strickland and fullback Harrison.

The play was broken from the snap. The interior of the Gamecock offensive line had collapsed, and Clemson's defensive ends were in the Gamecock backfield before Hagan could even turn to make the pitch. Hagan proceeded with the toss to Wadiak who was moving to his right across the backfield. Wadiak ran only a couple of steps before a Tiger defender grabbed his jersey slowing him down. Clemson's Johnny Poulos then rammed his shoulder into Wadiak's right arm, causing Steve to lose the football. Poulos chased the ball down and recovered it at the Clemson 12-yard line, putting an end to the Gamecock drive.

Moments earlier, the Gamecock fans were on their feet cheering wildly over the breakaway run by Wadiak. They had been silenced by his mistake. The fans knew how close they had come to finishing off their rivals—only to have their chance fumbled away by the normally sure-handed Wadiak.

As Steve trotted toward the sideline, he felt an enormous weight of disappointment. He had let his teammates down. He had let the fans down. He had let his coach down. He could only hope he would get a chance to redeem himself.

Clemson's next drive ended when Fred Cone's 23-yard field goal attempt sailed wide to the right, the miss allowing the Gamecocks to cling to a slim 7-6 lead with six minutes left in the game.

Carolina took over, hoping to keep the ball away from Clemson and secure the win. Unable to get a first down, Hagan dropped back to punt on fourth-and-one from the Gamecock 29-yard line. Against Mississippi State, Clemson had blocked a punt in a key situation. Hoping for another block, Coach Howard sent the Tiger defense on an all-out rush.

Once again, it was Phil Prince who came up with the big play for the Tigers. Prince shed his blocker and raced directly toward Hagan. He thrust both his arms straight up in the air as he neared Hagan and leaped toward the spot where he expected the kick to be launched. The ball caught Prince's arm just below his right wrist and ricocheted toward the end zone. Clemson's Oscar Thompson scooped up the ball and ran it in for the score, escorted by a handful of jubilant teammates. Clemson led 13-7 with four minutes to play.

On the USC sideline, Steve Wadiak buckled his chinstrap and readied himself for a chance to make up for his critical fumble. On the Gamecocks' first play of the ensuing series, Hagan under threw a pass down the sideline that was intercepted by Clemson's Bobby Gage. Clemson's 13-7 victory was secure. Steve Wadiak would have to wait another year for his chance at redemption.

As the deflated Gamecock fans exited the stadium, Wadiak sat slumped underneath the west stands, waiting for the bus to take the team back to its locker room at Carolina Field House. He had played hard, rushing for 91 yards on 10 attempts, but when he had the chance to secure a win for his team, he failed to deliver. He showered and went back to his room at the Preston dormitory, hoping he would wake up Friday morning and know it had all been a bad dream.

The Gamecocks could not recover from the devastation of the narrow loss to Clemson. They would manage only one victory in their final four games, finishing the year with a disappointing 3-5 record. Although he may not have seen it at the time, one of the few bright spots in the 1948 season was Wadiak's emergence as a future Gamecock star.

Starting with the first practice after the Clemson loss, Wadiak was driven by a desire to never again let his teammates down. He practiced with a vengeance, running every drill and play with all-out abandon. When practice ended, he remained on the field for extra work. At one point, Coach Enright approached Wadiak and told him he was practicing too hard, and he needed to dial back his intensity. This was something Enright could not recall ever having to tell another player.

After the Gamecocks lost 35-12 to West Virginia in Morgantown, Enright decided it was time for some personnel changes. Steve, still playing in a backup role, rushed for 57 yards and caught a 20-yard touchdown pass against the Mountaineers. Enright believed that Steve had earned a chance to be in the starting lineup, although typically he did not grant this status to a first-year player.

In the next game, Carolina's homecoming contest against Maryland, Wadiak received his first start at left halfback, ousting senior captain Jack Crouch from his starting role. The Gamecocks were outmanned against Maryland and lost the game 19-7, yet in Wadiak's first start, he rushed for 102 yards on eight attempts on a muddy playing field. Wadiak's rushing total was more than the combined rushing yards for the Maryland team. The highlight of the game for Carolina was a 70-yard breakaway run by Wadiak.

A 27-7 win at Tulsa featured another signature long-distance run by Steve—this one 67 yards. Wadiak finished the game with 106 yards, his second consecutive performance rushing for more than 100 yards.

The Gamecocks closed their 1948 campaign with a 38-0 loss to Wake Forest. Wadiak ended his freshman season as the leading ground gainer for the Gamecocks, rushing for 420 yards and an impressive 8.2 yards per carry. His yards per carry average in 1948 remains today as the highest for a single season in USC football history.

Clemson's season went the other direction as they finished undefeated and beat Missouri in the Gator Bowl 24-23, giving the Tigers their first perfect 11-0 record. The Tigers success made Carolina's loss to its rival all the more painful.

Gamecock fans quickly showed Steve that they had a short memory. While he struggled to shake the guilt from his fumble against Clemson, Gamecock fans became enamored with Wadiak's all-out running style. By the time the season ended, USC supporters were hopeful and looking forward to next season. The foundation for that hope was the powerful returning Gamecock backfield tandem of Wadiak and Strickland.

It took only a season for Steve to become one of the most recognized and well-liked students on the Carolina campus. One of his favorite hangouts was the canteen in the basement of the Maxcy dormitory. It was a gathering place where students could meet one another while they enjoyed their favorite soft drinks, coffee, or snacks. It was here that Steve made himself accessible to the student body.

Jim Jackson, sports editor of "The Gamecock" in 1948, summarized

Wadiak's status on campus as a freshman:

> *Steve Wadiak is a friendly, likeable fellow who loves to play football, has all the physical qualifications for doing so at almost any position and bids fair to become one of the school's outstanding athletes before he graduates.*

In 1941, two rival sororities, Pi Phi and Tri Delta, began a tradition of playing a highly competitive and well-promoted touch football game. The popular game was played on Melton Field and quickly became known as the "Powder Bowl." Tickets were sold for 50 cents apiece with all proceeds going to the Carolina Children's Orphanage Home.

Steve Wadiak (back row, far right) served as an assistant coach to head coach Joe Patrone (back row, far left) for the Pi Phi sorority in the annual USC Powder Bowl in March of 1949.

(Photo courtesy of USC Archives)

Two notable alumni were selected to coach the teams. In January 1949, Joe Patrone, a Gamecock guard from the '30s, was named coach of the Pi Phi team. Ed McMillian, a former Duke and Carolina back, was appointed as head coach of the Tri Delts. Each sorority also selected an assistant coach from the ranks of current Gamecock football players. It was a job that any player would gladly aspire to fill, as it provided the opportunity to work closely with a team full of co-eds in a series of practice sessions leading up to the game.

The Pi Phi ladies offered the highly coveted job of assistant coach to Steve Wadiak. He gladly accepted. For him, it was added confirmation that the Gamecock faithful held nothing against him for his critical fourth-quarter fumble against Clemson.

Under Coach Wadiak and Coach Patrone, the Pi Phi squad defeated the Tri Delts and remained unbeaten in all Powder Bowl contests. The star of the Pi Phi team was a shifty running back named Frances LaBorde. Fans, teammates, and the campus newspaper referred to Frances by her nickname, "Choo Choo." After the game, Coach Wadiak had no shortage of players on his team who wanted to be escorted by him to the celebration party.

13
Rex

In 1924, legendary football Coach Knute Rockne directed the Notre Dame Fighting Irish to a perfect 10-0 record and a national championship. Rockne's team was led by the talented backfield of Harry Stuhldreher, Don Miller, Jim Crowley, and Elmer Layden.

After Notre Dame's 13-7 win against Army that season, well-known sports writer Grantland Rice wrote poetically about the four members of the talented Irish backfield. Rice's lead paragraph in the his post-game account that appeared in the "New York Herald Tribune" forever immortalized the Notre Dame backfield in the annals of college football history.

> *Outlined against a blue-gray October sky, the Four Horsemen rode again. In dramatic lore their names are Death, Destruction, Pestilence, and Famine. But those are aliases. Their real names are: Stuhldreher, Crowley, Miller and Layden. They formed the crest of the South Bend cyclone before which another fighting Army team was swept over the precipice at the Polo Grounds this afternoon as 55,000 spectators peered down upon the bewildering panorama spread out upon the green plain below.*

Back on campus at South Bend, an industrious young Notre Dame publicist had the "Four Horsemen" pose in full football uniform saddled on the backs of four horses. The photo further cemented the image and legendary status of Notre Dame's 1924 backfield.

Fullback Elmer Layden's backup in 1924 was Rex Enright, a 6'2"

195-lb. junior from Rockford, Ill., who would eventually pursue a career as a college coach.

Born in 1901, Enright was a young boy when his father died suddenly. His mother was an aspiring vaudeville actress who was constantly on the road chasing her dream to become a star. Rex was left with his maternal grandparents, Swedish immigrants who operated a respectable boarding house in Rockford.

Enright's father was a devout Catholic, and his mother honored her late husband by insisting that Rex attend Catholic school as a young boy. Enright's mother and maternal grandparents were Lutheran, and Rex was raised attending Lutheran services every Sunday.

Rex was a good student who also had a passion for athletics. At Rockford's Central High School, he eventually became captain of the football team and played on the Illinois state champion basketball team of 1918. His skills on the football field caught the attention of the Notre Dame coaches, and he was offered a scholarship to play in South Bend.

At Notre Dame, Enright found himself among a team full of high school All-Americans. His playing time was limited in his early years and, due to injuries, he sat out his entire second season. After serving as the backup fullback for the Four Horsemen in 1924, Enright at last earned a starting berth during his senior year in 1925 and contributed significantly to the Irish's respectable 7-2-1 season. His best individual performance was against Northwestern when he rushed for a pair of touchdowns in a 13-10 win. Enright also kicked the extra point after his first score.

Enright's consistent play in 1925 earned him the honor of making the All-Western Football All-Star team, the only Irish player to earn a spot on the squad. Selection to this team came via the recommendation of Coach Rockne. Enright's backfield mate on the all-star squad was Red Grange, the talented runner from Illinois who later earned historic NFL fame with the Chicago Bears.

Enright also was a two-year letterman on the Notre Dame basketball team and contributed to the success of the 1925-26 Irish team that finished with a stellar 19-1 record.

After his college playing days concluded, Enright joined the Green Bay Packers of the National Football League for two seasons (1926-27). In Green Bay, he was united with fellow Notre Dame alum, Curly Lambeau, who served as the founder and player/coach of the Packers. In 1927, Enright scored five touchdowns for the 7-2-1 Packers and was an integral part of Green Bay's most successful season to date. Enright's five TDs included two pass receptions, two rushes, and a 40-yard interception return in the season opener against the Dayton Triangles. In his two seasons in Green Bay, Enright struggled with a series of nagging injuries and elected to retire from professional football after a brief 19-game career.

While playing for Green Bay, Enright used the off-season to complete his law degree at Notre Dame. His youngest daughter, Alice, confided that the law degree was something he pursued to appease his mother, but athletics was his first love; his real desire was to become a coach. During his lifetime, Enright never used his law degree in professional practice.

Enright obtained his first football coaching job as an assistant at the University of North Carolina in Chapel Hill, where he stayed until 1931, when he accepted an assistant coaching position at the University of Georgia. At Georgia, Enright also served as the head basketball coach for the Bulldogs. In six seasons as head basketball coach, he compiled a 62-54 record. On the football field, Enright assisted Head Coach Harry

Mehre, another Notre Dame graduate and Knute Rockne disciple.

In 1937, the USC football team finished a disappointing 5-6-1 and did not earn a victory against a Southern Conference opponent. After the season, Head Coach Don McAllister made a number of changes on his coaching staff, including the dismissal of his backfield and line coaches. Don McAllister began working to fill his open assistant coaching positions, and speculation swirled around campus that a number of top assistants from across the country were being interviewed, including Frank Howard, the current line coach at rival Clemson University. Shortly before Christmas, the USC Board of Trustees gave McAllister a one-year extension on his current coaching contract at a salary of $4,000 per year.

Neither the potential changes in the assistant coaching ranks or the contract extension sat well with Gamecock boosters and students. Before classes dismissed for winter break, a group of 200 students gathered to publicly express concern about McAllister's competence as head coach. One student said he overheard several of McAllister's players state that they had lost respect for their coach.

University President Rion McKissick began to receive unsolicited correspondence from Gamecock football supporters suggesting that he fire McAllister, who prior to his tenure at USC, had been a head coach only at the high school level. Correspondence in McKissick's personal files included specific recommendations for McAllister's replacement, including one from a fan who instructed McKissick to be sure to hire a coach from a Protestant religious faith. The unsigned typed letter dated Dec. 11, 1937, documented the recent trend among several Southern universities to hire coaches who were Catholic, most of whom were products of Notre Dame, and stated that South Carolina would be making a mistake by following suit. The anonymous fan detailed the records of a select number of Catholic head coaches in the South and compared them to the winning records of Alabama's Frank Thomas, a non-Catholic, in an effort to make his point clear to McKissick.

On the evening of Dec. 26, 1937, the Junior Alumni Association of the school met at the Hotel Columbia and voted formally to ask the Student Advisory Committee of the Board of Trustees to reconsider the board's recent decision regarding the continued employment of Coach McAllister. The Student Advisory Committee consisted of six board members who were responsible for overseeing activities such as the hiring of coaches. The committee was chaired by powerful Barnwell politician and South Carolina Speaker of the House of Representatives Solomon Blatt.

The day after the gathering at the Columbia Hotel, McAllister tendered his resignation as Carolina's head football coach. Concurrent with McAllister's resignation, USC announced the hiring of McAllister's replacement, clearly indicating that a significant amount of activity was occurring behind the scenes in the wake of the McAllister situation.

The committee's most likely first choice for the job was Georgia's head coach Harry Mehre, who had recently resigned from his position in Athens. In December, Mehre, a Notre Dame graduate, was invited to USC for an interview, and he brought along his most trusted and polished assistant, Rex Enright. During the interview process, the South Carolina officials took an immediate liking to the gentlemanly Enright and offered him the job as head coach football coach. Mehre became the head coach at Mississippi.

Enright signed a four-year contract for $5,500 per year. In current dollars, the amount would be approximately $90,000 per year. John A. Montgomery of "The State" described his initial impressions of Enright:

> *The former Notre Dame fullback is an affable personality. There was warmth in his initial greeting . . . Enright is 35 years old. Six feet tall (or more) a brunet and weighs over 200 pounds. He is old enough and experienced enough to know his business and young enough to be enthusiastic about advancement.*

At South Carolina, Enright inherited a football team on a downward spiral. The Gamecocks had lost four consecutive games to archrival Clemson by a combined score of 116-6. The Board of Trustees made it imminently clear to Enright that a performance such as his predecessor's against Clemson would lead to a brief tenure at USC.

Upon his arrival, Enright also learned that the USC athletic program was in dire financial straits. Its athletic facilities were antiquated and not up to par with other schools in the Southern Conference. Enright was promised that investments would be made in athletic facilities and programs—but first, the athletic budget needed to be balanced, and a roster of angry unpaid vendors needed to be addressed.

Enright immediately installed the only brand of football he knew—the Notre Dame football system. USC fans were excited about his bringing to Columbia the techniques and knowledge of the legendary Knute Rockne.

In his first season at the helm in 1938, Enright led the Gamecocks to an acceptable 6-4 record. It would take him four years, however, before he would garner his first victory over Clemson. After a win over the Tigers in 1942, elated Gamecock boosters gave Coach Enright a brand new Cadillac. They repeated the gift after Carolina's 1947 win over Clemson; this time, the gift was a new Chrysler.

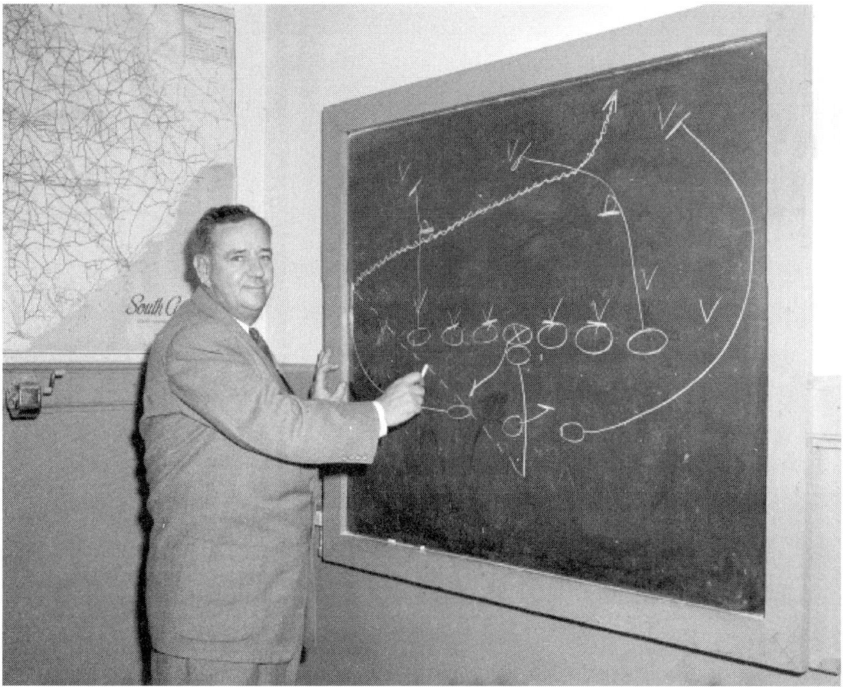

USC Head Football Coach Rex Enright diagrams a play.
(Photo courtesy of USC Archives)

Rex Enright is most often described by those who knew him well as a quiet and reserved gentleman. He earned a reputation as a classy coach and administrator who was loyal to his institution and the athletes who were a part of the scholarship program. He demonstrated care and compassion for the boys he recruited.

"Daddy used to do things for his players that you couldn't do in today's environment," Enright's youngest daughter, Alice, recalled. "I remember when one boy's mother had taken ill, and he needed to get home to see her, but he didn't have the bus money. Daddy just gave him the money out of his own pocket."

Another incident that highlighted Enright's compassion involved Dick Anderson, a high school player from Macon, Ga., who, in the late 1930s, was offered a full-contact tryout with the Gamecocks. During the tryout, Anderson severely injured his knee and was unable to complete the workout.

Later, Enright noticed Anderson walking down Greene Street carrying a suitcase. He flagged Anderson down and asked him where he was going. Anderson said he was headed home because he knew that no coach would want to give a scholarship to an injured player. Enright told Anderson that he had gotten hurt while trying out for his team, and he would find a way to make sure he received an education. Enright found administrative responsibilities for Anderson, who not only earned his degree from USC, but also stayed on to become the first full-time athletic ticket manager and served as executive director of the school's "Buck-a-Month" (BAM) Booster Club. Anderson remained employed by USC for more than 20 years in a variety of roles. Later, he furthered his education at Southern Methodist University and was subsequently appointed by President John F. Kennedy as the state director of the Federal Housing Administration in South Carolina.

Enright's concern for his boys was highlighted by his willingness to give a player a second chance. He saw the good in young men and took his role as a mentor in their lives seriously.

In 1953, Enright recruited Sam DeLuca, a talented offensive lineman from Brooklyn, N.Y. Shortly after arriving in Columbia, DeLuca was involved in an altercation with some students at the corner of Greene and Pickens Street. The street-savvy DeLuca reportedly did some serious physical damage to a couple of other students, and the USC administration pressured Enright to send DeLuca back to New York. Enright confided in a friend that he believed "that if ever there was a time that DeLuca needed someone to stand up for him, now was that time."

Enright gave DeLuca a second chance under the condition that DeLuca keep a promise to never again involve himself in behavior that might disgrace the university or the athletic department. DeLuca did not disappoint his coach. He became an outstanding college and professional football player and eventually was named to the USC Athletic Hall of Fame.

It wasn't just the superstars that Enright watched out for. Johnny Reeves was a freshman from Greenville and worked as a volunteer student trainer for the football team in 1951. Reeves recalled spending long hours in the locker room tending to injured athletes and cleaning the training room equipment and facilities. Enright took notice that Reeves often left the locker room after the school cafeteria had closed. Enright expressed concern to Reeves about his inability to eat dinner due to his long hours in the locker room.

Scholarship football players were fed at a separate training table that allowed for a flexible meal schedule. Midway through the 1951 season, Enright promised the hardworking Reeves that if the Gamecocks beat Clemson, he would ensure that Reeves would receive a place at the Gamecock training table with the players. After the South Carolina victory over Clemson, Enright honored his word, and Reeves no longer had to miss dinner after putting in long hours in the Gamecock locker room.

Enright's gracious demeanor endeared him to the media. In a day when the relationship between coaches and media was much less adversarial, Enright enjoyed the company of reporters. He gave them access, insight, and oftentimes friendship.

His closest media companion was Jake Penland, longtime sports editor of "The State." Penland and Enright regarded each other as friends—a relationship that was beneficial for Enright when things weren't going so well on the field. In the darkest of times, Penland used his pen to stand in the corner of his good friend.

Enright's life was consumed by his work. He didn't play golf, hunt, or fish, although he once took a fishing trip with some friends to Canada. On the trip, Enright reportedly got a hook stuck in his head and had to be taken to the hospital for stitches. This brought an abrupt end to his fishing adventures.

One of his few distractions from the pressure of his job was a game of cards. He enjoyed Bridge with his wife and other couples, as well as a friendly game of poker with the guys at the Elks Club in downtown Columbia.

Vacation consisted of an annual week or two at Ocean Drive on the Carolina coast, along with an annual trip to see family in Illinois. These were the only two breaks in an always busy schedule typically filled with practices, games, recruiting trips, booster meetings, and the academic duties he carried out while serving as the Dean of USC's Physical Education Department.

Enright is remembered as a devoted family man. Rex and his wife, Alice, had three daughters: Jean, Joyce, and Alice. In a 1948 interview with "The Gamecock," Joyce described her father at home: "He's never cross with any of the family. Although it is evident that at times, he is worried. Sometimes he fidgets—picking up a letter or scrap of paper to scribble plays on. Always, he says that the boys do their best. Sometimes, he has nightmares or dreams. He never forgets Mother's birthday and his wedding anniversary or any of the family's birthdays.

Whenever my friends come over, he talks to them as if he was one of them. I wouldn't have any other daddy in the world."

Alice Enright noted that her parents worked as a team, which was necessitated by her father's lack of domestic skills. "Daddy really wasn't much help around the house. He couldn't fix things. Once he tried to fix a doorknob, and it just fell in the floor, and we all got a big laugh. Mother hired someone to do the yard work because Daddy just didn't have time for that."

Alice also recalled that her father was committed to the faith of his childhood.

"We were in church every Sunday. We went to the Lutheran church downtown, but if we couldn't make it all the way down there for some reason, we would just go to the Methodist church across the street from our house. But we were going to be in church every Sunday," Alice said..

She added that not all of Sunday was occupied with church activities. "Later on Sunday afternoons during football season, we would always listen to the Washington Redskins on the radio."

Alice recalled fondly that she often dropped her father off at his office on campus so that she could take the car on to her high school. This left her father having to catch a ride home to his house on Heyward Street with one of the other coaches. He never complained.

"Daddy loved his job, and he loved his family," his daughter recalled.

By the time the 1948 football season ended, a special relationship began to develop between Steve Wadiak and his head coach. After that initial tryout, Enright simply promised Wadiak a chance. He had proven faithful to his word. By the time the season ended, Wadiak was permanently established as the starting left halfback for the Gamecocks. He believed that Enright's faith in him had opened up the opportunity of his lifetime, thus his loyalty to Coach Enright ran deep.

Neither Wadiak nor Enright was a big talker. Both were quiet and reserved, but the two men seemed to have a chemistry that didn't require unnecessary words. Enright knew he would always get a 100-percent effort from Wadiak, and Steve gave everything he had in practice, as well as in games. He listened attentively to instruction. He never questioned his coach's authority. He never complained. He never bad-mouthed a teammate or a coach. Wadiak was a coach's dream. Enright wished he had a team full of players like him.

In the Oct. 2, 1954 issue of "The Saturday Evening Post," Rex Enright authored an article about his former player Steve Wadiak. Enright, during 25 years of coaching up to that date, most likely had come in contact with well over 1,000 student athletes. He had coached All-Conference players as well as All-Americans. The title of the article summarized Enright's opinion of Wadiak's football ability—"The Greatest Player I Ever Coached."

Sixty years after that article was published, Enright's daughter Alice recalled the affection that her father held for Wadiak. She noted that he "went on about Wadiak unlike any other player he had ever coached." As the youngest of three daughters to Coach Enright, Alice aptly summarized her father's relationship with his star player: "Steve was like the son he never had."

14
Next Year

After a disappointing finish to the 1948 season, Gamecock football fans were restless. Head Coach Rex Enright had been at USC since 1938, and the execution of his plan to establish respectability in the Gamecock football program had been interrupted by World War II. After the 1942 season, Enright joined the Navy and coached military teams at the Athens, Ga. pre-flight station and also served as a coach and athletic director at the naval air station in Jacksonville, Fla. In his eight seasons at USC—five before the war and three after the war—Enright compiled a mediocre 31-37-5 record. Perhaps most importantly to the restless fans, he had won only three of his eight meetings with Clemson.

In the final game of the 1948 season, Wake Forest was on its way to a 38-0 drubbing of the Gamecocks. Many Gamecock fans in attendance that day began to publicly vent their frustrations over another disappointing season. The primary target of their verbal attacks was Head Coach Rex Enright. Sitting in the stands on that chilly afternoon was Coach Enright's wife, Alice. Her emotions began to boil with each insult hurled at her husband.

Mrs. Enright knew that her husband was a good man who was giving everything he had to turn the Gamecock football program into a consistent winner. She knew he had inherited a program with inferior facilities, an unbalanced budget, and no winning tradition. It was just too painful to sit and listen to inebriated fans yelling obscenities at her beloved husband.

At halftime, she left her seat, went underneath the west grandstand,

and proceeded to walk directly through the stadium exit. She'd walked a good portion of the nearly two miles to her home on Heyward Street when a neighbor spotted her and offered her a ride.

Near the end of the 1948 season, Van Newman, sports editor of "The Gamecock," laid the blame for the disappointing performance of the football team directly on Coach Enright. He wrote in his column the following critique:

> *After the Duke-Carolina game last year, Coach Wallace Wade of Duke, who isn't addicted to making excuses, commented that he would give anything to have the material on the Carolina squad.*
>
> *After the Maryland-Carolina clash Saturday, Jim Tatum said that Carolina had the finest backs he had seen all year.*
>
> *Apparently, the coaches in the nation have devised defenses that have caught up with and gotten ahead of the "T" as it was used primarily after its reintroduction several years ago. New variations, however, such as employed by Georgia Tech, Notre Dame and Army are still ahead of defensive strategy. Carolina obviously is not in this group.*
>
> *In short coaching seems to be the answer to the problem in this case. Enright, through his influence and contacts in the country, is a decided asset. However, we feel that he could be of far greater service as an athletic director than as a head coach, if we could afford both.*

An angry fan from Newberry, S.C., sent a postcard to "The State's" Jake Penland, expressing a sentiment that was common among many fans:

> *Why not give readers a break and tell them that Carolina could have a winner if Mr. Enright could coach the line to play offensive ball? He*

> *has the material, and if he is the coach that we pay for he could convert some backfield talent to play in the line. See if you can't help Carolina have a winning football team by really telling people how some things are.*

Penland publicly defended his good friend and told the reader in print that coaching a winning football team was not as easy as he might think.

Throughout a history of mediocrity on the football field, South Carolina football fans held to a simple slogan—*Wait 'til next year.* It was a slogan filled with the hope that Next Year would be the year that the Gamecock football program would at last rise above its long history of futility.

Hope in 1949 rested on the broad shoulders of the talented running tandem of Wadiak and Bishop Strickland, as well as the rifle arm of John Boyle, a highly recruited sophomore quarterback from Brooklyn, N.Y. While Boyle was in high school, former Gamecock standout and Brooklyn native Dominic Fusci encouraged the Gamecock coaches to try to recruit Boyle. Backfield coach Al Grygo was dispatched to Brooklyn to take a look at the prep star, and he returned to Columbia with a glowing report: "He's the greatest high school passer I have ever seen," Grygo claimed.

Boyle stood 6'4" and weighed 210 lbs. He had a powerful throwing arm that enabled him to fire passes often described as the kind that could "take the skin off of a receiver's hands." Boyle had successfully quarterbacked the 1948 Gamecock freshman team, referred to as "the Biddies." He quickly became a fan favorite among the Gamecock faithful, and writers for "The Gamecock" hyped his abilities to their readership, explaining why late in 1948 the freshman football games were more popular for fans than the varsity contests:

> *"The amazing passing of Boyle is the main factor in this crowd interest but the wide open type of offense that the Biddies use also helps to draw the fans from their radios and easy chairs . . . With the total collapse of the varsity, the student body has turned to the freshman for their football thrills and the Biddies are practically assured of having a large crowd on hand whenever they play.*

Against the Clemson freshman team, Boyle connected on 15 of 24 passes and might have completed more if his receivers had been able to hold on to all of his bullet-like passes. "The Gamecock" reported that Boyle's passing "left the Clemson team dazed with amazement."

Boyle was expected to be the catalyst for bringing some firepower to a lackluster Gamecock offense. It was hoped that under his leadership USC would develop a passing attack that would bring needed balance to the USC offense and keep opponents from stacking the line of scrimmage against the Gamecock running game.

While Boyle had plenty of raw physical skills, he lacked an understanding of the footwork and mechanics required to play the quarterback position. Enright knew he needed help in developing Boyle, so, during spring practice in 1948, he leaned on his Notre Dame connections to bring in a special tutor.

In March of 1948, the South Carolina campus was buzzing when former Notre Dame great Johnny Lujack showed up to lend a hand to the Gamecock coaches. Lujack was an All-American in every sense of the word. He had led the Fighting Irish to three national championships, including an undefeated 1947 season in which he received the coveted Heisman Trophy. His college career was interrupted for two years while he served as a Navy ensign on submarines that were assigned to locate German watercraft lurking in the English Channel. After graduating from Notre Dame, Lujack became the first round pick of the Chicago Bears. His popularity led him to also be featured in a 1949 ABC radio program, called the "The Adventures of Johnny Lujack."

Lujack's assignment in Columbia in the spring of 1948 was to help John Boyle become a complete quarterback, while also sharing the latest offensive innovations with the Gamecock coaching staff. Lujack quickly determined that Gamecocks' offensive scheme was severely outdated. He told one of the veteran players during spring practice, "You guys are running an offense that was run way back when. You need to get up with the times." Installing some new wrinkles in the Gamecock's offensive game would be easy. Training John Boyle would prove far more difficult.

Boyle's mechanical problems could easily be fixed with instruction and repetition. The greater challenge with Boyle stemmed from a poor attitude and his inability to mesh with his teammates. Boyle was the son of a New York policeman who died when Boyle was young, leaving John to be raised by his mother and grandmother. During his most formative years, he did not have the influence of a male authority figure in the home. Through adolescence, he grew bigger and stronger than most other teenagers, and his success in athletics brought him accolades he was not mature enough to handle.

Boyle believed he could succeed on his raw abilities and didn't like being told what to do. He knew only one way to throw the football—a hard line drive. Lujack showed Boyle how to deliver a pass with touch that would land softly into the hands of a moving receiver. Unfortunately, Lujack was wasting his time with Boyle, who only feigned an interest in Johnny's instruction.

Boyle showed up for fall practice in 1949 15 pounds overweight. He struggled with his weight throughout his tenure at USC, having developed a fondness for Southern cooking that far exceeded his appetite for conditioning. Despite the attitude issues and lack of discipline, Boyle still managed to earn the starting quarterback position for the Gamecocks 1949 opener against Baylor.

In the season opener, the Gamecocks traveled to Waco, Texas, and lost 20-6 to Baylor. Furman upset the Gamecocks in their home opener 14-7, a game in which Wadiak lost his front tooth in a collision with a Paladin tackler. In their third game of the season, the Gamecocks played respectably against All-American Charlie "Choo Choo" Justice and the sixth-ranked North Carolina Tar Heels, before losing 28-13. With Boyle at quarterback, the Gamecocks had proceeded to drop their first three games.

Coming into Big Thursday against Clemson, the Gamecocks were in need of a dramatic turnaround if they were to avenge their disappointing prior year loss to the Tigers. USC students developed a new cheer that drew attention to the periodic tradition of Gamecock boosters' purchasing a new car for Coach Rex Enright as reward for a win over archrival Clemson. During games, students chanted:

Rickety rack, rickety rack,
Give the ball to Wadiak!
Rickety rack, rickety rack,
Enright needs a Cadillac.

Jake Penland of "The State" permanently solidified Wadiak's nickname when he began to refer to him frequently as "Th' Cadillac."

A record crowd of 35,000 jammed into the recently expanded

Carolina Stadium. It was a beautiful fall afternoon, and the only clouds in the sky were created by the smoke from a squadron of P-80 USAF fighter jets from Sumter's Shaw Air Force Base that flew at a low altitude over the stadium just before the 2 p.m. kickoff.

Public address announcer William C. Ouzts told the capacity crowd that grandstand vendors could be identified by their white caps, and he detailed the prices of their sale items so fans could be certain they were not ripped off by an overly aggressive vendor. Soft drinks and peanuts were sold for 10 cents each. Ice cream went for 20 cents, and sandwiches and cigarettes were 25 cents.

The game started like it was headed for another disappointing Gamecock defeat. Aided by two interceptions of John Boyle passes, Clemson jumped out to an early 13-0 lead. Both of Boyle's interceptions were delivered directly into the hands of Clemson defenders. After the Tigers' second score, Steve Wadiak stood around his goal line awaiting the Clemson kickoff. He remembered the prior year and how his late-game fumble had contributed to the Gamecocks' loss. He did not want to relive that disappointment.

Wadiak received the kickoff and returned it 59 yards to the Clemson 39-yard line. Wadiak's exciting return brought a ray of hope to thousands of downcast Gamecock fans.

Earlier in the week, Coach Enright was bothered when he heard that the betting line on the game had shifted dramatically in favor of the Tigers. In 1949, betting on college football was nearly as popular as the game itself. It was big business, and it involved big money. When John Boyle fired two consecutive passes directly into the hands of the opposing team, the rumor Enright had heard in town about the shift in the betting line flashed through his head.

Coach Enright had lost confidence in Boyle. He decided to replace him with veteran quarterback Bo Hagan. Hagan had been a superstar for the Gamecocks in his freshman season in 1946, leading them to a 16-14 come-from-behind victory over Clemson and a 5-3 season. For the next two seasons, Hagan battled a series of injuries that diminished his effectiveness. Coming into the Clemson game, he had played sparingly in the first three games and once again spent more time in the training room than on the practice field. One local newspaper had reported earlier in the season that Hagan's playing days at USC were finished.

After Wadiak's long kickoff return, Hagan hobbled onto the playing field with instructions from Enright to get the Gamecock offense in gear. Wadiak was thankful to see his friend Hagan enter the huddle. Steve's football instincts told him they would have a much better chance against Clemson with an injured Hagan than with the temperamental Boyle at full capacity. Hagan was a leader and understood the role of a quarterback.

Hagan proceeded to lead the Gamecock offense to its first score. Two series later, Hagan directed another Gamecock scoring drive capped off by a two-yard TD run by Wadiak. The game was tied 13-13 at halftime.

Behind the quarterbacking of Hagan and the running of Wadiak, Strickland and sophomore fullback Chuck Prezioso, the Gamecocks dominated the second half. Hagan connected on a long touchdown strike to Jim Pinkerton for the go-ahead score and later scored himself on a six-yard run to clinch the victory. Wadiak finished the game as the leading ground gainer with 88 yards on 20 attempts. Strickland notched 83 yards on 17 tries, while Prezioso rushed for 68 yards on five attempts.

Bo Hagan's courageous performance earned him hero status in the game. He went from being written off as an injured player whose career was over to once again becoming the most popular man on campus.

His opportunity in the game came as a direct result of the poor performance of Boyle.

Gamecock players were not oblivious to the recent criticisms directed at their head coach. They wanted Enright to know that they had won this big game for him. At the end of the game, a handful of USC players spontaneously hoisted Enright up on their shoulders and carried

Head Coach Rex Enright is carried off the field after a Gamecock victory over Clemson.

(Photo courtesy of USC Archives)

him across the field. The practice of carrying the victorious coach across the field was just beginning to take hold in college football, and this show of post-game emotion caught the attention of the national media. A picture of Enright's victory march on his players' shoulders was carried in "Time" magazine.

Prior to the Clemson game, Enright received a vote of confidence from the board of trustees and was given an extension to his contract as athletic director and head football coach. Jake Penland, who had been receiving a steady flow of letters from fans critical of Enright, praised the board and its chairman, Rut Osborne, for its belief in the Gamecocks' coach:

> *Rut Osborne and his athletic committee are exceedingly high on their head coach and athletic director. But it is not a blind faith that makes them feel and think and act as they do. They know a lot more Rex Enright than the average man in the street. They know him as a capable coach who teaches sound football, as one of the best advertisements any university ever had, as a shrewd athletic director and as an all-American gentleman.*

At practice the following week, the short college career of John Boyle came to an abrupt end. During the team's Tuesday practice session, Enright attempted to correct Boyle over a mistake in practice. Boyle mouthed off to his coach, and the normally mild-mannered Enright reached his limit. In no uncertain terms, Enright instructed Boyle to go pack his bags and go home. Although surprised at the outburst by Enright, Boyle was clear on the certainty of his coach's decision. He retreated across the practice field toward the locker room at Carolina Field House.

Penland reported in "The State" that Enright gave Boyle the following parting message:

> *Enright told him, "You have been blessed with a wonderful arm and good vision. You could become a fine football player. But all along you have had the wrong attitude. To become great you'd have to work hard, get along with the other fellows and learn all you can. You haven't done your part."*

After Enright said farewell to Boyle, he searched the Gamecock locker room to find Steve Wadiak. He needed a reminder of how a real football player should carry himself—the kind of player who had the skill, the attitude, and the discipline, along with humility—the kind of player who could make a coach remember why he gave his life to his profession. Steve Wadiak was that kind of player.

The Gamecocks would break even in their final six games of 1949, with wins over Marquette, Wake Forest, and The Citadel and losses to Maryland, Miami, and Georgia Tech. They continued to struggle against teams that featured bigger, stronger lineman and a depth chart that allowed them to fully employ a two-platoon system. Enright's team had a history of hanging tough for one half of football, but their inferior depth wouldn't allow them to finish off a victory. Their final record of 4-6 overall and 3-3 in the Southern Conference once again left the Gamecock faithful looking toward the hope of "next year."

Wadiak in his sophomore year finished the season as the Gamecocks' leading rusher, with 775 yards on 152 carries. Backfield mates Strickland and Prezioso ran for 522 and 446 yards, respectively. Wadiak was named to the second team All-Southern Conference team, but was conspicuously missing from the All-State team.

Charlie "Choo Choo" Justice, to no one's surprise, was named the Southern Conference Player of the Year. The best team in the state of South Carolina in 1949 was the Wofford Terriers, who finished 11-0 and earned a bid to play in the Shrine Cigar Bowl against Florida State on January 2.

For Steve Wadiak, one game in 1949 held special significance. On November 5, the Gamecocks traveled to Milwaukee to play Marquette. Wadiak's brothers, Joe and Walter, had made the two-hour trip from Chicago to Milwaukee along with a handful of Wadiak's neighborhood friends. It was a rare opportunity for family and friends from the Burnside neighborhood to watch Steve play. Also in attendance at the game were a number of friends and family of Rockford, Ill. natives Pat Vella and Chuck Prezioso. Vella was named by Enright as the honorary captain for the game.

The Gamecocks' offense, unable to get on track against Marquette, suffered through numerous fumbles and penalties. Through three quarters of the game, South Carolina had crossed the 50-yard line only once.

Finally, in the final seconds of the third quarter, trailing 3-0, the Gamecocks mounted a drive that would turn out to be the difference in the game. Wadiak burst over left guard for a gain of 12 yards. Then, Prezioso took a handoff on a misdirection play and broke free down the left sideline. He galloped 30 yards to the Marquette 40-yard line before a Marquette defender dragged him down from behind.

On the first play of the fourth quarter, Hagan faked a handoff up the middle to Prezioso and quickly pitched the ball to Wadiak, who sprinted around the right end and beat the Marquette defenders to the corner. He turned it in high gear down the sideline and stopped suddenly around the 20-yard line, causing a defender to flail and miss him completely. Then, Wadiak burst forward and bounced off of three different tacklers before he was finally wrestled down at the 10-yard line. The members of the "Wadiak fan club" from the Burnside neighborhood jumped to their feet and screamed with delight over the spectacular run by their neighborhood hero and friend.

During the next series, Prezioso took a pitchout around left end, lowered his head, and bowled over one tackler before he was forced out of bounds at the one-foot line. Hagan sneaked the ball in for the score on the next play to give the Gamecocks a 6-3 lead, and that is all they would need to secure the win. Steve Wadiak, Pat Vella, and Chuck Prezioso were particularly happy to escape with that win in front of their friends and family members.

After the Marquette game, Coach Enright used his friendship with Curly Lambeau, head coach of the Green Bay Packers, to arrange for his team to travel to Chicago on Sunday and attend the Packers-Chicago Bears game at Wrigley Field. The Gamecock squad watched as the Bears defeated the Packers 24-3 behind the quarterbacking of an old friend of the Gamecocks—Johnny Lujack.

As Wadiak stood on the sideline in Wrigley Field, his mind and heart returned to his childhood. Memories of sitting in his den listening to the exploits of the Bears' Bronko Nagurski came flowing back to him. He recalled the hours he spent on the prairie near his childhood home, pretending to be the star of the Chicago Bears, hearing his name being called across the airways.

In a rare moment of self-focus for a guy known as the consummate teammate, Wadiak turned to a friend standing beside him, and as he looked around sold-out Wrigley Field, he said, "Someday, this is where I hope to be playing football."

This was Steve Wadiak's dream. He hoped it would become his destiny.

15
Friends

Steve Wadiak's popularity among the student body at USC reached celebrity status after the 1949 season. He became the most recognized student on campus, as well as on the city streets of Columbia. His electrifying runs eased the pain of Gamecock fans who suffered through some disappointing seasons.

Popularity did not alter the humble demeanor of the football star. Wadiak continued to be a regular patron of the student canteen in the basement of the Maxcy dormitory, and he enjoyed interacting with fellow classmates all across the campus. He hung out in the Preston dormitory with his friends and teammates, playing a friendly game of Gin Rummy or just carrying on in the manner of normal college boys.

Steve liked walking the streets of Columbia, usually on the way to one of his favorite eating places. At most local restaurants, Steve benefited from his superstar status and rarely paid for a meal. Proprietors understood that having "Th' Cadillac" dine in their establishment was always good for business.

Wadiak was approachable and genuine, exuding an air of accessibility that made everyone feel as though they knew him personally. Former teammate and friend Bill Rutledge recalled Wadiak's winsome nature.

"Steve's friendliness was impressive," Rutledge said. "He had this ability to meet people and show a real interest in them. It drew people to him. It was amazing to see."

Several former teammates commented that they never heard Wadiak complain or grumble about anyone or anything. They said when he would be in the company of a group that was bad-mouthing another person, he would listen but never join in the criticism.

Steve loved his new Carolina home. He enjoyed the milder weather, the friendliness of Southerners, and the tastiness of Southern cooking—but his greatest source of contentment came from the new friendships he had formed.

While Steve seemed to have a casual relationship with almost everyone, there were a few teammates and others with whom he shared a deeper friendship. He was more than 800 miles from his childhood best friend, Louie Guida, and his old neighborhood buddies, but teammates such as Pat Vella and Chuck Prezioso formed the nucleus of a new band of close companions.

Both Vella and Prezioso were from Rockford, Ill., just an hour or so northwest of Steve's Chicago home. On holidays, Steve sometimes hitched a ride back to Chicago with Vella and Prezioso. Vella recalled that they took turns driving, and on one trip home, Steve was behind the wheel during the wee hours of the morning when he neglected to pay attention to the car's gas needle. They ran out of gas on a desolate two-lane road, and Steve started to hitchhike toward the nearest town. Fortunately, a farmer in a pick-up truck spotted Steve and gave him a lift to the nearest gas station.

Vella remembers dropping Wadiak off at his home on University Avenue in Chicago and engaging each time in a lengthy conversation with Anna Wadiak, Steve's mother. She insisted that Vella provide her with details about her youngest son's activities in South Carolina.

Wadiak, Prezioso, and Vella were kindred spirits. On warm days, they often visited Columbia's Sesquicentennial State Park. "Sesqui," as it was known among the locals, was commissioned to be built in 1936 in honor of the 150th anniversary of the founding of the city of Columbia. Steve enjoyed swimming in the lake at Sesqui, an exercise for which he had developed a fondness as a youth swimming in Lake Michigan. The real draw to Sesqui for Steve and other male USC students was the abundance of co-eds who sunbathed along the shores of the 30-acre lake.

Steve Wadiak's close friends and teammates,
Pat Vella (left) and Chuck Prezioso, talk with Head Coach
Rex Enright (center) during a practice session at Melton Field.
All three were natives of Rockford, Illinois.

(Photo courtesy of Rose Vella)

Steve lived in a corner room on the first floor of the Preston dormitory. His roommate was Bayard Pickett, a Charleston native whose family were descendants of General George Pickett, leader of Pickett's Charge—the Confederate Army's last-ditch effort at the Battle of Gettysburg in 1863.

Prezioso lived in a room that shared a common bathroom with Wadiak and Pickett. Prezioso's roommate during his first two years was center Len Ekimoff. Upon Ekimoff's graduation in 1949, William "Hootie" Johnson, a highly recruited and promising young running back from Greenwood, S.C., moved in with Prezioso. Johnson later rose to national fame as the president of Augusta National Golf Club.

Wadiak was a sharp and fashionable dresser. His clothes were always neatly pressed, and he wore the latest fashions thanks to the benevolence of the owners of a couple of men's clothing stores in downtown Columbia. The proprietors saw the marketing value of having the most popular Gamecock athletes model their latest offerings.

Steve's dorm room closet and dresser overflowed with shirts, pants, shoes, and accessories. Many of these items remained in their plastic wrapping, as Wadiak had more clothes than he could possibly wear. His only peculiarity when it came to clothes was his distaste for ties. He had an unusually large neck, and wearing a tie was miserable for him.

Noticing that Wadiak had an excess supply of clothing, Bayard Pickett would often "borrow" some of his roommate's wares. One rainy day, Wadiak noticed Pickett walking across campus wearing a new overcoat that Wadiak had just received from Lourie's clothing store. Wadiak was upset that his new coat was getting damaged by the soaking rain.

"Hey, Bayard," Wadiak yelled at his roommate. "Take my coat off."

To which Pickett yelled back, "I can't do that, Steve. If I take your coat off, I'll get your suit wet."

On another occasion, however, Wadiak was not nearly as concerned about parting with his clothes. Prior to the 1950 season, Steve was introduced to Bob Korn, a freshman recruit who came from a West Virginia coal-mining family. The two men were standing in the locker room in the Carolina Field House, and Wadiak was moved by the tattered condition of Korn's clothes. He pulled the freshman aside where they would have some privacy, removed the new starched shirt he was wearing, and gave it to Korn. Laurie Blackmon, Korn's daughter, heard her father tell this story many times and says she will always remember Steve Wadiak as "the man who literally gave my father the shirt off his back."

Another teammate to whom Steve was immediately drawn was John LaTorre. As a slender 158-lb., 18-year-old recruit out of Charleston's Bishop England High School, LaTorre arrived in Columbia in September of 1948 with a head full of wavy sandy brown hair and a happy-go-lucky attitude. The upper classmen quickly took a razor to his hair, but that did nothing to extinguish LaTorre's likeable personality. LaTorre was recruited to USC primarily as a basketball player but was coaxed into playing freshman football, where he quickly demonstrated excellent defensive skills despite being undersized.

LaTorre was from a working class family in Charleston. His father spent most of his life working on the Charleston docks. Like so many of Wadiak's childhood friends, LaTorre also had a distinctive nickname. To this day, he is known by most as "Lip" LaTorre. He earned this moniker while playing basketball as a youth and constantly giving officials "lip" over calls with which he did not agree.

Adding to Steve's ability to enjoy his new found Carolina home was the fact that he rarely found himself short on cash. He was receiving $120 a month from the government for his service in the Navy, and his athletic scholarship entitled him to a small monthly stipend as well.

Also, it was not uncommon for Gamecock boosters to discreetly give cash to their favorite Gamecock football player. Teammate Bob "Moose" Kahle vividly recalls seeing one of these exchanges between a fan and Wadiak.

"I remember after one of our games, we were walking toward our bus to go back to the Field House, and this fan walked up to Steve and shook his hand," Kahle recalled. "When he shook Steve's hand, he slipped him a hundred-dollar bill."

Going into his junior year, Steve acquired an automobile—a new 1950 Pontiac Catalina. The car was two-toned, with an ivory body and a rust colored top. It featured thick whitewalls and plush leather upholstery. Its approximate sticker price in 1950 was $2,000.

The Pontiac gave Steve even greater freedom to enjoy all that Southern living had to offer. Steve's frequent sidekick was his good buddy Lip LaTorre.

"He would come down to my room and say, 'Come on and ride with me to the post office,' or we might go up to Cogburn's Steak House on Sumter Street, and they would fix us a late night breakfast. He was always getting me to go somewhere with him," LaTorre recalled.

Nearly every female on campus wanted to meet Steve. Repeatedly, Steve's teammates were being asked by co-eds to introduce them to "Th' Cadillac." During his junior year, Nancy Fulmer, a strikingly attractive blonde sophomore student from nearby Springfield, S.C., caught Steve's eye. Steve was smitten. The two became inseparable, and to the disappointment of hundreds of USC co-eds, the most popular male student on campus officially had a steady girl.

One of Steve and Nancy's most frequent dating destinations was the Carovets Apartments. The Carovets consisted of a group of prefabricated government buildings designed as living quarters for the families of military veterans attending USC. The complex was located off of Bull Street, a couple of miles north of the main campus. It included a playground, a clubhouse, and child care services. The Carovets provided a quiet place where Steve could visit friends while escaping from the constant attention he received on campus or in town.

After getting married, Pat Vella and his wife often called upon Steve and Nancy to babysit their children at their Carovets apartment on Confederate Avenue. Another Carovets resident, Moose Kahle, recalled that Steve and Nancy would spend evenings with them playing cards and eating popcorn. Sunday afternoons at the Carovets were filled with family dinners and touch football games. Steve and Nancy frequently joined in these activities.

One of Steve's favorite places to visit and hang out in Columbia was the Five Points district. Located a few blocks from campus down the sloping hill of Greene Street, Five Points featured a series of restaurants and retail outlets.

Bill Rutledge recalled his memories of Steve in Five Points: "I remember seeing Steve in Five Points one Sunday morning," Rutledge said. "He was petting a dog who had its head sticking out of a car window. Steve was just having a great time rubbing that little dog and playing with him."

On another occasion, Rutledge reminisced about sitting in a booth with Wadiak in what he referred to as a "beer hall" where athletes often gathered in Five Points.

"I remember we were all sitting there cutting up and having a good time," Rutledge said. "And I always remember that Steve never touched a thing . . . not even a beer. So I asked him, 'How in the heck do you sit here with all this yakking going on, and you seem to be having more fun than anybody and you aren't even drinking?'

I remember he just looked at me and smiled and didn't say a word. He just seemed incredibly happy and content to be right where he was," Rutledge said.

One spring afternoon in 1949, Steve was walking in Five Points, and he stopped and peered into an ABC Package Store at 726 Harden St. He noticed that the walls of the store were lined with black and white photos of current Gamecock football players. He stepped into the store and said hello to the proprietor, who quickly recognized Steve and invited him in.

The two men introduced themselves, and immediately, a chemistry emerged that would forge a new friendship. The owner was Frank Chibbaro, a native of New Brunswick, N.J., and a fellow USC student. He, like Wadiak, had been transplanted to Columbia via a football scholarship from Rex Enright. Chibbaro earned a starting guard position on the 1941 Gamecock freshman squad and was then redshirted for his sophomore season. His college tenure was interrupted by a four-year stint in the Navy during World War II. After the war, he returned to USC but elected to have the GI Bill fund the remaining portion of his education and chose to use his spare time to work a series of jobs instead of playing football.

Frank reminded Steve of his old neighborhood friends. He was the sixth child of Italian immigrants and the only member of his family to graduate high school, much less attend college. Frank's family was poor, and football had provided a way to a better life. The two men swapped stories about their childhoods and enjoyed recalling the good times from their old neighborhoods.

Sometimes they would run into each other while attending Mass at St. Peter's Catholic Church on Assembly Street. Frequently, they met outside of Frank's store in Five Points and would sit and talk about everything from football to food to girls. Shortly after they began their friendship, Wadiak did what was only customary for him to do with a good friend—he gave Frank a nickname. Steve changed his new friend's name from Frank to "Franco."

As Franco told Steve about his childhood, the two were drawn closer by the similarities of their respective life experiences. Franco told Steve about scraping enough money together as a kid to go to the movies on a Saturday to watch Tom Mix or Gene Autry in their serial Westerns. Steve relayed his childhood experiences of going to see his favorite Westerns at the Avalon Theater in Chicago and his childhood dreams about being the next great hero of the Wild West.

Upon entering high school, the boys' participation in the sport of football was a source of displeasure for their immigrant parents. Steve had to hide his dirty football equipment from his disapproving mother, while Frank threatened to run away from home if his parents would not sign a form giving him permission to play on his high school football team.

Life in Carolina was good for both Franco and Steve—almost too good to be true.

Both men had moved a long way from their meager beginnings. They had both survived the war. They were discovered by USC's coaches while playing football in the obscure sandlots of their hometowns. Both had been given chances that their siblings had not, and they each carried with them a deep sense of gratitude and appreciation for the opportunities that had been afforded them in their new South Carolina home.

One day, Franco shared with Steve that he had never owned a pair of shoes that were exclusively his until he came to the University of South Carolina. He explained how he had worn his brother's hand-medowns all his life and how he had put cardboard inside them to cover up the worn places in the soles. Today, at age 93, Frank's feet show the scars of wearing poorly fitted shoes for most of his younger years. As a survivor of the Great Depression, Frank knew that having a new pair of shoes was a blessing rather than an entitlement.

By comparison, the equipment manager for the Gamecock football team once expressed confusion over Wadiak's unwillingness to wear anything new. Steve enjoyed wearing torn jerseys, and unlike so many of his teammates, he never asked for anything new. During the peak of Wadiak's football career at USC, his football cleats were badly worn and held together by athletic tape. Maybe it was superstition that caused him to hold on to his worn-out shoes, or perhaps it was just gratitude and humility.

After all, for some, new shoes were a luxury.

Steve Wadiak holds a pair of worn-out football cleats while standing in Carolina Field House.

(Photo courtesy of Safran's Antiques and The Gamecock Shop)

16
Prelude

The 1950 South Carolina Gamecock team graduated its best quarterback, Bo Hagan, and its four-time All-State end, Red Wilson, along with its two most experienced linebackers. Coming out of spring practice, Coach Enright was not optimistic about his team's chances to improve on its 4-6 record from the previous season.

"After watching the boys doing all that blocking, tackling, and hard work in spring training, I know we're going to have a squad that'll never quit," Enright told "The Gamecock." "I'm a football coach, and they are going to say I'm moaning, but we just haven't got what it takes to come out on top in the win-loss column."

The Gamecocks would continue to operate their offense from the T-formation, and the backfield would feature the proven talent of Wadiak at left halfback, Bishop Strickland at right halfback, and Chuck Prezioso at fullback. Larry Smith was expected to be All-Conference at center. Other than these few known potential stars, Enright referred to the remainder of the talent on the 1950 squad as "unclassified," and he made sure Gamecock fans understood that football games were not won "on halfbacks alone."

Mordecai Persky, a staff writer for "The Gamecock," wrote a poem entitled "Steve Fever" that appeared in the student paper on March 10, 1950. It did nothing but add to Steve Wadiak's growing iconic status around campus. The poem included the following excerpt:

Spring practice out on Melton Field—
And eyes and tongues have not concealed

Their interest in Wadiak—
They see his shoulders, chest, and back,
But only heels and dust he shows
To mightiest Gamecock foes
What makes these football monsters grieve?
You've got your answer kid, it's Steve!
All the way Wadiak—
Enright wants a Cadillac!

Fifty varsity players wearing shorts and T-shirts lined up for calisthenics on Melton Field at 6:15 on a steamy September 1, 1950 morning. The Gamecocks began a series of two-a-day workouts and had only three weeks to prepare for their September 23 home opener against the Duke Blue Devils.

USC's offense continued to be an Achilles heel for Rex Enright's Carolina teams. In an effort to bring life to his lackluster offense, Enright added a new backfield coach to his staff. Once again relying on his Notre Dame connections, Enright hired George Terlep, a star performer on the 1943 national championship Fighting Irish team and a former professional football player. In his final two seasons as a pro, Terlep played for the Cleveland Browns under legendary coach Paul Brown. Terlep had first met Brown while playing for him on the Great Lakes Naval Station football team during the war.

Terlep was young and inexperienced as a coach, but he had an excellent football pedigree. His familiarity with the Notre Dame system of football would make his transition to Enright's staff an easy one. Terlep inherited a stable of talented and proven running backs, but he quickly surmised that his greatest challenge would be dealing with an undersized line with a history of struggling to open up the holes needed to unleash the skills of Gamecock running backs.

Through the early days of contact drills, the Gamecocks suffered a number of key injuries that weakened their already thin depth chart. Fullback Prezioso injured his knee in a scrimmage, an injury that plagued him for the remainder of his USC career.

Ed Pasky, a senior from Erie, Penn., began to emerge as the apparent successor to Bo Hagan at quarterback. Pasky would also be relied upon to play defensive back. Dick Balka, a sophomore from South Bend, Ind., became the backup signal caller. The Gamecock offensive line was led by Lamar Collie, a senior from Augusta, Ga., who had been the most consistent blocker on the 1949 squad. Collie, an excellent student, also served as president of the USC student body.

The Duke Blue Devils provided a stern test for USC in its season opener. Coached by longtime Head Coach Wallace Wade, Duke was a two-touchdown favorite to beat USC and was expected by most prognosticators to finish atop the Southern Conference standings.

Quarterback Billy Cox captained the Blue Devil offense, and his favorite passing target was Mike Souchak, a talented end, who after his time at Duke, would become a successful PGA Tour golfer, winning 15 tournaments and representing the United States in two Ryder Cup competitions.

Despite a number of pleas from university officials in the local papers, advance ticket sales for the home opener against Duke were disappointing. USC Board of Trustees Chairman Rut Osborne wrote an open letter to USC fans that was published in "The State." The chairman's letter questioned whether or not Gamecock fans really wanted big-time football in Columbia. In an attempt to instill some competitive rivalry among the fans, he compared the attendance figures at schools like Duke, North Carolina, and Georgia to the average USC attendance.

Despite Osborne's impassioned plea, only 24,000 out of a possible 34,000 seats were filled in the recently expanded Carolina Stadium on September 23 for the 2 p.m. kickoff to the 1950 season.

The Gamecocks' season began on a sour note when Bishop Strickland fumbled on the first offensive play of the game. Duke recovered on the Carolina 15-yard line and four plays later scored a touchdown to give them a lead they would never relinquish.

Coach Wade instructed his top defender, end Blaine Earon, to key on Wadiak. Earon shadowed Wadiak throughout the game, leading the Blue Devil defense to hold Wadiak to 68 yards on 16 rushing attempts. The Gamecock offense fumbled the ball three times, and its passing game was limited to a mere 21 yards.

Despite the ineffectiveness of their offense, the Gamecocks fought hard and earned the respect of their opponent. Duke's Coach Wade commented after the game, "If South Carolina had not fumbled on the opening play, it may have been an entirely different ball game."

Next up for the Gamecocks was a trip to Atlanta to face Georgia Tech, where once again, the Gamecocks entered the contest as a significant underdog. Tech was coached by Bobby Dodd, who was in his sixth year of what became a legendary 21-year tenure as head coach of the Yellow Jackets. During his time at Tech, his teams made 13 bowl appearances, and his undefeated 1952 team won the college football national championship.

Prior to the game, Coach Enright received a timely phone call from an old coaching friend, Frank Moseley, who was working as an assistant under Paul "Bear" Bryant at Kentucky. Moseley had been sent to scout Georgia Tech in its opening game against SMU, and he advised his old friend that the key to winning the game would be USC's ability to stop Georgia Tech's powerful running game.

Enright leaned on Ted Petoskey, his trusted defensive assistant coach, to devise a plan to stop the Jackets' running attack. Petoskey, a former All-American end on back-to-back national championship teams at the University of Michigan in 1932 and '33, was a brilliant defensive strategist with an innate ability to study the tendencies of an opponent and devise a scheme that would put his players in the best possible position to stop that opponent.

Petoskey was remembered by his former players as an intense motivator, although he was never one to lose control of his emotions. His former pupils recalled how Petoskey would never use profanity but instead relied on his go-to "G-rated" phrase of "Gol Darnit" whenever he saw something he didn't like or wanted to emphasize a point.

The Gamecock defense executed Petoskey's plan to perfection as it limited Georgia Tech rushers to a meager 42 yards and held the Jackets scoreless. USC needed only a single score to win, and the Gamecocks' winning drive was begun after defensive end Don Earley intercepted a Yellow Jacket pass at the Carolina nine-yard line near the end of the third quarter. The Gamecock offense, led by backup quarterback Dick Balka, began to move the football with consecutive pass completions to Moose Kahle and Fred Duckett.

With the ball on the Tech 40-yard line, Balka handed off to Wadiak, who found very little running room at the line of scrimmage. He was immediately swarmed by a group of Tech defenders but somehow broke free and weaved and twisted his way downfield, changing directions and cutting across the field a number of times. He was finally wrestled out of bounds at the Tech five-yard line.

"It was probably the greatest run I ever saw him make," sports publicist Don Barton recalled. "He probably ran 100 yards to get the 35 he gained."

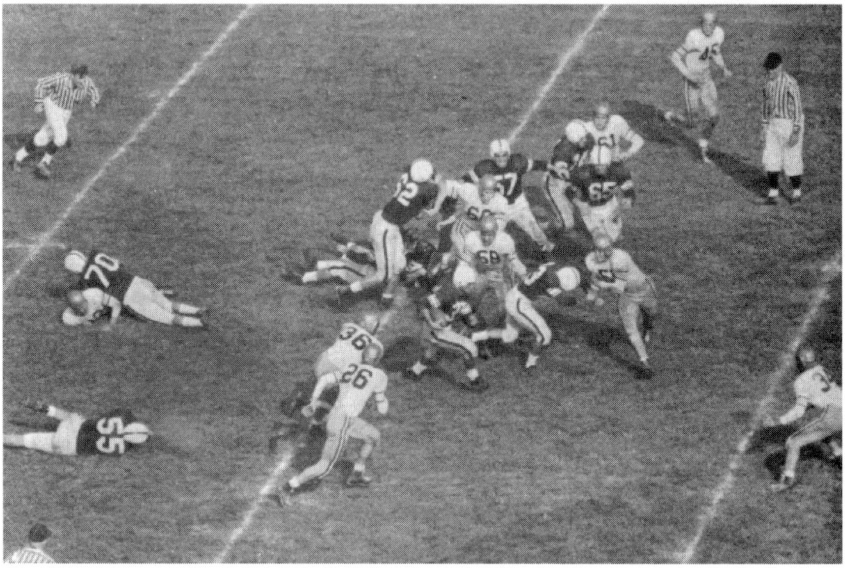

Wadiak explodes through an open hole against Georgia Tech in a 7-0 Gamecock victory in 1950.

(Photo courtesy of "Garnet and Black" yearbook)

More than one experienced sportswriter in attendance at Grant Field that day referred to Wadiak's 35-yard jaunt as one of the greatest runs he had ever witnessed. Later the next week, local movie theaters in Columbia showed a highlight of the game to give Gamecock fans the opportunity to view the spectacular run.

Three plays later, Wadiak took a handoff from Balka and ran behind his left guard, Vince Gargano, toward the end zone. Wadiak was swarmed by four Yellow Jacket defenders at the two-yard line but kept churning his powerful legs and carried the defenders with him into the end zone. Bill Killoy's extra point gave the Gamecocks a 7-0 lead, and that is all they needed to secure the upset win over Georgia Tech.

Following the Tech victory, the Gamecocks earned a 21-6 win over Furman before a sold-out crowd of 15,500 at Greenville's Sirrine

Stadium. Both Wadiak and teammate Bishop Strickland rushed for over 100 yards in the game.

In the third quarter, Wadiak scored on a sideline TD run. After the play was over, a Furman player sneaked up on Bishop Strickland, ripped his helmet off, and gave him a wallop on the back of the head. Strickland quickly retaliated, and an all-out brawl that cleared both benches ensued. It was the second time in a row that the Gamecocks' game against Furman, played in Greenville, had been marred by fisticuffs. Local police were brought onto the field to separate the two teams and restore order, and as a result of the skirmish, officials assessed a 15-yard penalty against the Gamecocks. Strickland was ejected from the game.

In his game story, Jake Penland from "The State" penned a new verb in his description of Wadiak's performance. In reference to Wadiak's nickname, Penland wrote that Wadiak took a handoff and "Cadillaced" to the 27-yard line. Later, in his account of the game, he once again used his newfound verb to explain how Wadiak ran around end and "Cadillaced" down the sideline.

The Gamecock defense was emerging as the strength of the team. It had yielded only 20 points in their first three contests. Contributing to the strong line play was 6'1" 210-lb. sophomore tackle, Hugh Merck. A native of Liberty, S.C., Merck earned All-State high school honors four consecutive years. After participating in the Shrine Bowl—the annual affair pitting the prep All-Stars from North and South Carolina against one another—Merck received 23 scholarship offers. He narrowed his choices to Clemson, Georgia, and South Carolina.

Merck's hometown of Liberty was located less than 20 miles from the Clemson campus, and Merck had grown up a Clemson fan. It was generally assumed that the talented lineman would continue his football career at Clemson and play for legendary Coach Frank Howard.

Merck said he was anxious about meeting the famous "Baron of Barlow Bend," a title Coach Howard had been given in reference to his Alabama birthplace. Ironically, it was that first meeting with Coach Howard that helped Merck realize Clemson was not the school for him.

"He (Howard) sent Banks McFadden to pick me up at my house in Liberty," Merck recalled. "He drove me over to Frank Howard's office, and I walked into an office that was 12-by-14 and had a big wooden desk and two wooden chairs sitting in front of the desk. There was a large picture of a tiger behind his desk. It wasn't very palatial, and it was pretty intimidating. Howard had a big ol' chew of tobacco in his mouth and a spittoon sitting in the corner of his office. He grabbed a chair and got right up in my face and began to curse at me. He looked right at me and said, 'Merck, you ain't nothing but a snotty nosed linthead . . . You would be stupid to consider going anywhere else but here.

. . . 'cause you're one of us.'

I knew right then that if he talked to me like that as a recruit, there was no way I could ever play for him."

The next week, Merck signed his scholarship agreement with Rex Enright, the gentlemanly, soft-spoken head coach of the Gamecocks.

The Gamecocks held a promising 2-1 record entering the 1950 Clemson game on Big Thursday, and Steve Wadiak's performance in the first three games had been outstanding. Gamecock fans were hoping it was a prelude to what he might do against Clemson.

Meanwhile, Clemson had dominated its first three opponents—Presbyterian, Missouri, and N.C. State—by a combined score of 115-0. The Tigers' equivalent of Steve Wadiak was their senior fullback, Fred Cone. While Coach Howard may have let local star Hugh Merck slip through his grasp, he used his keen football insight, along with some good fortune to uncover a rare hidden talent in Fred Cone.

Cone was born in 1926, the same year as Wadiak, and like his Gamecock counterpart, Cone's football career began in relative obscurity. He grew up in the small farming community of Pine Apple, Ala., located a few miles south of Montgomery.

Cone did not play high school football for the simple reason that Moore Academy, his small Alabama high school, did not have a football team. He played on the school's basketball team, which played its home games on an outdoor clay court lit by a string of spotlights.

After high school, Cone enlisted in the U.S. Army and spent time in Japan as a paratrooper with the elite 11th Airborne Division. After the war ended, Cone happened to be visiting his sister in Biloxi, Miss., and had an experience that would forever change his life.

The next-door neighbor and best friend of Cone's sister in Biloxi was Hazel Howard, the sister of Clemson Coach Frank Howard. Hazel took note of Cone's solid build and athleticism while observing him jumping off a diving board at a nearby swimming pool. She petitioned her brother to give Fred a chance to attend Clemson. Howard happened to have one scholarship left to give in 1947, and out of his respect for his sister, he sent Fred Cone an invitation from Clemson with a chance to earn that final spot on his team.

Quickly, Cone proved to be a gritty and talented football player who blossomed under the tutelage of Coach Howard and his staff. He had natural instincts and a physical toughness that would become the trademark of his career. In his sophomore season in 1948, Cone was a key contributor to Clemson's first undefeated season.

By the time his senior season arrived in 1950, Cone was regarded as one of the nation's top running backs. His contributions to the Clemson football program earned him an eventual place in Clemson's Ring of Honor, the highest and most prestigious award that a Clemson athlete can receive from the school. After graduating from Clemson, Cone played seven years for the Green Bay Packers as a running back and place kicker, eventually earning a spot in the Green Bay Packer Hall of Fame. After one year with the expansion Dallas Cowboys, Cone returned to Clemson in 1961 as the director of football recruiting, working for his old coach, Frank Howard.

After three games, Gamecock fans began to tout Steve Wadiak as the next Gamecock All-American, but All-Americans in Gamecock football were about as rare as Republican governors in the South. Gamecock publicity man Don Barton knew he would have his work cut out for him if Wadiak were to gain coveted All-American status.

Barton had extra photographs printed of the Gamecock superstar, and he sent them to as many local and national media outlets as possible. He touted Wadiak's statistics and exploits to anyone who would listen.

One day, Cliff Turner, the developmentally disabled young man who followed every movement of the Gamecocks football team, tracked Barton down and made an emphatic request.

"I want picture Wadiak," Cliff insisted.

Barton was in the midst of an extremely busy day and wasn't really sure he could spare one of his media prints for Cliff, so he put Cliff off by simply telling him if he would come back to see him in two months, he would give him a picture of his hero, Steve Wadiak.

Barton said that two months to the day, Cliff showed up at his office requesting the picture he had been promised. Barton obliged and gave Steve's biggest fan a photo of his hero. Cliff left Barton's office with a broad smile, clutching his new valued possession. Cliff had no way of knowing that the "street value" of a Steve Wadiak photo was about to increase significantly.

Publicity photo of Steve Wadiak—1951

(Photo courtesy of USC Archives)

17
The Game

In November of 1970, an 11-year-old Gamecock fan was excited that his father had promised to take him to the Carolina-Clemson game. The boy's father had attended every Carolina-Clemson game since 1941, with the exception of the three he missed while serving in the military during World War II.

The young boy enjoyed his father's stories about former Gamecock heroes. There were many tales about the "great Steve Wadiak." In the middle of the week leading up to the 1970 Carolina-Clemson contest, the boy made a request of his father: "Dad, will you tell me the story about *the game*?"

Immediately, the boy's father knew which story his son was requesting. With exacting detail, his father relayed his memories of the 1950 Carolina-Clemson game.

Heavy rains fell on Columbia in the hours leading up to the 2 p.m. Saturday kickoff. The rains were the lingering effects of Hurricane King, a Category 3 hurricane that had made a direct hit on downtown Miami a few days before. Packing 125 mph winds, Hurricane King caused $27 million of property damage in southern Florida and claimed the lives of seven people.

The weather did not deter South Carolinians from attending the most significant social event of the year. A capacity crowd of 35,000 fans filled Carolina Stadium shortly before kickoff.

The storm did, however, significantly alter the typical fall fashion show that took place as part of the rivalry game. Instead of their finest fall attire, spectators covered themselves in raincoats, ponchos, rubber hats, and boots—anything that might protect them from the winds and rains that pummeled the Midlands. Fortunately, the rain subsided about 20 minutes before game time, and as the teams walked onto the field for the kickoff, the sun began to peek through the overcast skies.

Twenty-nine newspapers were represented in the wooden press box atop the west stands of Carolina Stadium. Five networks were on hand to broadcast the game, which would air on 46 stations across the region. The broadcast also was transmitted to the Armed Forces Network and aired on a number of military bases in Korea, where U.S. troops remained heavily engaged in the Korean Conflict.

As the Gamecocks dressed in the basement of Carolina Field House, players were handed shoes that featured extra-long spikes. With the consistent rains that had fallen, Gamecock coaches knew that the field would be a quagmire. The spikes would give Gamecock players a better chance to find footing on the treacherous playing field.

Clemson was dressed in white jerseys trimmed with orange numbers. The Tigers wore burnt orange helmets and purple pants. South Carolina wore white pants, garnet jerseys with white numerals, and white helmets trimmed in garnet. Within a few minutes of action, nearly all of the players' uniforms were covered in mud, making it difficult to distinguish individual numbers.

With a record of 3-0, Clemson entered the contest ranked 12th in the nation, and the Tigers were a solid seven-point favorite over the 2-1 Gamecocks.

The physical intensity of the rivalry was on display early in the game. On Clemson's second possession, star fullback Fred Cone took a direct snap from center and started to execute a "spinner" play, in which he attempted to confuse the Gamecock defenders by spinning 90 degrees after taking the snap and handing off to wingback Ray Matthews. After spinning and executing the handoff, Cone was immediately blindsided by Don Earley, the Gamecocks' left tackle. Earley, a 6'1" 210-lb. sophomore from Vandergrift, Pa., threw a violent forearm and elbow directly to the unprotected face of Cone. The Tiger star collapsed to the ground, his face gushing blood.

Sixty-three years after the incident, 86-year-old Cone watched a replay of the hit delivered on him by Earley, acknowledging that he had never been told the name of the player who had leveled him.

"What was his number? Who was he?" Cone joked as he watched the game film. "I'd like to know where he is today."

Cone managed to get up after the play and stayed in the game to punt for the Tigers on the very next play. When he reached the sideline, trainers immediately stitched the open wound in his face. Known for his toughness, Cone refused to allow the injury to keep him out of the Tiger lineup. The blow to the face and the stitches seemed to do nothing but inspire him to an even greater level of intensity.

Cone's attacker, Don Earley, fractured his hand on the play. He recalled that the break was so severe, a bone in his hand was protruding from the skin. He went to the sideline, had his hand taped up, and played the remainder of the game. Remembering the play in which he injured Cone as well as himself, Earley was apologetic.

"I didn't intend to hurt him," Earley recalled. "I knew after he handed off that he would become a blocker, and so I needed to hit him, but I honestly wasn't trying to hurt him."

Like Cone, who followed his playing days with a long-term career as a coach, Earley spent over 30 years as a successful high school football, track, and basketball coach in Western Pennsylvania.

Neither team mounted any offense in their first three possessions. In their fourth possession, the Gamecocks faced a second-and-eight from their seven-yard line. Quarterback Eddie Pasky pitched the ball to Wadiak, who swept toward the right side of the field. Backfield mates Bishop Strickland and Tony Garrafalo executed textbook blocks that gave Wadiak some daylight on the corner.

At the 20-yard line, a Tiger defender closed in for the tackle. As he began to reach for Wadiak, he was hit in the face by a sledgehammer. Steve quickly thrust his left arm toward the defender, jamming the heel of his palm directly into the face of the oncoming tackler and knocking him to the ground. Wadiak sprinted down the sideline before he was finally pushed out of bounds at the Clemson 25-yard line, completing an electrifying 66-yard run.

Gamecock fans erupted. They sensed that their team was going to make a game of it with the favored Tigers. Six plays later, with the ball on the Clemson five-yard line, Wadiak took a handoff and bowled straight up the middle, running over a couple of would-be tacklers on his way to the first score of the game. Bill Killoy's extra point gave the Gamecocks a 7-0 lead in the early minutes of the second quarter. The scoring drive covered 89 yards. Wadiak's efforts accounted for 81 of them.

On their next possession, the Gamecocks moved the football down the field again behind the running of Wadiak and Strickland. Their drive stalled on the Clemson 37-yard line, and Bill Killoy's field goal attempt sailed underneath the cross bar.

Throughout the first half, the Gamecock defense played superbly. Linebackers Ashley Phillips, Roy Skinner, and Harry Jabbusch, tackles Don Earley and Hugh Merck, and ends John "Lip" LaTorre and Spec Granger led a Gamecock defense that was not fooled by the trickery of

Clemson's single wing. They played disciplined, spirited football and frustrated the Tiger runners throughout the first half.

On offense, Clemson's coaches knew they had to change something. Midway through the second quarter, with first down on its 44-yard line, Ray Matthews fired a long pass down the sideline toward Billy Hair. The Clemson receiver was surrounded by three Gamecock defenders, all of whom appeared to leap in unison in an attempt to deflect the pass.

USC's Tommy Woodlee came the closest to touching the ball, but it slipped through his outstretched fingers and fell into the hands of Clemson's Hair. Quickly, Hair secured the ball and turned upfield, realizing that he was now behind all of the Gamecock defenders who had overcommitted on the interception attempt. Hair sprinted untouched into the Tiger end zone. The PAT sent the teams into the locker room tied at 7-7.

The pageantry of the annual event was showcased at halftime. Visiting dignitaries and their wives paraded across the muddy field and waved to the fans. Included in the entourage was Governor Strom Thurmond and Governor-elect James F. Byrnes, as well as the presidents of both schools.

Late in the third quarter, South Carolina took possession after a Clemson punt on their 27-yard line. On the first-down play, Pasky handed off to Wadiak, who followed his blocking up the middle, just left of center. He appeared to be stopped three yards past the line of scrimmage, disappearing from view for a moment, when all of a sudden, he broke free and turned on his open field speed.

Two Clemson defenders stood ahead of him but were caught flat-footed as they assumed the play had been stopped. With a full head of steam, Wadiak streaked passed them and raced 73 yards for the go-ahead touchdown. When he crossed the goal line, there were no Tiger defensemen within 15 yards of him. Killoy's extra point kick gave the Gamecocks a 14-7 lead heading into the final quarter.

At the start of the fourth quarter, Blackie Kincaid intercepted a pass from Clemson quarterback Jackie Calvert and returned it 15 yards to the Clemson 42-yard line. Gamecock fans could sense that victory was within their collective grasp.

The Gamecock ground attack moved the ball down to the Clemson 23-yard line on three consecutive runs. The Gamecock runners were churning the clock and moving the football steadily downfield. A Gamecock score would secure the upset win for Carolina.

Facing second-and-three, Enright called a pass play. It was unsuccessful. On third down and short yardage, once again, the Gamecocks called for a pass. This time Pasky's throw was intercepted by Clemson's Jimmy Ward at the Clemson five-yard line. On that day, South Carolina would attempt nine passes and complete none, and two of their aerials were snagged by their opponents.

The decision to go to the air at that point in the game left Gamecock fans wondering, given the daylong success of their running game. After the interception, Clemson was stopped once again and had to punt.

The Gamecocks moved the ball into Clemson territory but were stalled at the 30-yard line. Out of field goal range, the Gamecocks went into punt formation. Punter Tommy Woodlee attempted a pass on a fake punt, but the pass slipped through the hands of Bishop Strickland and Clemson took over on its 30-yard line.

Sensing that the game was on the line, Clemson began to feed the ball to its workhorse fullback, Fred Cone. After an 11-yard completion from Billy Hair to Glen Smith, Cone exploded through the line of scrimmage for a 12-yard gain.

The Tigers were on the move. Cone caught a 14-yard pass from Ray Matthews. An untimely piling-on penalty against the Gamecock moved the ball to the Gamecock 28-yard line. Four plays later, Cone bullied his way into the end zone on a short run. In the Tigers nine-play, 70-yard scoring drive, Cone handled the ball six of the nine plays and accounted for 40 of the 70 yards. Cone finished the game with 117 rushing yards on 29 attempts.

Charlie Radcliff came on to kick the all-important extra point for the Tigers. His kick sailed wide. South Carolina held a slim lead, 14-13, but one of the officials stood beside a flag he had thrown. The Gamecocks were offside on the play, giving Radcliff a mulligan for his miss. This time, the extra point sailed through the middle of the uprights, and the game was tied at 14 with a minute and 45 seconds to play.

The Gamecocks had one chance remaining. All day, Wadiak had carried the Gamecock offense on his back, and he was now more determined than ever to finish the task. Wadiak grabbed Cone's kickoff at the 18-yard line and ran it back to the 34-yard line. On the next play, Wadiak took a pitch and headed around right end with some running room. He cut back horizontally across the field and made a dash toward the Gamecock sideline.

Gamecock fans leapt to their feet, anticipating another explosive run from their star back. This time, however, Clemson's Jackie Calvert caught up with Wadiak and shoved him out of bounds at the Clemson 28-yard line. It was a 38-yard gain and another highlight run by Wadiak.

Pasky attempted a quarterback keeper with no gain, and Bishop Strickland ran a reverse that pushed the ball to the Tiger 20-yard line. Wadiak then bowled over a guard on a quickie and picked up the first down, but a penalty nullified the run.

Pasky attempted a pass over the middle, but the throw was off target and fell incomplete. Facing fourth down as time was running out, Gamecock coaches sent in Bill Killoy to try a game-winning field goal. His hurried 38-yard attempt fell well short of the goal post.

The game ended in a 14-14 tie. Jake Penland of "The State" described the mood in the stadium as time expired:

> *There was little hilarity in the stands. It was an unusual situation. Clemson's followers came to the stadium expecting to see their team win and retain its high national ranking. The fact that the Tigers were outplayed—and fortunate to gain a tie near the end of the game and see time run out with the Gamecocks threatening—does not inspire them to cheers. Followers of the Gamecocks had seen their team take a first half lead only to lose it with less than two minutes of the second half remaining. And then with their team again in the lead and victory less than two minutes away, they saw that lead kicked away. They should have been happy to secure a 14-14 tie, but they were almost glum because they felt they had been cheated out of a sweet victory.*

The opposing coaches had differing perspectives on the outcome.

"Well, on the basis of our performance, we could easily have won," South Carolina's Enright told reporters after the tie. "Some unfortunate penalties kept us from doing that. But those boys played their hearts out, and we are holding our heads high."

The Gamecocks were penalized 115 yards in the game. During Clemson's final scoring drive, a 15-yard piling-on penalty gave the Tigers a needed boost of momentum. After the contest, the culprit of the penalty tearfully apologized to Coach Enright.

On the other side of the field, Coach Howard saw the result in a different light. "We lost a game," Howard bemoaned. "They outplayed us throughout the game."

When asked if the wet field gave USC an advantage, Howard refused to make excuses.

"Hell no," he told reporters. "We both played on the same field, didn't we?"

The tie with the Gamecocks turned out to be the only blemish on Clemson's 1950 9-0-1 record. The Tigers earned a berth in the Orange Bowl, where they defeated Missouri 15-14 and closed out the season as the 10th-ranked team in the country.

The performance of the Gamecock defense was overshadowed by Wadiak's incredible day, however, in four games, the Gamecock defenders had given up only one rushing touchdown and had shut out two of its four opponents.

Steve Wadiak, No. 37, gains yardage against Clemson in the 1950 rivalry game.

(Photo courtesy of "Garnet and Black" yearbook)

Wadiak's performance was the single greatest offensive performance to date in the 58-year history of Gamecock football. He rushed for 256 yards on 19 attempts and scored two touchdowns against a defense that finished the season ranked seventh in the nation.

Wadiak's single game rushing record stood until 1973 when USC quarterback Jeff Grantz rushed for 260 yards against Ohio University. In 1991, Brandon Bennett eclipsed Grantz's record by rushing for 278 yards against East Tennessee State. To put Wadiak's performance in perspective, it occurred on a muddy field against a team that finished 9-0-1 and featured one of the stingiest defenses in the country. Ohio University in 1973 finished 5-5 and East Tennessee State completed its 1991 season with a 4-7 record primarily against Division II opponents.

Furman Bisher, covering the game for "The Atlanta Constitution," wrote of Wadiak's performance: "The hurricane moved out and Wadiak moved in. Give the gentleman a slither of daylight, and he'll take advantage of you."

Bob Quincy of the "Charlotte Observer" acknowledged the performance of both Wadiak and his counterpart Fred Cone: "Get Wadiak the Cadillac, but get Cone something nice too."

Steve Wadiak's remarkable performance in the 1950 contest further propelled his iconic status among Gamecock fans. It was a performance that those in attendance would share with their children and grandchildren for years to come. To some, it would always be referred to as "The Game."

18
MVP

On the Thursday following the 1950 Clemson game, the Gamecock football team boarded a charter flight that took them to Washington, D.C., for a Friday night game against the George Washington University Colonels. The match-up between the two Southern Conference schools was to be played at historic Griffith Stadium, home of the NFL's Washington Redskins and the American League's perennial doormat, the Washington Senators.

A small but vocal band of Gamecock fans made the trip to D.C. and were accompanied by the Carolina cheerleaders. A homecoming crowd of 13,497 filled about half of the wooden seats at Griffith Stadium.

The game against the Colonels provided the Gamecocks exposure to the influential D.C. media market. Gamecock publicist Don Barton recognized the importance of this exposure in his efforts to get Steve Wadiak the postseason recognition he deserved. Barton pumped local media outlets in advance of the game with a steady flow of material on Wadiak's exploits. The D.C. papers responded by hyping the USC runner throughout the days prior to the game. Steve responded well to the added attention.

After battling to a 7-7 halftime tie, South Carolina erupted for 27 points in the second half to soundly defeat GW 34-20. The Colonels were unable to stop the potent backfield tandem of Wadiak and Bishop Strickland.

The highlight of the game came on the first play of the fourth quarter. With the Gamecocks ahead 14-7 and backed up near their end zone, quarterback Ed Pasky called "left quickie" in the Gamecock huddle. It was a play designed for Wadiak to follow his left guard and try to nudge the ball out a few yards in order to provide some breathing room for punter Tommy Woodlee.

As Wadiak approached the line of scrimmage, he saw a small crease open between his left guard and left tackle. He exploded through the opening, juked one tackler just past the line of scrimmage, and darted toward the left sideline. A lone GW defender had an angle on him and closed in for the stop. Steve picked him up out of the corner of his eye, slowed his pace slightly, and braced his sturdy frame for contact.

As the tackler neared within an arm's distance, Steve thrust his right arm outward and upward with such exertion that Wadiak's feet actually left the ground. The blow caught the defender directly under his chin, and he fell to the ground.

The GW player became another victim of what many referred to as the most dangerous offensive weapon in the Southern Conference—Steve Wadiak's stiff arm.

Steve's powerful upper body, combined with his perfect technique, made it extremely difficult for a solo tackler to bring him down. Steve enjoyed ramming his open palm into the unprotected face of would-be tacklers and using the momentum of the stiff arm to propel himself farther downfield.

After escaping the last GW defender, Wadiak sprinted, untouched, 96 yards for a Gamecock touchdown. The TD run stands today as the South Carolina school record for the longest run from scrimmage.

The high profile game in Washington, D.C., may have been one of Wadiak's best all around games. He rushed for 182 yards on 24 attempts and also completed an 11-yard halfback option pass for a touchdown to his running mate Bishop Strickland. The D.C. media took note of the performance, which brought a smile to the face of Gamecock press man Don Barton.

Perhaps one of the least known but more defining moments of Wadiak's career came late in the game against the Colonels. The Gamecocks held a 27-13 lead and were driving for a final score. With first-and-goal from the one-yard line, quarterback Ed Pasky called for a dive play for Wadiak. In the huddle, Wadiak looked at Pasky and said, "Let's give someone else a chance to score. I already got mine," referring to the fact that he had already scored twice in the game.

The guys in the huddle were not at all surprised by the unselfishness of their star back. It was consistent with the humility they had seen him display since the day he arrived on the USC campus. On the next play, Pasky kept the ball on a quarterback sneak and scored his first touchdown of the game.

As the game drew to a close, a frustrated George Washington player took a swing at the Gamecocks' Tommy Woodlee, which incited an all-out slugfest between the two teams. A number of fans ran onto the field and got in on the action, turning the melee into a near riot scene.

An older female GW fan walloped Gamecock lineman Harry Stewart in the back of his head with her purse, shouting at him as she hit him, "Go back where you came from, you damn rebels."

Stewart, who hailed from Benton, Ill., retreated from his assailant and told her, "Lady, where I come from, we call people in Washington, D.C., rebels."

The fighting lasted about five minutes before coaches and police managed to break it up, and the two teams retreated to their respective locker rooms.

Five games into the 1950 season, Wadiak had firmly established himself as one of the most prolific backs in the country. Furman Bisher of "The Atlanta Constitution" called Wadiak and SMU's Kyle Rote "the two most effective backs I've seen this year."

Steve's 706 yards rushing though the season's first five games ranked him fourth in the nation in total yards.

NCAA Collegiate Rushing Statistics—November 1, 1950

Player	School	Yards	Attempts	Games
White	Arizona State	1013	118	6
Bright	Drake	868	129	7
Reynolds	Nebraska	835	103	5
Wadiak	South Carolina	706	94	5

USC's record was a respectable 3-1-1 as the team returned home and prepared to host Marquette in a Friday night match-up at Carolina Stadium. The Gamecocks battled the Hilltoppers to a 13-13 tie, and Wadiak notched his third consecutive 100-yard plus rushing game as he gained 108 yards on 25 attempts. Late in the game, Steve crossed the 2,000-yard career rushing mark.

Next up for the Gamecocks was the Citadel in Charleston. During the previous season, the Gamecocks romped over the Bulldogs 42-0, leaving a bad taste in the mouths of Bulldog players.

The Gamecocks arrived early on Friday afternoon and checked into the Francis Marion Hotel. Steve and his good friend John LaTorre, along with a handful other teammates, walked down King Street, where John, a Charleston native, showed them a few of his favorite men's clothing stores. After the players returned to the Francis Marion, LaTorre's father stopped by the hotel for a visit with his son. The elder LaTorre offered a warning to his son and the Gamecocks who were gathered in the hotel room.

"He told us we had better watch out, that they (the Citadel team) were fired up," John recalled. "He said that the Citadel boys were really out to get us this year."

The words of LaTorre's father proved prophetic. The Bulldogs played inspired football and utilized two blocked punts to defeat the heavily favored Gamecocks 19-7 in front of 10,000 surprised spectators. The Citadel's center, Sam Rubino, blocked a Tommy Woodlee punt in the first quarter, scooped up the ball, and ran it in for a score. Lightning struck again when Rubino crashed through to block a second Woodlee punt. This time, teammate Paul Drews ran it in for a touchdown, giving the Bulldogs a 12-0 halftime lead over the stunned Gamecocks.

It was the first time The Citadel had defeated USC since 1926. Wadiak was held to under 100 yards for only the second time in the season, rushing for 96 yards on 17 attempts.

Citadel Coach Quinn Decker commented on the significance of the win for his Bulldog team. "We'd rather beat the Gamecocks than anybody on our schedule," he said. "Our play against South Carolina was the best performance of any team I have coached in my 19 years at The Citadel."

Following the disappointing loss to The Citadel, the Gamecocks returned to Columbia for a homecoming match-up against North Carolina. USC entered the afternoon game a seven-point underdog. Starting quarterback Ed Pasky was unavailable to play due to a leg injury, so the starting nod went to Dick Balka, a redshirt transfer from Notre Dame.

UNC Head Coach Carl Snavely reinforced a simple message to his team as they prepared for USC—stop the running game of Wadiak and Strickland. The Tar Heel defense was anchored by its captain, Irvin "Huck" Holdash. Snavely asked Holdash to hone in on Wadiak and appealed to him as the leader of the team to shut down USC's star runner.

Holdash was the first athlete from his small hometown of Austintown, Ohio, to receive a scholarship to a major university. He was a hardnosed football player to whom Wadiak referred at the end of the 1950 season as the best defensive player he faced all year.

The Tar Heel defenders were physical and tough. Both Wadiak and Strickland received injuries during the first half of the game, rendering them less than 100 percent for the remainder of the contest. As the Gamecocks' passing attack continued to be inept, the Tar Heels stacked their defensive line in anticipation of the run.

Steve Wadiak's teammate, Bob "Moose" Kahle, poses with the official's penalty flag that Wadiak handed to him in the huddle of the USC-UNC game in 1950. Bob passed away in December 2013.

Everywhere Wadiak turned, UNC defenders were waiting for him. Frustration mounted. Finally, in the third quarter, Wadiak broke free for a 16-yard run only to see a penalty flag laying on the ground as he walked back to the huddle. As the referees huddled to discuss the call, Wadiak leaned over, picked up the flag, and brought it back to the huddle, unseen by the officials. He handed the flag to teammate Moose Kahle and instructed him to hide it in his pants.

On an otherwise dismal day, the Gamecock players were able to get a laugh as they watched the officials searching frantically for the missing flag. The officials never found the flag that Moose kept stuffed in his pants for the remainder of the game. Kahle, who passed away in 2013, kept the flag as a treasured reminder of his playing days with Wadiak.

The Gamecocks closed the season with a disappointing 14-7 home loss to Coach Peahead Walker's Wake Forest Demon Deacons. South Carolina finished with a 3-4-2 record. If not for the impressive performance against a powerful Clemson team, Gamecock fans would have likely been demanding a coaching change. Wadiak finished with 998 yards rushing on 163 attempts, while playing only nine games. Gamecock publicist Don Barton regrets to this day that he did not send word to the sideline during the season's final game that Steve was only two yards short of reaching 1,000 yards rushing. Wadiak's 998 yards broke the single-season rushing record in the Southern Conference, a record previously held by UNC's Choo Choo Justice.

Teammate Don Earley, who spent more than 30 years coaching high school football in Pennsylvania, noted, "I would have loved to have seen what Steve could have done in an I-formation as a tailback. He played in the straight T all four years at Carolina, and he had to share the football with two other running backs. There is no telling how many yards he would have gained as a tailback."

While Wadiak was still known to most as Th' Cadillac, writers handed out a number of other nicknames including "Stout Steve," "Steamboat

Steve," and "the Chicago Comet." The origin of Steamboat Steve was either a result of Wadiak's service in the Navy or the fact that he was observed making a snorting sound as he ran the football. One of his teammates said he sounded like a "steamboat" when he ran.

As the season neared its end, Don Barton continued to promote Wadiak to the press corps. He sent out a questionnaire with a series of football trivia questions, all of which had the same correct answer—Steve Wadiak. Each question was designed to raise awareness about one of Wadiak's many accomplishments.

The coveted Most Valuable Player award in the Southern Conference was scheduled to be given out at the D.C. Touchdown Club after the completion of the college bowl games. Wadiak was a dark-horse candidate to win the award, given the somewhat dismal record of his Gamecock team. Maryland's Bob Ward was the favorite, with UNC's Holdash and Duke's Billy Cox expected to give Ward some competition.

In anticipation of Ward's winning the award, publicity photos of him were taken in advance. When all the votes were tallied, however, the winner of the coveted MVP award was Steve Wadiak.

Barton recalled getting an urgent phone call from the program director of the awards banquet requesting that he get a photo of Steve in a tuxedo posing like he was reaching to receive a trophy. Barton obliged and sent the photo to D.C. to be included in the program for the banquet.

It was the first time a South Carolina football player had been named the most valuable football player in the Southern Conference. Wadiak flew to Washington, D.C., to attend the Touchdown Club's annual awards banquet on Sat., Jan. 5, 1951. He arrived three days early and was treated like royalty by the club's sponsors.

The D.C. Touchdown Club was founded by Arthur "Dutch"

Bergman in 1934. Bergman was a former running back at Notre Dame in the 1920s alongside the famous George Gipp. He later coached football at Minnesota, New Mexico, and Catholic University. He founded the club in an effort to recognize the nation's top athletes and to raise money for various charities.

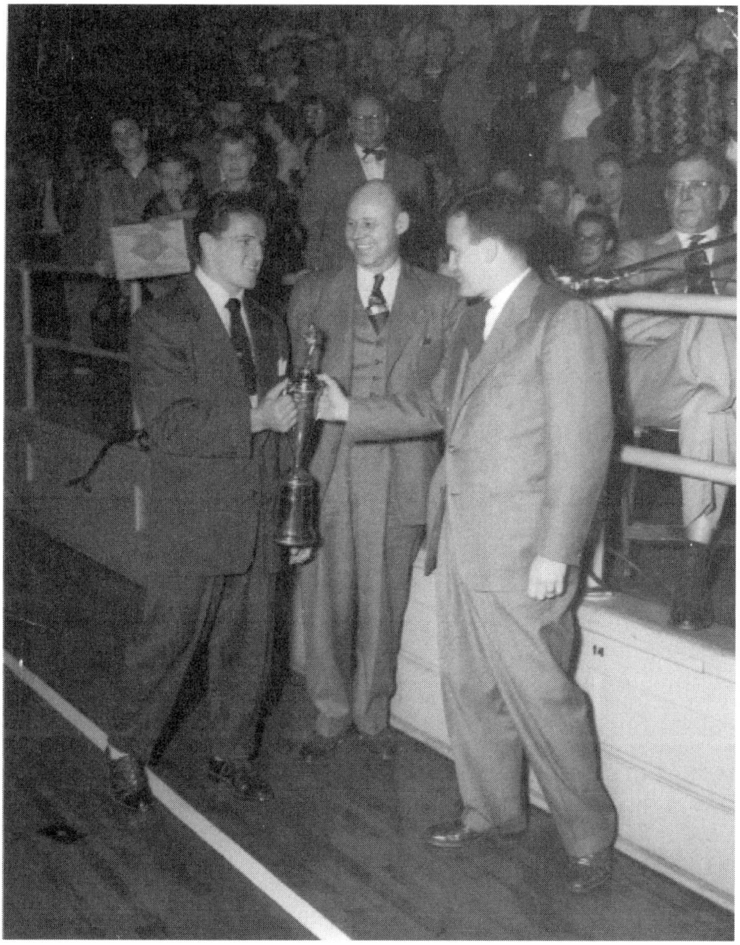

Steve Wadiak is presented his 1950 Southern Conference Most Valuable Player trophy at halftime of a USC basketball game in Carolina Field House.

(Photo courtesy of USC Archives)

The annual awards banquet was a black-tie affair held at D.C.'s Statler Hotel. The 1,200-person guest list read like a who's who in American sports. "Sports Illustrated" called it the "granddaddy of all sports banquets." Sports-minded politicians also flocked to the event, and the 1951 gathering included Supreme Court Chief Justice Fred Vinson and Speaker of the House of Representatives Sam Rayburn. During the week of the event, D.C. became the sports capital of America, with more than 200 of the nation's top coaches and athletes attending the gala, including former heavyweight champion Jack Dempsey and New York Yankee shortstop, Phil Rizzuto.

A photo from "The Washington Times Herald" featured Wadiak standing between NFL Player of the Year Bob Waterfield and legendary Oklahoma Coach Bud Wilkinson. "The Washington Post" featured a large photo of all of the banquet's 14 award winners and displayed Wadiak in his tuxedo standing next to Kentucky's Babe Parilli, who received the Walter Camp Award as the nation's top collegiate back.

Sixteen years after Wadiak was honored by the Washington, D.C. Touchdown Club, another outstanding college football player with connections to the University of South Carolina was invited to attend the same banquet. This University of Florida senior earned college football's most coveted award in 1967—The Heisman Trophy. A press photo from the 1967 banquet shows the athlete standing alongside Sonny Jurgensen, NFL player of the year in 1966. The banquet honoree went on to become the winningest coach in the history of USC football—Stephen O. Spurrier.

19
Suspended

After the 1950 season, Steve Wadiak accumulated a number of postseason accolades. He was named captain of the Associated Press's All-Southern team by virtue of receiving the most votes of any player. He was selected for two prestigious All-South Teams: "Collier's Magazine" and the International News Service (predecessor of United Press International). These teams were comprised of players from the Southern and Southeastern Conferences, as well as independents. Steve was also the top vote getter on the South Carolina All-State team.

Wadiak was considered by most as the "Mr. Football" of the South, a player predicted to be a leading candidate for All-American honors going into the 1951 season. After his record-breaking junior season, professional scouts took notice of his talents.

Upon receiving the 1950 Southern Conference MVP award, Wadiak, acting with his typical humility, acknowledged the role of his coach and teammates in his success, stating: "All I have today, I owe to my teammates and to the finest coach a man could have—Rex Enright."

In three short years, Wadiak had risen from an unknown Chicago sandlot player to the most iconic superstar in the history of USC athletics. Requests for his public appearances were numerous. He was not comfortable being the center of attention, but he never refused when asked to give his time. It was his way of displaying gratitude for the good fortune he had experienced in Columbia.

Steve preferred spending time outside of the public eye—going on a date with his girlfriend, Nancy Fulmer, or simply cruising around town in his 1950 Pontiac. He was always courteous when someone recognized him, yet secretly he wished he were not so noticeable.

Other than the occasional invasion of privacy from an adoring fan, Steve Wadiak was living a dream. He was playing the sport he loved in a community that had become his home. He recalled how a few short years before he had returned from the war without any real direction or opportunity for his life. Now, he was living a life that seemed almost too good to be true.

In February of 1951, Steve's dream-like existence was interrupted by a mysterious ordeal that would become a lone black mark on his otherwise untarnished legend.

On the morning of March 1, 1951, Gamecock fans across the state opened their local newspapers to read a short but shocking wire service story from Columbia.

> *Columbia (AP)—Steve Wadiak, University of South Carolina halfback, has been suspended from the university for the remainder of the school semester.*
>
> *The action was taken yesterday by a faculty discipline committee after what Coach Rex Enright called an "infraction of university rules." A university spokesman said, however, that it will be possible for Wadiak to attend summer school and be eligible to play with the Gamecocks next fall.*
>
> *"Steve Wadiak has always been a hardworking, clean living football player," Coach Rex Enright said. "He does not drink or smoke in season or out of season. He is now involved in an infraction of the university rules. When he is permitted to return to the university, he will certainly be welcomed on the football squad."*

Fans across the state were stunned. How could this be? The life-blood of the Gamecock football team, the hero of every schoolboy in the state, the humble superstar who always had a kind greeting for everyone—suspended. There had to be some kind of mistake.

The events that led to Steve's suspension from school began on Sunday evening, Feb. 25, 1951, when a young man showed up at USC's Sims dormitory looking for Miss Nancy Claire Fulmer. He was informed that Miss Fulmer was out on a date, so he asked if he could speak with the person who was in charge of the dormitory. He was told that the person was sick, so he began to explain the purpose of his visit to the hostess on duty.

The man reached into his pocket and pulled out a marriage certificate dated December 1947, which showed that he and Nancy Fulmer were married. He told the hostess at the dorm that the marriage had been kept secret, but Nancy's parents were aware of it. He went on to explain that he had been the principal at Nancy's high school while she was a student there, but he was now working as a manager of a Piggly Wiggly store in Walterboro, S.C.

He then demanded that something be done about the relationship between Steve Wadiak and the woman he claimed was his wife, Nancy Fulmer. He told the hostess that not only were Wadiak and Fulmer dating, but also that Wadiak had taken Fulmer on two weekend out-of-town trips. The man also asserted that Coach Enright and many of Nancy's friends at the Sims dorm were aware of his marriage to Nancy, as well as her current relationship with Wadiak.

On Tues., February 27, Mrs. A.B. Childs, the university's dean of women, called Nancy in for an interview related to the man's claims. The following is taken from the official transcript of that interview:

Dean Childs: Are you married?

Miss Fulmer: In a sense.

Dean Childs: Are you married in the eyes of the law?

Miss Fulmer: Yes.

Dean Childs: When were you married?

Miss Fulmer: When I was 15 years old, just turning 16, 4 years ago. I never lived with him –there was only a marriage ceremony. I didn't want to tell my mother. We had decided to wait to tell her, wait until this summer. But we told her last year, in April. The lawyer we had said to wait to do anything about it until after school was over, that this summer we would do whatever we could.

Dean Childs: When did your mother find out?

Miss Fulmer: Last April, at Easter, there was no choice but to tell her. We got into a predicament. After Mother found out, we went to our lawyer, Senator Brown, and asked him if he thought it was necessary to tell the school officials. He said that since I was established there as Nancy Fulmer, I should go along as I was. If anything came up, he would take care of it. He assured Mother and me that it was all right.

Dean Childs: Have you told your friends and other people here about your marriage?

Miss Fulmer: Yes. I haven't offered, but if they asked, I told them.

Female students at the university were required to sign out whenever they left the dormitories in the evenings.

Dean Childs: When you go out and come home at about 10:30, signing out for supper and a show, are you out with Steve Wadiak?

Miss Fulmer: I'm often with friends, girls from Columbia College.

Dean Childs: Here is your engagement card showing you out six nights,

until 10 and 11 o'clock at night. Was this with these girlfriends, or are you with Steve Wadiak often during the evening?
Miss Fulmer: I do see him when I go out with friends. I don't consider seeing him that way dating.

After establishing that Miss Fulmer was in fact married to the man who had visited the Sims dormitory and that she was at least a friend of Steve Wadiak, Dean Childs began to question Nancy about the alleged trips to Florida.

Dean Childs: Have you ever been to Florida?
Miss Fulmer: Yes. Two or three times.
Dean Childs: Under what circumstances?
Miss Fulmer: Last Easter, the boy I married asked me to come home for Easter. He wanted me to come home. I had asked him to help me. I needed his help on what to do about the situation. I had planned to, but felt I couldn't go home to him. He wanted me to live with him and let everybody know we were married. I didn't care anything about him, and he kept running around telling everybody about it—said if I didn't tell them, it would be up to him to tell them. When I felt I just couldn't go home, Steve Wadiak told me some of them were going to Charleston. If I wanted to go with them—that it would be a way of getting away from going home. I didn't realize at the time what it meant. Some of them were going to Florida and a couple from Cheraw were going along with them to Florida. I didn't tell Mother I was going to Florida. I wrote the boy (husband) a letter I just couldn't take him any longer. He told my mother, went around talking to everybody, then my mother came to the university and found out I was in Florida and got me. She thought I should change schools, should not come back to the university, but I

wanted to come back here to school.

Dean Childs: You have gone off with Steve Wadiak twice?

Miss Fulmer: No, only once. That boy (husband) said he would see that the talk go around, that he would tell everybody. He told my mother he had spent $6,000 on my schooling. He did offer to do things, but I couldn't think it was right to accept since I disliked him. He even told the superintendent at home that he paid my tuition. That isn't true because my mother paid it.

Dean Childs: Do you think the Athletic Department knows about Steve?

Miss Fulmer: Yes, I know they do, since last Easter. My mother went to see Coach Enright when she found out I wasn't in Charleston. Mother thought maybe I was with Steve there. She found out from Mr. Enright where I was.

At 5 p.m. on February 27, the eight-person Discipline Committee consisting of Mrs. Childs, Dean F.W. Bradley, Professor T.M. Stubbs, Mrs. Grace Sweeny, Professor G.W. Tomlin, Professor H.H. Turney-High, Dean J.B. Jackson, and Joe Ingram (student representative) met to discuss the matter involving the two students. Steve Wadiak and Nancy Fulmer were also present at the meeting.

The transcript of the interview with Nancy was read into the record of the meeting. Both Wadiak and Fulmer agreed to the facts. The committee asked further questions about the trip to Daytona Beach that had reportedly occurred April 7-11, 1950. It was explained that friends, a married couple form Cheraw, S.C., had rented an apartment in Daytona Beach, Fla., two weeks earlier and had invited Wadiak to join them.

When Fulmer did not return home at Easter, Nancy's husband,

brother, and mother came to Columbia and visited Coach Enright at his home. Enright assisted them in determining that Fulmer was with Wadiak. Fulmer's three family members traveled to Daytona Beach, found Nancy, and immediately brought her back to South Carolina with them.

After the incident, Enright said he advised Nancy to go and live with her husband and asked Steve to cease dating her. The minutes of the meeting documented that Coach Enright had not relayed any of this information to the dean of women or to other university officials at the time it was made known to him.

After listening to the various reports, the Discipline Committee deliberated for an extended period of time. No doubt, consideration was given to the significant amount of attention and acclaim that Steve Wadiak had brought to the school. No athlete in the school's history had ever been as well-recognized in the national media or more well-known in the Carolina community.

The Committee reached its final conclusion:

> *The committee felt that such improper conduct could not be condoned: otherwise, the good name of the university and the good reputation of its students would be injured.*
>
> *It was the unanimous opinion of the committee that Mr. Wadiak be suspended for the remainder of the semester for improper conduct, and that Miss Fulmer be suspended indefinitely, but that she may be re-admitted when her marital situation, in the opinion of the university, has been cleared up.*

After the ruling, Nancy moved off campus into Cornell Arms, a nearby apartment complex at the corner of Sumter and Pendleton streets. Steve returned to his home in Chicago.

Concern for Wadiak and the impact of his suspension on the football team escalated throughout the student body, the fans, and influential supporters of the school. On March 2, 1951, University President Norman Smith received the following letter from influential board member Sol Blatt, Jr.

Dear President Smith:

I have learned from what I consider a most authoritative source the grounds upon which the Discipline Committee recently suspended Steve Wadiak. When I first read of this action by the Discipline Committee I felt sure that Steve must have committed some particularly bad offense as far as the university rules and regulations were concerned, because ordinarily he would be entitled to every break that the university could give him. In my opinion, his conduct both on and off the field has brought considerable credit to the university and his participating in various outside activities on behalf of the university has been to my mind most advantageous. When I learned the true grounds for the suspension given him, I was really quite shocked. It appears to me, if my information is correct, that the committee in order to prove to the public that it was not showing favoritism has gone far to the other extreme and has done him quite an injustice. In view of this fact, I intend to present the matter before the board when it meets this month and I would appreciate you having the file available when we meet in the event that the board votes to hear the matter.

With the very best wishes, I am,

Sincerely,

Sol Blatt, Jr.

President Smith was keenly aware of the power Blatt and his constituency yielded within the state, so he took Blatt's request to heart. He had the dean of men, J.B. Jackson, prepare a detailed account of all the events surrounding the suspension and sent this account to Blatt in advance of the upcoming March 20 board meeting.

The summary document concluded that Wadiak's most serious offense was that he had taken Fulmer to Florida without the consent of her parents. At the time of the trip, Wadiak was 25 years old, while Fulmer was 19.

While never mentioned directly in any of the documents detailing the disciplinary hearing, the seriousness of taking an underage female across state lines was connected to a well-known federal statue. Passed in 1910, the Mann Act was used for a variety of enforcement activities including the illegal transport of underage females across state lines.

The report noted that, after the trip, Wadiak was asked by Enright to cease his relationship with Fulmer. After a lapse of time, it was noted that Wadiak continued his relationship with Nancy.

Even the powerful influence of Sol Blatt, Jr. could not keep the decision of the Discipline Committee from being upheld.

To this day, mystery surrounds the accuracy of the reports about the events and circumstances that led to Steve's suspension from the football team. Newspapers carried little or no coverage of the suspension other than the standard wire service report. When spring practice started in March of 1951, Wadiak was conspicuously missing, yet few teammates even to this day can recall the reason behind his absence.

Steve's close friend and sidekick John LaTorre recalled being on one trip with Steve to Florida that involved Nancy.

"One weekend, Steve and I drove to Gainesville, Florida, and we spent the night there," LaTorre recalled. "The next day, we picked up

Nancy and her sister, who was a student at the University of Florida, and we drove to Daytona Beach for the day."

LaTorre has an old faded photograph showing himself, Wadiak, Nancy, and her sister wearing bathing suits, standing on Daytona Beach in front of the six-story Sheraton Plaza hotel. He cannot recall the exact date of the trip, but he does not believe it was that trip that led to Steve's suspension, given that Nancy and her sister were already in Florida when the two of them met up with Steve and John.

Wadiak regretted the ordeal but was also confused by the severity of his punishment. He was 25 years old. He had served his country in World War II. He had done everything his university had asked of him, including making numerous appearances at a myriad of charity events. He was different from his teammates, who were frequently guilty of disorderly conduct, which often led to arrest, destruction of property, and embarrassment to the school and the team.

He had been a model student, teammate, and citizen. He had followed the rules, however when it came to matters of the heart, he did not believe that it was the university's place to tell him what he could and could not do. His affection for Nancy was more powerful than his sense of duty to these rules. It was the one thing that was even stronger than his willingness to submit to the authority of his mentor and coach, Rex Enright.

The harshness of the sentence left Steve feeling abandoned by a school and a community he had grown to love.

He confided to a friend, "If it were not for all that Coach Enright had done for me, I would just go back to Chicago, and tell them what to do with all this mess."

However, Wadiak's loyalty to his coach drove him to accept his punishment.

The March 22, 1951 issue of "The Gamecock" brought hope to the Gamecock faithful regarding the plight of their fallen star when it printed the following update.

> *"Steve is definitely coming back." Those were the words of Rex Enright when we asked him about the possibility of Wadiak's playing next year.*
>
> *We don't pretend to know the facts involved in Steve's suspension, but we're glad he has decided to return. It is definite that he will enroll for summer school, a necessity if he is to be eligible for football next fall.*

Steve relaxes in his family's Chicago home with two of his nieces, Cassie and Connie.

(Photo courtesy of Jeanette Wadiak Korlin)

After accepting the suspension, Steve made a long, lonely drive home to Chicago. He parked his shiny two-toned 1950 Pontiac, bearing South Carolina license plates, in front of his childhood home at 9322 University Ave. The conspicuous presence of his car caused the residents of the close-knit Burnside community to wonder why Steve had returned home from college in the middle of a semester.

This would not be a hero's welcome for one of the nation's top-rated college football players. Steve had to explain to his family the reason for his leaving school. There would be numerous private discussions between Steve and his two older brothers, Walter and Joe, about the events leading up to the suspension and the best course of action for Steve's future. His only consolation was that the suspension gave him time to reconnect with his family. He occupied his time by taking long runs through the prairie behind his home and along the sandy shores of Lake Michigan. These runs helped him escape frequent questions from curious neighbors and friends and also kept him in shape for his eventual return to the gridiron.

The entire ordeal was difficult and embarrassing to explain, and Steve counted the days until he could return to his beloved Carolina home.

Wadiak returned to Columbia in June of 1951 and signed up for 10 semester hours of summer school. He earned a B, two C plusses, and a C in his four summer courses and was declared eligible to play for the 1951 Gamecock football team.

While in Columbia for summer school, 25-year-old Wadiak had a will prepared by a local attorney. It was filed with the probate court of Richland County on July 25, 1951. The simple five-paragraph document bequeathed his 1950 Pontiac to his close friend John LaTorre. All his other assets were left to Nancy Fulmer, who was also listed as the executrix of the will. Steve placed a folded copy of his will in his wallet.

On Sept. 7, 1951, Nancy visited with Dean Childs and let her know that her divorce was complete, and she requested permission to return to the university. Dean Childs told her she could return as a day student if she would agree to be as inconspicuous on campus as possible.

Nancy returned to USC as a student in the fall of 1951. However, her affections for the most well-known and popular student on campus would make it very difficult for her to remain inconspicuous.

20
Pain

In the fall of 1951, the war on communism was raging throughout Korea. In October, UN troops defeated the North Koreans and Chinese in a decisive and bloody month-long battle in an area known as Heartbreak Ridge. Despite this significant victory, the Korean Conflict continued for another two years and provided an interruption to the college football careers of several of Steve Wadiak's Gamecock teammates.

In the world of entertainment, blue-eyed crooner Frank Sinatra made his Las Vegas debut, appearing as the headliner at the Desert Inn. Nat King Cole featured his silky soft baritone voice in recording two of the year's top singles—"Unforgettable" and "Too Young."

Moviegoers were flocking to see Humphrey Bogart and Katherine Hepburn in "The African Queen," and one of the most talked about films of the year was the adaptation of Tennessee Williams's Pulitzer Prize-winning play, "A Streetcar Named Desire." Alfred Hitchcock terrorized viewers with "Strangers on a Train," while Gene Kelly and Leslie Caron lifted the spirits of audiences in the romantic musical "An American in Paris." The first soap opera, "Search for Tomorrow," along with the ever-popular "I Love Lucy" show debuted on CBS TV in the fall of 1951.

In the sporting world, New York City was buzzing about two gifted rookie outfielders who were leading their teams on pennant drives—Mickey Mantle for the New York Yankees and Willie Mays for the New York Giants. In golf, Ben Hogan had returned from near fatal injuries sustained in a head-on collision with a Greyhound bus and won both the Masters and the U.S. Open golf championships. Rocky Marciano defeated Joe Louis for the world heavyweight boxing title, and the Cleveland Browns were on their way to winning the 1951 NFL championship.

It was against this backdrop in the fall of 1951 that Steve Wadiak began his fourth and final season of college football. He was expected by many to become a college football All-American. The South Carolina Football Media Guide, referred to as "The Little Red Book" featured Steve on its cover, with a photo and the headline All-American Bound!

In 1951, Topps chewing gum company produced one of its first sets of sports cards, a 75-card set featuring outstanding college football players. The set was referred to as a Topps Magic Set because the backs of the cards contained a "scratch-off" feature that revealed the mascot of the player's college. Steve was featured on card No. 36 in the set, and the inscription on the back of the card read as follows: *Snake hipping his way to 998 yards, Steve is rated as one of the nation's top 10 runners.*

Practice for the 1951 Gamecocks began at 7 a.m. on a sweltering September day. Steve had missed spring drills due to his suspension and felt as though he had let his teammates down. He began practice determined to make his final season his best. He also hoped that a successful senior year would lead to his lifelong dream of playing professional football.

These motivations fueled an intense desire within the heart and soul of Wadiak—a desire he translated into running every drill to perfection, staying after practice for extra conditioning and treating intra-squad scrimmages as though they were the Carolina-Clemson game.

Despite his absence from spring drills, Wadiak was clearly the undisputed leader of the 1951 Gamecock squad. It was a position that the soft-spoken hero had earned through his example. Coach Enright, as a matter of principle, historically had withheld bestowing the official title of team captain until the end of the season, believing that it was an honor that had to be earned by performance and leadership. Prior to the opening game of 1951, Enright abandoned this longstanding practice and named Wadiak as the official captain of the 1951 Gamecock squad. Enright knew it was a decision that no teammate, coach, or reporter could possibly second guess. Three years of heroic performances and leadership by example had earned Wadiak the right to be named team captain.

Steve Wadiak's longtime running mate, Bishop Strickland, had graduated and moved on to the NFL, where he would play one season for the San Francisco 49ers. The 1951 Gamecock offense revolved around their All-American candidate, Steve Wadiak. Expected to join Wadiak in the starting backfield were junior Hootie Johnson at right halfback, sophomore Bobby Drawdy at fullback, and sophomore Johnny Gramling at quarterback, all very talented and promising, yet all unproven.

Enright had been working all summer on a way to create a more balanced offensive attack in order to take some of the pressure and attention off Wadiak. Enright's Gamecock teams were never known for their ability to move the football through the air, and in the previous season, they completed only 13 of 30 passes for a meager 175 yards. Enright was highly respected as a defensive tactician who had fielded several outstanding defensive teams. However, his teams consistently lacked offensive firepower.

Searching for anything that might improve his offense, Enright implemented a new wrinkle to his straight-T backfield formation: He moved the fullback a step in front of the two halfbacks. He referred to this as the TV-formation and predicted that the minor change would provide new opportunities to move the ball through the airways. Two weeks before USC's opening game against Duke, Enright's offensive strategy would be dealt a sudden blow.

In a routine controlled scrimmage, Steve received a handoff and charged through an open hole in the line and took a direct hit in the unprotected area of his rib cage. The Gamecock captain collapsed to the ground, gasping for breath. The pain caused by the hit from his teammate was as severe as anything Steve had ever experienced.

In three previous seasons, Wadiak had never missed a game and rarely missed a practice due to injury, despite being punished and pounded relentlessly by opposing defenders. When he fell to the ground in practice and failed to get up, his teammates knew it was serious.

Trainer Jess Alderman rushed onto the field and helped the Gamecock superstar to his feet. Steve grimaced as each movement of his body sent waves of excruciating pain through his core. Wadiak's teammates removed their helmets as practice came to a halt and a silence fell over the practice field. Spiritually minded teammates offered a prayer for their fallen hero.

Everyone watched anxiously as their leader walked gingerly toward the training room at Carolina Field House. Enright began to imagine a Gamecock backfield without No. 37. It was a nightmarish thought for the 50-year-old coach.

With the centerpiece of the Gamecock offense missing, it was difficult to continue with practice.

Wadiak was diagnosed and treated for badly bruised ribs. No official release was issued to the media regarding the seriousness of his injury. Enright feared letting an opponent know about Wadiak's damaged ribs would do nothing but paint an even larger bull's-eye on the back of his star runner.

As the team continued to prepare for the opener against Duke, Wadiak attempted to go through some light non-contact workouts. The pain in his ribs was agonizing and relentless, yet he never complained. Even taking a deep breath reminded Wadiak of the tenderness in his rib cage, although most of his teammates remained unaware of the severity of his injury.

Steve knew the importance of his presence to the fortunes of the Gamecock team. He also was keenly aware that having a successful senior year was critical to his personal aspirations. There was no way he would allow an injury to keep him from being on the field when the season opened against Duke.

Longtime assistant trainer J.C. Sullivan, nicknamed "Him," applied his "secret salve" to Wadiak's ribs in an effort to ease the star's pain. Sullivan had been a part of the Gamecock football staff for several years and lived in a small house adjacent to Carolina Stadium, where he doubled as custodian and groundskeeper. He was a self-proclaimed master of "home remedies," and he tried every trick in his medicine bag in an effort to help the ailing superstar. Unfortunately, even J.C's wizardry had little effect on Steve's constant pain.

Wadiak asked head trainer Jess Alderman to do whatever he could to get him ready to play against Duke. Coach Enright was not a proponent of pain-killing injections, but he wasn't aware of everything that went on in the training room.

Prior to the Duke game, Wadiak insisted that Alderman give him an injection to numb the pain in his ribs. Alderman obliged and also wrapped Wadiak's rib cage tightly with athletic tape. As Steve waited for the painkiller to take effect, he asked a manager to assist him with putting

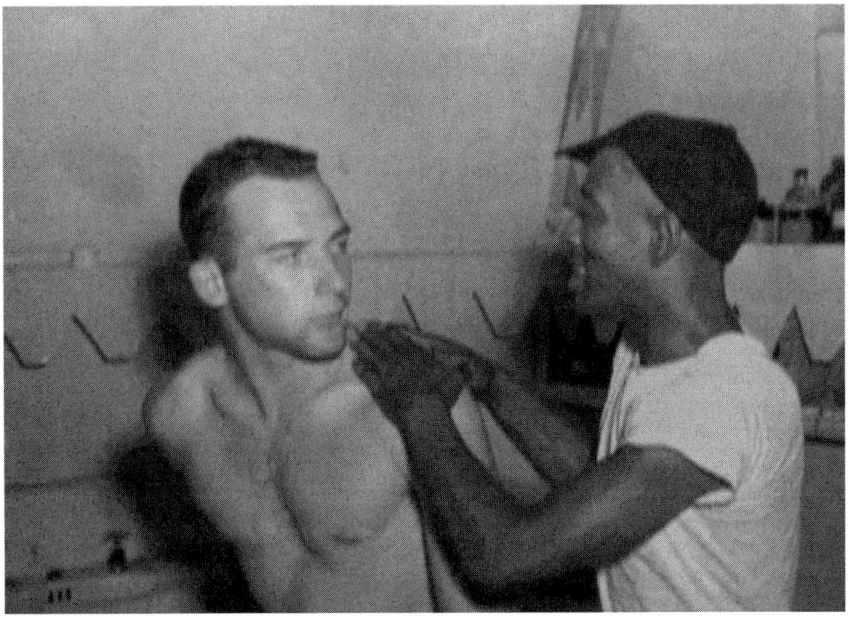

Longtime Assistant Trainer and stadium custodian
J.C. "Him" Sullivan works on the shoulder of
USC All-American Lou Sossamon (circa 1942).

(Photo courtesy of Lou Sossamon)

on his shoulder pads and jersey. The pain of simply raising his arms above his head was unbearable.

South Carolina's opening opponent, the Duke Blue Devils, entered the game as heavy favorites. South Carolina had not scored against Duke in its previous three meetings. Optimism about the Blue Devils' chances centered around a 75-0 preseason massacre of a talented military team from Camp LeJeune.

Duke's longtime coach Wallace Wade had relinquished his head-coaching role to become commissioner of the Southern Conference. Former Delaware coach and Duke alumnus Bill Murray took over as the Blue Devils' leader and abandoned Wade's time-honored single-wing offense, installing in its place a split T-formation.

A crowd of approximately 25,000 showed up for the 2:30 p.m. kickoff at Carolina Stadium on September 22. Captain Steve Wadiak met Duke Captain Jim Gibson at midfield for the coin toss. The Gamecocks won the toss and elected to kick to the Blue Devils. Duke quickly proceeded to dominate all aspects of the contest and trounced the Gamecocks 34-7.

Duke's defensive game plan was simple—shut down Steve Wadiak. Duke loaded its defensive line of scrimmage with as many as 10 players, daring the Gamecocks to beat them through the air. With the added hindrance of his painful rib injury and a poor blocking performance by the offensive line, Wadiak's opening day performance was unproductive. He was limited to a mere 26 yards rushing on 18 attempts.

Wadiak did, however, manage to make an exciting 51-yard kickoff return that helped set up the Gamecocks' lone score of the day—a 42-yard touchdown scamper by fullback Bobby Drawdy.

In their next game, South Carolina successfully avenged its prior season upset loss to the Citadel Bulldogs with a 26-7 victory. Wadiak, still ailing from his rib injury, gritted his way to 81 yards on the ground and scored a pair of rushing touchdowns.

Two games into the 1951 season, with his body hampered by the lingering effects of his injury, Steve was not living up to his preseason All-American hype. His dream of becoming a professional football player was in jeopardy, and he did not have a Plan B.

The following week was homecoming at USC, and across campus, decorations sprouted in garnet and black as the school readied itself for a weekend of festivities and pageantry. Nominations for the 1951 homecoming court added an off-the-field distraction and additional pressure to Wadiak's frustrating senior season.

One of the co-eds who had been nominated for the homecoming

court by her fellow students was Nancy Fulmer, Steve's girlfriend. Although Nancy was divorced, the embarrassment caused by her relationship with Steve had not been forgotten by the university's administrators.

Upon returning to the university, Nancy was instructed by USC's dean of women to keep a low profile around campus. Being a part of the homecoming court clearly did not meet the school's definition of "low profile." Nancy was informed by the Student Discipline Committee that if she were to appear in public as a sponsor or attendant at homecoming, she would be immediately expelled from school.

This Discipline Committee's threat created an uproar among students, who petitioned Student Body President Floyd Spence to speak on behalf of Nancy.

Spence arranged a meeting with school President Norman Smith and shared with him the students' sentiment that both Fulmer and Wadiak had suffered enough over last spring's incident, and they should not continue to be punished.

The administration refused to give in and allow Nancy's name to appear on the homecoming ballot, but a compromise was reached: Nancy would be allowed to accompany Wadiak to the homecoming dance and would also be permitted to represent him as his sponsor when the senior players were recognized at the upcoming Big Thursday game with Clemson.

Wadiak was deeply appreciative of the support he and Nancy received from the student body, but he was frustrated by the hard-line stance taken by the school's administration. Wadiak, on the advice of his coach, remained silent and simply channeled his frustration into his preparation for the homecoming game against Furman.

Against the Paladins, Steve released his pent-up anger, rushing for

147 yards on 23 attempts. He also scored a pair of touchdowns in leading USC to a solid 21-6 homecoming win before 12,000 fans on a warm September afternoon in Columbia. Gamecock fans were relieved to see Steve return to his heroic form.

Steve's success, however, was short-lived. The Gamecocks traveled to Chapel Hill to face the UNC Tar Heels, where Steve was held to a season low 22 yards rushing by a Tar Heel defense that shadowed his every move. It was his lowest rushing total since his freshman year. The Gamecocks were defeated 21-6, but the South Carolina defense, led by Steve's close friend John LaTorre, played one of its best games of the season. LaTorre played courageously at defensive end, refusing to leave the game despite a badly bruised and swollen left eye.

The Tar Heels were resolute in their desire to completely neutralize Wadiak's influence. UNC employed what one writer referred to as "the Wadiak shift," which was designed to overload the line of scrimmage in the direction of Wadiak's most likely point of attack. As a result, Wadiak was typically surrounded by a horde of Tar Heel tacklers as he approached the line of scrimmage.

On the UNC sideline for the game was Charlie "Choo Choo" Justice, the Tar Heels' newest assistant coach, whose Southern Conference single-season rushing record Wadiak had eclipsed during the previous season.

After the North Carolina game, a statement was released from the athletic department detailing the extent of Wadiak's preseason injury. It was the first public mention of Wadiak's ailment. "The Gamecock" reported:

> *Stout Steve Wadiak has been sharply below the rushing pace that led him to a new Southern Conference record last year, yet when the*

story is known that he has been suffering from a broken rib, it may show what a truly great athlete he really is.

Steve was hurt in a scrimmage prior to the opener with Duke. Since that time he had not participated in any of the contact work during the practice sessions. Yet, despite the broken rib, he was wrapped in approximately a half mile of tape and played banged-up ball in four games. Better, in fact, than the average good college back does when in good shape.

The story wasn't released while he was suffering from the injury because it was figured that some of the teams may be laying for him, trying to put him out permanently. He has now recovered and will be able to go full speed against the terrible Tigers from Clemson.

One local newspaper account also reported that Wadiak had actually suffered four fractured ribs.

With Wadiak fully recovered from his injury, the Gamecocks began their preparation for the 1951 Big Thursday match against Clemson. As always, Enright and his staff were meticulous in their preparation for the Tigers. Practice was once again moved to Columbia's City Stadium during the week preceding the rivalry game, where the surrounding outfield wall and grandstands provided a protective border from any potential enemy spying activities.

Clemson again was heavily favored. The Tigers had won 15 of their last 16 games, including a victory over Miami in the 1951 Orange Bowl. An increased hostility between USC and Clemson was present, thanks in part to some boastful and derogatory comments that Clemson's Coach Frank Howard made over the summer at a high school coaches' clinic. Despite Clemson's far greater overall football success under Coach Howard, Enright held a 4-3-1 record against Howard's teams, and this aggravated Clemson's head coach.

It would be Steve's last chance to play in a Big Thursday game. In the previous year's game against the Tigers, he turned in the single greatest offensive performance in the history of the school. Judging from all other games thus far in 1951, he knew he would be the primary target of the Tiger defense.

No longer was Steve the unknown Navy veteran from Chicago. Everybody knew Th' Cadillac. As he walked around campus, students encouraged him to have another big game against the Tigers. Off campus, he was one of the most recognizable faces in Columbia. Well-wishers greeted him everywhere he went and frequently added a comment to the effect of, "Make sure you stick it to Clemson this year." These comments burdened Steve with additional pressure, unlike any he had felt.

With running mate Bishop Strickland gone and the Gamecock offensive line underperforming, Steve had recurring nightmares about being tackled by 11 members of an opposing team. To do what he did best, he needed daylight, and in 1951, daylight was very hard to find.

On Sunday night before Big Thursday, Steve had trouble sleeping in his Preston dormitory room. He lay awake and stared at the plaster ceiling as his mind raced with thoughts about how he would help lead his team to a win over its hated rival.

Unable to fall back asleep, Steve quietly slipped out of his first floor room and walked across a deserted Greene Street toward Melton Field. He walked through the gate of the practice field and found his way to the empty rows of wooden bleachers.

Alone with his thoughts on a clear, cool October evening, Steve stared up at the stars and realized that his success had not come without a price. He felt a heaviness in his chest when he thought about all the people who were depending on him to play well on Thursday.

His memory took him back to a time when playing football was much simpler. He recalled the game he had played as a youth on the prairie behind his Chicago home with his neighborhood buddies. The equipment was sparse, the ground rugged, and the weather often raw, but the game was fun. Steve and his buddies played hard, and they played to win, but they played in isolation. Mistakes were not written in local newspapers. Losses were forgotten the next day. It was just a game—nothing more, nothing less.

Football in South Carolina in 1951 was far more than just a game. Thousands of dollars were illegally wagered on the outcome of each game. Coaching careers and the livelihood of a coach's family teetered in the balance of wins and losses. Players like Steve hoped their performances would yield a ticket to the NFL.

As Steve sat alone in the bleachers of a deserted Melton Field that night, he felt the weight of a team, a university, and a community, as well as the weight of his own future, resting squarely on his broad shoulders. No wonder he couldn't sleep.

21
Visitors

During the days preceding the 1951 Big Thursday game between Carolina and Clemson, USC President Norman Smith agonized over a mountain of ticket requests. Politicians, judges, military leaders, and a host of other well-known dignitaries wanted to be inside Carolina Stadium for the big game.

President Smith faced the impossible task of trying to dole out a limited supply of complimentary tickets. He had been president of the university for the past seven and a half years, and the task of allocating this scarce resource had become increasingly difficult.

Prior to the game, venerable Clemson Head Coach Frank Howard fueled the hatred between the two schools by boldly predicting that his Tigers were a sure bet to beat the Gamecocks this year. Howard's confident prediction drove demand for tickets to an all-time high.

President Smith maintained a detailed schedule that tracked the distribution of his 490 complimentary football tickets. As he allocated the tickets, he hoped his decisions would have a favorable impact on the political landscape that directly influenced the strategic and financial direction of his school.

Once all of the available tickets had been distributed, Smith would then dictate a series of personal letters to the dignitaries who would not be receiving tickets to this year's game. He would tactfully choose his words, and as a consolation, he would offer the requester the opportunity to attend a different USC home football game. His letters of regret typically contained an explanation similar to the following:

I am informed that this year more complaints than usual have been received deploring the scarcity of tickets—a situation that will be corrected only by construction of a larger stadium. As there are no Carolina-Clemson seats available, your check is being returned herewith.

Recipients of Smith's letters of denial would often respond to him in writing with feelings of anger and disappointment over his ticket allocation process. Shortly before the 1951 game, Smith announced that he would be retiring at the end of the school year. The responsibility for handing out a limited supply of Carolina-Clemson tickets to the who's who among state officials and other elite parties would be the part of his job he'd miss the least.

Officially, Carolina Stadium had 34,533 seats in 1951. Clemson was provided 13,271 tickets, including 2,569 for students. Tickets were sold at a face value of $3.60. In 1951, Coach Enright was given 268 tickets to allocate among Gamecock football players, coaches, staff, and recruits. Each member of the team was provided with two tickets for the game. Many of the out-of-town players whose families or friends could not attend the game would sell their Clemson game tickets at a premium to scalpers.

On most occasions, Chicago native Steve Wadiak had little need for his complimentary tickets, but the 1951 Carolina-Clemson game proved to be an exception for him. He would not only need his two tickets but also procure an additional ticket for the game. Much to his surprise, his sister Jeanette and her husband, Vern Korlin, were driving from their home in Indiana to attend the game. Accompanying them was Steve's biggest fan—his mother, Anna Wadiak. It would be her first and only opportunity to see her son play college football.

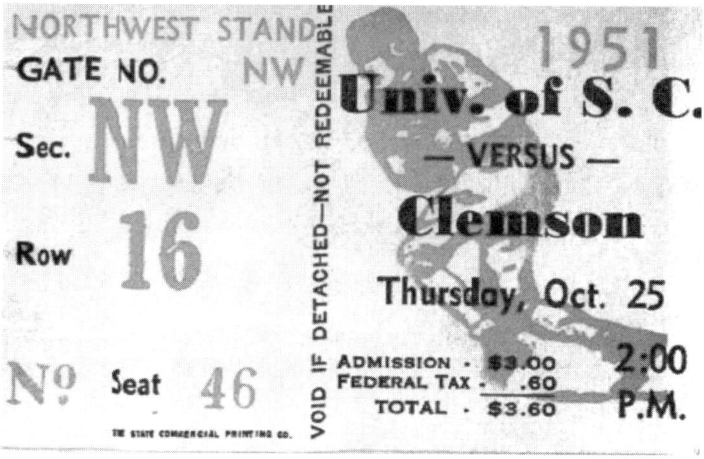

Jeanette Wadiak Korlin's ticket stub from the 1951 Carolina-Clemson game

(Photo courtesy of Jeanette Wadiak Korlin)

Steve had not seen his mother since the previous spring and was very grateful for her effort to visit him in South Carolina. His only regret was his hectic schedule—classes, extended practice times, and other demands placed on the Gamecock star during Big Thursday week—meant that Steve struggled to find time to visit with his relatives once they arrived in Columbia.

In the time he was able to spend with them, Steve showed his loved ones around the campus and the city of Columbia. He walked them across the grounds of the Capitol, where he had once been the guest of the governor. Everywhere he went, he was recognized. Local restaurant owners treated Steve and his guests with a level of attention and service typically reserved for influential politicians and business leaders.

The night before the big game, Steve took his guests to the South Carolina State Fair. Since 1869, the State Fair had been held in October in Columbia, with the Big Thursday football game between Carolina and Clemson occurring in the middle of the week's festivities. In 1904, the fair was moved from its original location off Elmwood Avenue to its current location on Bluff Road adjacent to Carolina Stadium. The fair drew visitors from all over the state and featured livestock exhibits, live entertainment, amusement rides, and carnival games.

Steve had purchased a garnet wool sweater for his mother, and she wore it proudly as she walked with Steve through the crowds of people attending the fair. The crisp autumn evening air was full of the smell of sawdust, cotton candy, and popcorn.

Steve and his family had trouble making their way through the fairgrounds without Steve being recognized and interrupted. Anna, Jeanette, and Vern waited patiently as Steve signed autographs for adoring youngsters and spoke kindly and patiently with a constant flow of well-wishers.

Anna marveled at the affection that her son garnered. This was her baby boy—the little boy whose winsome and energetic personality had stolen the hearts of the adults in the Burnside neighborhood of his childhood. Steve had secured a special place in the hearts of South Carolinians. Anna could not fully understand how or why all of that attention resulted from Steve's ability to play the game of football. Regardless, she marveled at how her son had risen from his humble beginnings to being treated like royalty in his new Carolina home.

While visiting with his family on the evening before Big Thursday, Steve pulled his brother-in-law, Vern, aside for a private conversation. He shared with him how fortunate he believed he was to enjoy such a dreamlike existence in Columbia, but he was apprehensive about his future. He did not feel deserving of the life he was leading and did not believe it could continue forever.

The exact details of the conversation between Steve and his brother-in-law are not known, but in a vulnerable moment, Steve shared with Vern that he did not expect that he would play professional football. He also confided in his brother-in-law that over the summer, with the help of a local attorney, he had drawn up a personal last will and testament.

It was an odd conversation for Vern to have with his brother-in-law. He was witnessing Steve living in Utopia—not wanting for anything and being worshiped by all. Steve appeared to be grappling with his own mortality, despite the fact that all those around him seemed to

Steve Wadiak's mother, Anna, outside Carolina Stadium on Big Thursday, October 25, 1951

(Photo courtesy of Jeanette Wadiak Korlin)

view him as immortal.

The night before the game, Steve gave his mother and sister beautiful corsages trimmed with garnet and black ribbons. With pride and affection for their loved one, the ladies planned to wear the corsages to the game the next day.

As Frank Howard prepared his team to avenge the prior year's disappointing 14-14 tie with South Carolina, he stressed to his defense that under no circumstances were they to allow Steve Wadiak to single-handedly beat them. He instructed his defense to at all times be aware of Wadiak's whereabouts and to key their point of attack around his every move.

USC's Enright knew that Wadiak had embarrassed the Clemson defense in the prior year when he ripped up the Tiger defense for 256 rushing yards. He also knew Coach Howard would not allow that to happen again. Enright designed his offensive game plan to use Wadiak principally as a decoy to help divert the attention of the Clemson defense.

Enright and his staff drilled their team with precision during their week and a half of practice leading up to Big Thursday. The Gamecocks would employ a 7-2-1-1 defensive formation against Clemson's single-wing offense. Starting quarterback Johnny Gramling, in Don Barton's book, "They Wore Garnet and Black," recalled Enright's mastery over Coach Howard.

"If anybody had anybody's number, Coach Enright had Coach Howard's number," Gramling said. "When it came to defending the single wing, they just did an excellent job of scouting from a standpoint of what they (Clemson) did with personnel.

"I can remember Coach Enright telling Don Earley (defensive tackle), 'Now we're gonna put you here, and if you don't make 90 percent of the tackles that come your way, you aren't worth your salt. There's no way they can block you.'"

A capacity crowd of over 35,000 jammed Carolina Stadium on a warm fall afternoon to witness the civil war between the Tigers and the Gamecocks. The betting line prior to the game held Clemson as a solid seven-point favorite over the Gamecocks.

From the start, the Gamecock defense took control of the game, holding Clemson to minus seven yards rushing in the first quarter. The defense was led by the superb play of linemen Bob "Moose" Kahle, Don Earley, Harry Jabbusch, Leon Cunningham, and defensive back Bill Stephens. Stephens, a third string quarterback from Wrightsville, Ga., who was pressed into duty as a safety, electrified the Gamecock crowd with a 76-yard punt return for a touchdown late in the first quarter.

Wadiak, used mostly as a decoy throughout the game, rushed for 69 yards on 20 attempts, with Larry Smith opening up many of his running lanes from his center position.

Defensively, Stephens was all over the field, intercepting a pass, recovering a fumble and breaking up two long Clemson pass attempts. The Gamecock defenders played a nearly flawless game as they led Carolina to a stunning 20-0 upset over the Tigers. Stephens's play would earn him the distinction of being named the game's Most Valuable Player.

It was the first time in 40 games, dating to a 1947 loss to N.C. State, that Howard's Tigers had been held scoreless.

"Greenville News" Sports Editor Scoop Latimer gave credit to Enright and his coaching genius: "Carolina outplayed, outfought, and outsmarted Clemson to win the game as a tribute to Coach Enright's perfect preparedness and his team's aggressiveness on offense and defense."

After the game, a smiling Enright was hoisted on the shoulders of his players and carried across the field amidst jubilant teammates and fans.

Clemson's star tailback Billy Hair, who would set a Clemson school single-season record for total offense in 1951, was held to a net 20 yards rushing and 24 yards passing. Gamecock end Moose Kahle played what Enright called the best game of his career and credited him with shutting down Hair.

A few hours after his team's disappointing loss, Coach Howard sat slumped in a chair in a Columbia hotel dining room. A reporter approached him and asked him about the whereabouts of his star tailback, Billy Hair. Howard told him he believed Hair was in his hotel room. The reporter then asked, "Is that Kahle fellow (in reference to USC's Moose Kahle) still with him? 'Cause he sure didn't leave his side all day today!" Howard was not amused.

Later, a well-meaning fan approached Howard and attempted to cheer him up by telling him, "In defeat, you gain strength." Howard looked at the fan and grunted, "Well, meet the strongest man in South Carolina 'cause I just got the hell beat out of me."

The day after the game, Anna Wadiak and Vern and Jeanette Korlin stood outside Preston dormitory on Greene Street and said farewell to their famous loved one. Steve told his family there was a high likelihood that he would be asked to participate in a couple of postseason All-Star games which would require him to be away from home over the Christmas holidays. They embraced and said their goodbyes.

On the drive back to Chicago, Anna sat in the back seat of her son-in-law's late-model Plymouth sedan and contemplated the past few days of visiting her youngest child in his new South Carolina home. She had dreamed that her children would be blessed with opportunity greater than her own. Her desire for her children to have a better life than she had experienced motivated her as a teenager to endure a treacherous journey across the Atlantic. It drove her to work tirelessly to help support her family. It shaped her prayer life.

In a Southern community that was unknown to her, Anna's son had become a hero. She realized that her dreams for him had been fulfilled; her prayers, answered.

Anna's heart filled with joy as she recalled a stadium full of people cheering for her son. She remembered countless little boys looking up at Steve with wide eyes, and with gratitude, she reflected on a community of people who went out of their way to make sure that her son wanted for nothing.

As Anna stared out the window during her ride home, the joy she felt for her son's success turned bittersweet. She knew all too well the pattern of Steve's life. Just as she had left the Ukrainian neighborhood of her youth in pursuit of her American dream, Steve had moved far from his childhood home to pursue his dreams. Anna would never return to Ukraine, and in her heart, she knew that Steve would not likely be returning to the Burnside neighborhood of his youth. He had found a new home, and in many ways, he had found a new family.

Anna Wadiak did not know when she would see her baby boy again.

22
Final Act

After the 1951 Big Thursday game, the fortunes of the Clemson and South Carolina football teams went different directions. Clemson won all of its remaining four games and earned a trip to the Gator Bowl. South Carolina followed its upset win over the Tigers with familiar inconsistent play, showing only flashes of potential as to what might have been.

The Gamecocks' next game was a home contest against the George Washington Colonels, a team that USC had defeated soundly on the road in the prior season. GW entered the game having won only once in six attempts and was a 12-point underdog to the Gamecocks.

The Colonels' offensive attack was led by tailback Andy Davis and fullback Bino Barreira. Standing only 5'6" and weighing 150 lbs., Barreira was a spark plug for the Colonels offense, and the Gamecocks would struggle all day to contain the diminutive back.

On the first play of the game, a George Washington player stepped squarely on the leg of Steve Wadiak. The player's metal cleats cut a deep gash into Steve's leg, and blood began to pour through his white football pants. Reporters commented after the game that Steve's blood-stained pants were clearly visible all the way from the wooden press box atop the west stands of Carolina Stadium. Gamecock trainers wrapped and taped the cut, and Wadiak continued to play throughout the contest.

Steve commented after the game that he didn't even realize what had happened, and he understood the seriousness of the injury only when he reached the sideline. "When I pulled the cut open, I could see all the way to the bone," he said. After the game, a doctor would sew six stitches into Steve's leg.

USC Quarterback Dick Balka, playing in place of sophomore Johnny Gramling, connected with end Walt Shea for a 20-yard touchdown pass to put the Gamecocks ahead 14-8 with only 6:50 left to play. After the ensuing kickoff, GW mounted an impressive 92-yard scoring drive behind the crisp passing combination of Davis to Barreira. GW missed their extra point, leaving the game tied at 14-14 with 2:45 left to play.

On the next offensive series, Balka attempted a long second-down pass that was intercepted by the Colonels on their 42-yard line. Once again, Davis and Barreira went to work through the air, moving the ball at ease through an overly cautious Gamecock defense. On the final play of the game, GW pushed the ball over from the one-yard line to give the Colonels a stunning come-from-behind 20-14 win over the Gamecocks. Gamecock players, coaches, and fans were shocked at the outcome of the game, as they witnessed their opponent score twice in the game's waning minutes to steal the victory.

GW gained 243 yards through the air, while the Gamecocks completed only four passes for 42 yards. The tiny Barreira caught nine passes for 160 yards and was clearly the star of the game.

Despite the painful gash in his leg, Wadiak turned in a solid performance, gaining 109 yards on 21 attempts. His yardage gave him a career total of 2,647 and pushed him ahead of Charlie "Choo Choo" Justice as the all-time leading rusher in Southern Conference history.

Next up for the Gamecocks was a trip to Morgantown, W.Va., to face a 5-1 West Virginia team. The Mountaineers' only loss to date was a narrow 13-7 road decision to a powerful Penn State team. The Gamecocks rebounded from the shocking home loss to George Washington and played a near perfect game, upsetting West Virginia 34-13 before a homecoming crowd of 18,000.

The Gamecock defense played superbly, holding West Virginia to minus 12 yards rushing in the second half. Ends John LaTorre and Don Earley repeatedly stopped the Mountaineer runners for losses throughout the game, and Harry Jabbusch played a stellar game from his linebacker position.

Quarterback Balka played the best all around game of his career, passing for 106 yards, including a 53-yard touchdown strike to Walt Shea. Wadiak gained 77 yards and scored a touchdown against a West Virginia defense that had held its opponents to under 70 yards rushing per game in its previous six contests.

The following week, the Gamecocks traveled to Charlottesville, Va., to face a 6-1 Virginia team whom Rex Enright referred to as Carolina's toughest opponent of the year. Quarterbacking the Cavaliers was Charleston, S.C. native Rufus Barkley, who—eight years after the unexpected death of his father—would take the helm of his family's longtime Charleston-based business, Cameron & Barkley Co. Barkley became one of South Carolina's most well-known and respected business leaders.

Virginia had defeated Duke and North Carolina, who had previously trounced the Gamecocks, and Virginia was a 13-point favorite over USC. During the week leading up to the game, Wadiak missed two days of practice while he waited for the deep cut on his leg to heal.

South Carolina jumped to a 20-7 second-half lead and was driving for another score late in the third quarter when Wadiak was stopped only inches short of a touchdown on a fourth-down play. Eyewitnesses recalled that Wadiak's uniform bore the chalk of the goal line, but officials ruled that he had not crossed the plane.

The defensive stop for the Cavaliers changed the momentum of the game. A partisan crowd of 12,000 in Scott Stadium watched as Virginia went on to score three fourth-quarter touchdowns to notch a 28-27 come-from-behind victory over a disheartened Gamecock team.

Wadiak played an excellent all around game, rushing for 81 yards and a touchdown. He also returned three kicks for 87 yards and added 44 receiving yards.

After the game, the team returned to their Charlottesville hotel to gather their belongings and head to the train station for the trip back to Columbia. As Wadiak passed through the hotel lobby, he noticed "The State's" sports editor, Jake Penland, struggling to carry his luggage. Wadiak offered a helping hand and ended up carrying Penland's typewriter to the train station—an act of kindness that Penland would never forget.

Wadiak's final game of his college football career would be a home contest against the Wake Forest Demon Deacons on the Saturday following Thanksgiving. The Deacons had also previously defeated North Carolina and Duke and were heavily favored against the Gamecocks.

The weekend of the game coincided with an annual Boy Scout convention. Over 4,000 young boys from across North Carolina, South Carolina, and Georgia, dressed in either their olive Boy Scout or blue Cub Scout uniforms, migrated to Columbia for the weekend. On Friday, the Scouts were scheduled to hear from S.C. Governor James Byrnes, but a bad cold kept him from attending, and Steve Wadiak was asked to stand in for the governor. Wadiak's appearance further elevated his heroic status with the 4,000 wide-eyed youths.

The next day, the Scouts filed into the north end zone of Carolina Stadium to watch their hero attempt to lead the Gamecocks to victory. "The State" reported: "The man of the hour to the Scouts was Wadiak by a mile, and every time 'The Cadillac' would scratch his ear, the Boy

Scouts would send up a roar of approval."

The Gamecock defense led USC to a 21-6 upset win over the Demon Deacons in front of a home crowd of 19,000. Harry Jabbusch intercepted two passes and recovered a fumble in leading a Gamecock defense that caused 10 Wake Forest turnovers on the day.

"The Columbia Record" ran a photo of the jubilant Gamecock team celebrating their final win of the season with Coach Enright. Across the page, a contrasting story highlighted archrival Clemson's 34-0 win over Auburn and Clemson's expected invitation to the Gator Bowl. The Gamecocks would wrap up their season with a mediocre 5-4 record, despite having outscored their opponents 175-135. The Gamecocks' heartbreaking losses to George Washington and Virginia likely cost them a chance at a postseason bowl bid.

The Gamecocks celebrate underneath the stands at Carolina Stadium after their 1951 win over Wake Forest. From left are Billy Stephens (25), John "Lip" LaTorre, Steve Wadiak (37), Vince Gargano, Larry Smith, Coach Rex Enright, Harry Stewart, Louis Harrelson, Chuck Prezioso, Billy Renfrew, Harry Jabbusch (41), Paul Stephens, and Al Kavounis (53).

(Photo courtesy of "Garnet and Black" yearbook)

Wadiak finished the game with 73 yards on 22 attempts and scored a pair of touchdowns. His season rushing total was 685 yards, well short of what many fans and pundits had expected from the Gamecock star. It was the end of a somewhat disappointing senior season marked by high expectations, injuries, and obsessive attention from opposing defenses.

Wadiak's career rushing total of 2,878 yards would stand as the most of any back in the history of the Southern Conference and would remain a USC school record until 1980, when it was eclipsed by Heisman Trophy winner George Rogers. All four years at USC, Wadiak led his team in scoring as he scored 25 career touchdowns.

During Wadiak's four seasons, the Gamecocks' combined record was 15-19-2. During this time, the Gamecocks were 2-1-1 against Clemson teams that had an overall four-year record of 31-7-3. The Tigers finished two of the four seasons during the Wadiak era without a loss and appeared in three postseason bowl games.

Although his body was spent with exhaustion from the hard-fought final game of his career, Wadiak honored a commitment he had made to a young Gamecock fan. Six-year-old Dickie Warren of Columbia had received a new football uniform from his parents and requested that the jersey carry the numerals of his hero, Steve Wadiak. Dickie also asked his parents to arrange for him to have a picture made with Wadiak.

Steve sent word for Dickie to meet him after the game and posed for the photograph with his young fan.

"The State" ran a picture of Wadiak in his dirtied white uniform standing near the tunnel of the south end zone, shaking hands with young Dickie Warren. The boy was wearing a garnet jersey bearing the number 37, along with his football helmet. Dickie's parents were smiling proudly as they watched their son meet his hero. The photograph was titled "A Pair of 37s."

After greeting his young fan and the boy's family, Steve boarded the bus that would carry the team back to their locker room at Carolina Field House. Sitting on a stool in front of his locker, Steve peeled off his jersey and tossed it across the room into a pile of dirty uniforms. It would mark the final time that the number 37 would be worn by a South Carolina Gamecock football player.

23
Saturday's Hero

Steve Wadiak was walking along the 1200 block of Main Street in Columbia in the fall of 1951 when a framed movie poster at the Carolina Theater caught his attention. The poster portrayed a full-color image of a well-built shirtless man wearing football pants and holding a football helmet in his left hand. The billboard was promoting "Saturday's Hero," a recently released movie from Columbia Pictures. The tag line below the film title was, "This movie minces no words about big-time college football."

The movie starred John Derek as Steve Novak, a fictional college football player in the 1950s, who was caught up in the pressures of big-time college athletics. Donna Reed, who played George Bailey's wife in "It's a Wonderful Life," starred opposite Novak as his devoted girlfriend.

Novak was depicted as a rags-to-riches story—the son of immigrant parents who rose to fame as a result of his football skills and earned a scholarship to a prestigious college. The movie displayed Novak's struggle to balance the pressures of performing on the football field with getting an education and maintaining some semblance of a personal life.

The movie contained an eerie number of similarities to Steve's life. Steve had become "Saturday's Hero" in South Carolina. He faced the pressures of an expectant and adoring public while also carrying the burden of celebrity status.

As the 1951 Carolina football season came to an end, the athletic office received a steady stream of requests for Gamecock athletes to participate in local charity events. Many of the requests specifically asked for Steve's attendance. Wadiak rarely refused when asked to use his influence for a charitable cause. He felt he had been incredibly blessed by the opportunities that had been given to him, and it was his way of giving back.

On the evening of Dec. 3, 1951, Wadiak was the guest of honor at a father-son dinner at the Sims Park recreation building. A photo in "The State" newspaper showed Steve receiving a pair of new cuff links from a young boy who was the captain of the Sims Park Blue Devils.

Annually, the USC Block C Club held its Christmas party at the Carolina Children's Orphanage Home. A group photo in "The State" shows Steve gathered with several USC athletes giving attention to a handful of children. In the photo, Steve is standing with his hands placed affectionately on the shoulders of one of the young boys.

Another photo that appeared in "The State" shows Steve, along with teammates Jess Berry and Harry Stewart, as well as basketball player Jim Slaughter, attending the annual March of Dimes dance held at Columbia's Valley Park. The photo shows Steve—dressed in light pants and a plaid sweater vest—smiling down at a little girl who is holding herself up on a pair of crutches.

Steve's popularity on campus and around the state of South Carolina continued to soar. June Walker was a student at USC in 1951, and her mailbox at the campus post office was adjacent to Steve's. Walker, who later married Wadiak's teammate Bob Korn, recalled how Steve's mailbox was always jammed full of mail. "I couldn't believe that one man could receive so much mail," she said. "He was the most popular man on campus, but he never once acted like he was something special."

Whether he was attending a charity function or simply walking down a Columbia street, Wadiak was always in the public eye. There were few places Steve could go where he would not be noticed and asked for an autograph or to say a few words to some admiring fans. Steve was always obliging, yet it was never his desire to be the center of attention. At times, he longed for privacy and a sense of anonymity that was now nearly impossible for him to obtain in South Carolina.

Perhaps it was Steve's desire for a simpler and more private life that led him to a unique and somewhat mysterious friendship. Steve met Peggy Shealy, a 19-year-old college student, during the summer before his senior year while Peggy was working as a waitress at The Market restaurant on Assembly Street. The Market was in some ways the unofficial training table for the USC football team. Whenever Steward Dining Hall on campus was closed, athletes were allowed access to The Market, where they were treated to some of Columbia's finest food. A full menu of steaks, seafood, chicken, and veal, along with the restaurant's famous strawberry shortcake, was made available to Gamecock athletes.

During the summer of 1951, Steve and some of his friends were dining at The Market. Steve struck up a conversation with Peggy, who was waiting on their table. He found out that she was a native of West Columbia and was a rising sophomore at Winthrop College, an all-girls school located in Rock Hill, S.C.

Steve dined frequently at The Market that summer and began to ask that Peggy wait on his table. Unlike most co-eds around the USC campus, Peggy was not awestruck by the presence of Th' Cadillac. In fact, she initially had no idea who he was. It wasn't until some of her co-workers informed her that she was waiting on the famous Steve Wadiak that she became aware of his celebrity status. She had never seen him play football, and to her, he was just another customer, albeit a handsome one.

Peggy found Steve friendly and respectful. He found her attractive, wholesome, and winsome. A friendship would develop between the two. Sixty years after meeting Wadiak at The Market, Peggy described her relationship with Steve.

"I wouldn't call what we had 'romantic.' It was just a friendship," she said. "We enjoyed each other's company."

None of Steve's friends or teammates can recall Steve's mentioning his friendship with Peggy, nor can anyone recall if perhaps it occurred during a time when he and his steady girlfriend, Nancy Fulmer, were not seeing each other. Peggy was aware of Steve's relationship with Nancy and therefore assumed up front he was not looking for a steady girlfriend.

The first time Steve drove his Pontiac to Peggy's parents' home at 600 Center St. in West Columbia, he sat in his car and quietly admired the tranquility of the surroundings. The white ranch style home with its neatly landscaped yard seemed distant from the heart of the USC campus and the incessant craziness of dorm life.

Steve enjoyed visiting with Peggy and her family in their home and felt relaxed and comfortable around them. Peggy's mother adored him, not because he was a big-time football hero, but because he was a courteous and respectful young man. Peggy's younger sister, Norma, was captivated by the thought of having Steve Wadiak in her house, and Steve always gave her a fair share of attention.

The Shealys became a surrogate family for Steve while he was far from his loved ones. Their home was a place where no demands were placed on him. He could relax and just be himself—a task that became increasingly more difficult for him with each touchdown he scored or each award he garnered as a famous USC football player.

Steve would call on Peggy in the most gentlemanly way. He would visit her at her parents' home, and the two of them would sit outside in a swing and simply talk for hours. They might take a leisurely drive around Columbia in Steve's Pontiac. After the summer ended and Peggy returned to Winthrop, they remained faithful pen pals. Steve sent her a postcard from Charlottesville prior to the UVA game. The front of the linen card showed a picture of the medical school and hospital at the University of Virginia. The back of the card read:

> *Hi, have a few minutes before we play, so I thought I'd drop you a card. Wasn't that nice! Sure is cold here. I have my long underpants on.*
> *Steve*

In February of 1952, Steve and some of his friends, at Peggy's invitation, made a road trip to Rock Hill to attend a formal dance held at Winthrop. The following is an excerpt from a letter Steve sent to Peggy prior to attending the dance. It was fairly typical of the correspondence between the two friends.

> *Hi there,*
>
> *Hope this letter finds you in the best of health. As for me, I'm fine. I started to write you in class today, but the prof showed us a movie and I thought you would have a hard time reading my letter if I wrote it in the dark.*
>
> *I went to the fights last night and South Carolina and Miami tied. Tonight there is a basketball game going on and I guess I'll take that in.*
>
> *Some of the fellows from the dorm are planning on coming to the dance . . . I pity Winthrop with all us devils running around loose.*
>
> *Well I guess there isn't much more to say, so I'll close for now and I'll let you know as soon as possible about the 23rd. Be good and drop me a line when you have time.*
> *Steve*

P.S. One of the fellows that rooms next to me asked me if you could get him a date. He's a good-looking boy and I'll let you know before hand so you can see what you can do. He is on the basketball team and if he doesn't have to go on a trip on the 23rd, he said he is going. I'll let you know something definite in a few days.

Steve and Peggy Shealy take a walk down Main Street in Columbia in 1952.

(Photo courtesy of Jeanette Wadiak Korlin)

Steve's friendship with Peggy and her family provided him a respite, a safe haven where he was free from the weight of being "Saturday's Hero."

While many of Steve's acts of charity and kindness were displayed in the public eye and documented in local papers, some were not. He was touched by the plight of the children at the Carolina Orphanage, but other than offering a kind word and a smile, there wasn't really much he could do about their future. He was empathetic toward the crippled children he met at the March of Dimes dance, but he did not have the power to heal their physical ailments. However, there was one situation in which he would utilize his influence to make a small yet measurable difference in a young boy's life.

When Wadiak arrived in Columbia, he stepped into a culture very different from the one in which he was raised. The majority of students attending USC were from south of the Mason-Dixon line. To them, Northerners were outsiders and were to be treated with skepticism. One of Steve's friends from New Jersey shared a story with Steve about his experience during his first year in Columbia in 1941.

"If I was walking down a sidewalk on campus and some of the Southern boys saw me coming, they would immediately cross over to the other side," Steve's Northern friend recalled. "Finally, I asked one of them why they did that, and they let me know that they did not want to be caught on the same side of the street with a Yankee."

General Robert E. Lee had surrendered to the Union Army on April 12, 1865, at Appomattox, Va., but apparently, word of the Confederate surrender had not reached all parts of the South. For many, the War

Between the States was still being fought on the streets of many Southern cities, such as Columbia, S.C., in the 1950s.

In the early '50s, local newspapers frequently carried reports of Ku Klux Klan rallies being held in various cities throughout South Carolina. Steve had heard some of his Southern teammates speaking harshly about blacks, and he knew the issue of race was an explosive topic in the Deep South.

None of it made sense to Steve. He grew up in a multi-ethnic neighborhood where everyone got along. He was raised to treat everyone fairly, regardless of birthplace or skin color. Prejudice bothered him, but he was smart enough to realize that he could not single-handedly eradicate a few hundred years of unjust behavior. In a small but courageous way, he made a statement about how he felt about some of the prejudice he observed.

At football practice, Steve observed a young black boy who regularly sat outside the gates of USC's practice facility at Melton Field. Other boys—white youngsters—often wandered in and around Melton Field, but this young boy sat curiously outside the fence, never passing through the unlocked gates. College football had been integrated on a limited basis in 1951, and "Jim Crow" ruled the Deep South.

One day as Steve was walking toward Melton Field, he noticed the boy in his usual spot, staring through the fence at some Gamecock players tossing a football around before practice. Steve couldn't take it any longer.

"Why don't you come in and watch us from inside the fence?" Steve asked.

Steve's question paralyzed the young boy. It confused him. He knew he could never set foot on a field full of white people. Stepping inside the fence would be about as a crazy as sitting in the front of a bus or drinking out of a water fountain clearly marked "For Whites Only."

Sensing his fear, Steve put his arm around the boy and guided him through the gate and onto the practice field. Steve and the boy walked over to one of the team's managers who was busy unpacking a duffel bag of equipment.

"Can you give this young man a job as a water boy?" Steve asked the manager.

The manager looked confused by Steve's request. Other than J.C. Sullivan, the longtime assistant trainer and stadium custodian, there were no persons of color anywhere on the Gamecock staff. Steve glared at the manager and didn't say a word. The manager had seen Steve break would-be tacklers' noses with a simple stiff arm. He knew better than to try to argue with him. The manager would allow the young boy to serve as an unofficial water boy, and if anyone asked any questions, he would simply refer them to Th' Cadillac.

On this day on Melton Field, a black youth had been temporarily emancipated by one of the most powerful men in Columbia, a man who in many ways had become more than just "Saturday's Hero."

24
The Future

When the final 1951 All-American football teams were revealed, Steve Wadiak did not find his name on any of the first team squads. Princeton's Dick Kazmaier, considered the premier back in college football, was the runaway winner of the 1951 Heisman Trophy. Kazmaier was joined by three other future College Football Hall of Famers—USC's Frank Gifford, Washington's Hugh McElhenny, and Tennessee's Hank Lauricella—in the first team backfields of most All-American teams.

While Wadiak failed to make first team All-American as many had predicted, he did complete his career as one of the most decorated players in the history of South Carolina football. For the second year in a row, he was named first team All-Southern Conference. He was also the only unanimous choice for the All-State team in South Carolina and the only player to receive a first team vote from all 28 coaches and sports writers who selected the team. He was named to the prestigious Colliers All-South football team and was selected to the second team of the Helms Foundation's All-American squad. The 1952 edition of "Who's Who in Sports" named him the best college running back in the nation.

In late November of 1951, Wadiak, along with teammate Larry Smith, received personal letters of invitation from Champ Pickens, the general manager of the 14th annual Blue-Gray All-Star game, scheduled to be played in Montgomery on December 29. The envelope containing the letter also held a check to cover the players' travel expenses to Montgomery. Pickens instructed the players to bring football shoes, head gear, and pads when they arrived at practice. Around the same time, Wadiak and Smith also received invitations to play in the third annual Senior Bowl, played in Mobile on Jan. 5, 1952.

The two All-Star contests provided Steve the opportunity to showcase his skills and improve his stock in the upcoming NFL draft, but participating in the games meant he would not be with his family in Chicago over the Christmas holidays.

Wadiak and Smith arrived in Montgomery a week prior to the game and were greeted by a familiar face—their head coach from USC, Rex Enright, who had been asked to serve as an assistant coach for the Gray squad. Enright was extremely proud of his two star players and looked forward to putting them on display in front of a national audience.

The Gray squad held two-a-day workouts on a practice field at Montgomery's Maxwell Air Force Base. When the players weren't practicing, the Blue-Gray organizing committee kept them busy throughout Christmas week with a series of public appearances, including luncheons at the Montgomery Kiwanis and Lions Clubs. The players were given gifts commemorating their participation in the game. One of the gifts was a leather wallet engraved with the logo from the Blue-Gray game. Steve was in need of a new wallet, and he immediately changed out his old one for the shiny new one.

While resting in his room at Montgomery's Greystone Hotel on the day after Christmas, Steve used a piece of hotel stationary and drafted a letter to his friend Peggy Shealy in Columbia. In the letter, he described the odd feeling of spending Christmas away from family and friends.

> *Peggy,*
>
> *. . . Hope this letter finds you in the best of health. As for me I'm getting plenty tired practicing twice a day . . . I sure do miss the feeling of Christmas because here it just seems like another day . . .*

Blue-Gray game day festivities began on Sat., Dec. 29, with a morning parade, featuring several marching bands and a string of 28 decorative floats, rolling down the streets of Montgomery. A surprise rain shower soaked the parade attendees, but by game time, the rain had subsided, and fans and players alike enjoyed a mild overcast afternoon.

The game was played in Montgomery's Cramton Bowl, a stadium originally constructed in 1922 as a baseball venue. In its early years, the Cramton Bowl served as the home of a minor league baseball team as well as the spring training site for the American League's Philadelphia Athletics. The stadium also became a home field for selected games of the University of Alabama Crimson Tide football team. Between 1922 and 1954, Alabama played 20 times in the Cramton Bowl.

At the time of the 1951 Blue-Gray game, the Cramton Bowl held approximately 22,000 fans, and officials expected a sellout. Attendees paid $4 to reserve a seat and watch the collection of college All-Stars compete. The tickets featured caricatures of Confederate General Robert E. Lee and Union military leader and former U.S. President General Ulysses S. Grant, along with the Union and Rebel flags.

A ticket stub from the 1951 Blue-Gray All-Star game

Forty-eight players representing 29 different colleges were scheduled to participate in the game. Four players from the nation's number two-ranked team, Michigan State, were featured on the Blue squad, while LSU had three players on the Gray team. Joining Wadiak and Smith from the state of South Carolina was Wofford quarterback Jack Beeler, who earlier in the year had set a pass completion record in the Cramton Bowl in a game against Auburn.

Scouts representing seven NFL teams were in attendance, including Weeb Ewbank of the Cleveland Browns, who went on to coach the victorious New York Jets in Super Bowl III, and Tim Mara, founder of the New York Giants.

The game aired nationally over the Mutual Broadcast Network, with veteran broadcaster Harry Wisner calling the action. The Wadiak family invited a living room full of interested Burnside neighborhood residents to listen to the game in their home on University Avenue in Chicago.

The Blue team was a slight favorite as its roster included more "marquee" names, and it quickly jumped to a 7-0 halftime lead. In the second half, the Gray squad inserted SMU's Fred Benners at quarterback. Benners emerged as the hero of the game, completing 14 of 21 passes for 272 yards and leading the Gray squad to a 20-14 come-from-behind win. His most sensational play of the game was a 60-yard aerial strike to Wofford's Beeler, who had been moved from quarterback to receiver. The win for the Gray squad was its ninth in 14 Blue-Gray contests.

Rex Enright commented after the game: "I never thought I would see a day when two All-Star squads would put on such a show. It was a colorful and exciting game with the outcome hanging in the balance right up until the end."

Wadiak was praised as one of the unsung stars of the game, having unselfishly volunteered to play defensive back, a position he had not played since early in his college career. Wadiak made six unassisted tackles, and he also rushed the ball three times for 18 yards and caught one pass for 13 yards.

After the game, the players were invited to make their final public appearance in Montgomery at the annual Blue-Gray Ball. The formal event held at the Montgomery Country Club was a high society affair that included music, dancing, and a fireworks show. Guests celebrated and danced late into the evening to the "sweet musical sounds" of the popular Blue Baron and his orchestra. Baron began his musical career in the 1940s during the Big Band Era and enjoyed popularity across the U.S. during the '40s and '50s. Baron's song, "Cruising Down the River (on a Sunday afternoon)" hit number one on the pop music charts in 1949.

Steve attended the ball with his teammates and received a steady stream of congratulations from the predominately Southern crowd who were festively enjoying the Gray's victory over their "Northern aggressors."

On Sunday, following the Blue-Gray contest, Steve and teammate Larry Smith headed to Mobile for the Senior Bowl. This game would mark a college player's official transition from amateur to professional status, as participants in the Senior Bowl were paid to play in the game. Each member of the winning team would receive a check for $500, while the losers received $400 each.

The talent pool in the Senior Bowl was even richer than that of the Blue-Gray contest, as several players who had participated in New Year's Day bowl games were now available to play. The coaches for the event were well-known NFL coaches Paul Brown (North) of the Cleveland Browns and Steve Owen (South) of the New York Giants. Midway through the practice week, Brown was summoned to coach in the NFL's

Pro Bowl in Los Angeles, leaving the North squad in the hands of two of his Cleveland Brown assistants, Weeb Ewbank and Fritz Heisler.

Fifty of college football's top stars were in Mobile to play in the game, and for convenience, the two teams were listed as North and South, although promoters ignored the geographic origins of the players and simply divided the players equally to balance the power between the two teams. Steve was placed on the South squad while his Gamecock teammate Smith would play for the North.

Wadiak impressed his coaches during practice and earned a starting spot at left halfback for the South squad. Joining Wadiak in the South backfield were a pair of talented quarterbacks, Vanderbilt's Billy Wade and Kentucky's Babe Parilli. Southern Cal's Frank Gifford was moved to quarterback for the game and also served as co-captain of the North squad.

The game was played at Mobile's Ladd Memorial Stadium, and an enthusiastic crowd of 20,236 showed up on a cloudy and cool January afternoon to see the third annual Senior Bowl. The South team had won both previous games, but the North squad was favored slightly in the 1952 contest.

The South fumbled the ball five times in a sloppily played, scoreless first half. In the second half, the North capitalized on a pair of additional South turnovers to stake a commanding 14-0 lead and held on to secure a 20-6 win. The South managed its lone score in the fourth quarter when Wadiak found the end zone on a two-yard run.

Game accounts in the "Mobile Register" credited Wadiak as the lone bright spot in an otherwise dismal offensive performance by the South:

> *What little ground offense the South was able to engender was wrapped up in the legs of Steve Wadiak, the crack South Carolina back. Wadiak*

made almost all of the South's yardage on the ground . . .

After the game, Wadiak shared with a reporter his experience of playing in the star-studded event.

"They're all—both teams—a great bunch of guys," he said. "Maybe if we (the South team) had worked a little longer together, we'd have been able to win this one."

Wadiak referred to the coaches in the event as the finest he'd ever seen and expressed his gratitude for what he considered "a fine opportunity to meet and play with or against all these great boys."

"All of 'em are great football players," he commented. "The game," continued Wadiak, "is one of the greatest things for seniors out of college yet." According to Wadiak, it gave the boys a "chance to show themselves." Then, with a wink, he mentioned the financial benefits of participating in the game.

The Senior Bowl was broadcast nationally by the CBS radio network with legendary announcer Red Barber handling the play by play. When Barber announced Wadiak's fourth-quarter touchdown score, shouts could be heard up and down University Avenue.

Nearly two months after the game, Steve received a letter from Ron Schuessler, the vice president of the Senior Bowl, letting him know that the organizing committee had agreed to distribute additional profits from the game to the players. Enclosed with the letter was an additional check for $51.07, bringing Steve's compensation for his participation in the Senior Bowl to $451.07. In today's dollars, that amount would equate to approximately $3,600. Steve hoped that this compensation for his football efforts would be a foreshadowing of things to come as he moved closer to a career in the NFL.

After he returned from the two postseason bowl games, Steve wrote his mother about his experience.

> *Mom,*
>
> *I'm glad you enjoyed the football games we played in Alabama. While there, we stayed at the best hotels and ate like kings. I just wished there were more games like that . . .*

Wadiak had impressed the scouts—many did not know much about him before the two All-Star games. His effort and intensity in practice had earned him a starting berth in both games. His versatility as a runner, receiver, and defensive back made him a worthwhile investment for a professional team. He was a seasoned, tough football player, and there was no doubt in anyone's mind that he had earned the opportunity to play at the next level.

In January of 1952, representatives of the 13 current NFL teams gathered for the NFL draft in the ballroom of New York's Statler Hotel, across the street from Penn Station. The Los Angeles Rams made Vanderbilt quarterback Billy Wade the number one pick in the draft. Steve was passed over in the first and second rounds, but was eventually selected as the 30th overall pick in round three by the Pittsburgh Steelers.

The Steelers were the perennial doormat of the NFL. In their 18-year history, they held an unimpressive 72-126-10 record and had advanced to the postseason playoffs only once. The failures of their early years would eventually give way to their later glory years when they would become the first team to capture six Super Bowl championships. In 1952, however, they were a long way from discovering a formula for success in the NFL.

The Steelers had recently announced a decision to abandon their single-wing offensive scheme and convert to the T-formation. Wadiak had run from the T-formation for four years at USC. The Steelers' first round pick was Ed Modzelewski, a bruising fullback from Maryland. The Steelers were excited about the prospects of a backfield that would feature the power running of Modzelewski alongside the shifty and speedy Wadiak.

Steve was also being courted by the Montreal Alouettes of the Canadian Football League. The Alouettes were coached by former Wake Forest Head Coach Douglas Clyde "Peahead" Walker. As coach of the Demon Deacons, Walker had at least three opportunities to watch Wadiak perform and was confident the Gamecock star could play for his professional team. The money in Canada was enticing to Steve, plus Walker was a personal friend of Gamecock Head Coach Rex Enright. Steve knew he would have to give careful consideration to the offer from Montreal.

Steve confided in a letter to Peggy Shealy his disappointment about being drafted by the Steelers.

> *Peggy:*
>
> *I received a telegram from Pittsburgh saying I've been drafted by them for pro football. I was sort of hoping to get on the coast, but as usual my luck is bad. It sure will be a change for me from the fresh air of Columbia to the smoky city of Pittsburgh. I'm getting so used to Columbia that I hate to leave it . . .*

Back in school, Steve found it difficult to concentrate on his course work. He was enrolled in only four classes and was not on track to graduate in the spring, as he had fallen behind due to the semester he missed in the spring of 1951. He figured his degree would be necessary only if his primary dream did not pan out. Since his childhood days of imitating Bears great Bronko Nagurski on the sandlots of Chicago, Steve longed to make a career out of playing the game he loved, a game he was born to play. His dream was nearing reality. It was all he could think about.

Steve wrote a brief letter to his mother from Columbia in January of 1952:

Mom,

I'm enclosing $100 for you . . . I hope you had a nice Christmas and New Year. I've been reading it's really been snowing in Chicago. The weather here stays about the same all the time. I'm going to go and eat now but will write you later. Hope the money comes in handy for you.

Love,

Steve

Anna Wadiak held the crisp hundred-dollar bill in one hand and the letter in the other. She was thankful for the money, but she had not seen her son since she visited him in Columbia for the Clemson game in October. Christmas in the Wadiak home was not the same without Steve. She would have gladly exchanged the $100 for a chance to wrap her arms around her youngest son.

25
Highway 215

On Thursday evening, March 6, 1952, South Carolina Head Football Coach Rex Enright was resting in his room at the Sir Walter Raleigh Hotel in downtown Raleigh. He had spent the day at Reynolds Coliseum on the campus of North Carolina State University watching the opening round of the Southern Conference Basketball Tournament. A small group of coaches, including Maryland's Jim Tatum, gathered in Enright's room for a nightcap. Jake Penland, sports editor of "The State" was also in the room.

Peahead Walker, the former Wake Forest football coach and current head coach of the Montreal Alouettes of the Canadian Football League, stopped in to pay Enright and his former colleagues a visit. Known for his robust sense of humor, Walker had the room rolling in laughter as he spun stories about his coaching days in the Southern Conference.

Before he retired for the evening, Walker made a serious request of Enright. "I would really like to have that boy of yours, Wadiak, and I'll appreciate anything you can do to get him to sign with us," Walker pleaded. "I'll make him a mighty attractive proposition."

Eager to secure the services of Wadiak, Walker made a suggestion to Enright. "Why don't you do this? Why don't you get him (Wadiak) to fly up to Raleigh and talk to me this weekend?"

Enright respected Walker and knew he would keep his promise to look after his prized pupil. The next day, Enright placed a call to Steve back in Columbia to see if he would be available to fly up to Raleigh to meet with Coach Walker. Steve respectfully told his coach that he had made plans for the weekend, and it would be difficult for him to alter them.

Enright did not press Steve to change his weekend agenda. He told Steve to enjoy the weekend and that he would talk to him about his discussions with Coach Walker when he returned to Columbia the following week. Steve trusted his coach implicitly, and if Enright told him that his best professional opportunity was in Montreal, Steve knew he would be headed north of the border.

Steve had scheduled a full weekend of activities. Local restaurant owner and friend Doug Broome had invited him to join a large contingent headed to Augusta, Ga., for Broome's private birthday celebration. While he was away on Saturday, Steve promised his girlfriend, Nancy Fulmer, that she could borrow his car to visit her family in Springfield. On Sunday, Steve had planned to drive to Charleston to visit the family of his close friend John LaTorre. It would be a busy but fun weekend.

On Saturday afternoon, Steve walked down the hallway on the first floor of the Preston dormitory and noticed George Clauson lying on his bed in his room. Clauson was the son of Swedish immigrants and had been raised in South Bend, Ind. In high school, he excelled in basketball, baseball, and tennis and was recruited to USC as a basketball player. As a freshman, he tried out for the football team, but after one day of painful contact drills, he decided to play only basketball and tennis while at Carolina.

Steve extended his friendship to Clauson upon his arrival in Columbia, and as a result, the South Bend native was quickly accepted as a member of the unofficial fraternity of Gamecock athletes. Clauson remembered Wadiak as "an easygoing fella but a very tough football player."

Sensing that Clauson had little to do on the weekend, Steve invited him to go along with him to Broome's party in Augusta. Clauson agreed to go, and the two of them hitched a ride out to Doug Broome's drive-in on North Main Street early on Saturday evening.

Steve and George made small talk with the female curb hops and ate hamburgers while they waited patiently for the drive-in to close. After closing time, a group of five or six cars carrying approximately 25 people left the North Main Street location to make the 75-mile, late night drive to Augusta.

On the trip to Augusta, Steve rode with Doug Broome in Doug's vehicle. Saturday was Broome's 32nd birthday, and an all-out celebration at a private establishment along the Savannah River had been planned in his honor. Broome was thankful and proud that "The Cadillac" had made time to attend his party.

The evening's festivities began shortly after midnight, just after the caravan of Columbians arrived. A stocky man, who looked like an ex-football player, guarded the entrance of the private club, making sure that only Broome's invited guests were allowed inside.

Clauson—who passed away in 2011—recalled that Steve appeared genuinely interested in attending the party held in honor of his friend. He remembered that Steve was reserved and guarded in his public behavior, and his actions that night were consistent with that public persona. Clauson recalled that Steve did not drink or gamble as others did at the party, and although he was cordial to all of the women in attendance, he made no advances or attempts to pick up any of the female guests.

The party scene was not Wadiak's comfort zone. He simply had been invited to an event honoring his friend, and his sense of loyalty drove him to make the effort to attend. At dawn, the party began to break up, and a portion of the Columbia contingent decided to head home. Broome stayed behind, leaving Steve to travel back in a different car.

Two cars from the original traveling party pulled up to the front door of the club and began to load up with passengers. Steve moved toward the first car but sensed that it was full, so he walked back to the second car, a 1950 Buick Series 50 Tourback Sedan. Steve slipped into the empty front passenger seat, across from the driver, 23-year-old Joel Clinton Ray, manager of Broome's North Main Street Drive-In. Sitting between Ray and Wadiak in the front bench style seat was 28-year-old Lois Hull, who worked as a waitress at the drive-in.

Sixty years after that night, Hull made certain to point out that she was not a "curb hop," but rather an inside waitress. She explained that the two roles were dramatically different in the culture of a 1950s drive-in. She knew who Steve was because of his frequent visits to the North Main Street restaurant. She also remembered that the driver, Ray, was a likeable guy, who oversaw the operation of the North Main store and also served as head chef.

Seated in the back, directly behind Wadiak, was Clauson. Alongside Clauson were Goldie Rhoden and Betty Dugger, who worked as car hops at the drive-in. Other than Wadiak, Clauson had never met any of the car's occupants before that night.

Ray maneuvered his car out of the parking lot and followed the other car as they headed out of Augusta and toward Aiken, S.C., on their way home to Columbia. Ray drove through the deserted streets of downtown Aiken. It was early Sunday morning, and it would be a few hours before the streets were populated with well-dressed churchgoers.

The car cruised out of downtown Aiken on Highway 4, which soon turned into Highway 215 just outside the Aiken city limits. Highway 215 is a two-lane stretch of road that moves through the South Carolina countryside between Aiken and Columbia. The road was subsequently renumbered and today is known as Highway 302.

As the car headed northeast, the sun peeked over the horizon, and Ray and Wadiak pulled down their visors to block the bright glare from the early morning sun. It had been a long night, and everyone was ready to get home. Clauson dozed off to sleep, and his head fell limply against the shoulder of one of the female car hops in the back seat. Steve stared out the window, eager to get back to Columbia and catch a few hours of sleep before he headed to Charleston for his visit with the LaTorre family.

Ray stepped on the accelerator, and the 124-horsepower engine of his Buick revved as the car moved along a straightaway section of the highway. Sensing the sudden acceleration, Wadiak turned and looked at Ray, whose hands clutched the steering wheel tightly. Steve suggested that Ray slow down. Ray did not respond, and his vehicle continued to roar past the desolate farmland bordering Highway 215.

About seven miles outside of town, the Buick sedan picked up speed as it raced down a steep hill. At the bottom of the hill, just before a bridge, a road sign warned of a sharp curve ahead. The posted speed limit for the curve was 45 mph. If Ray saw the sign, he ignored it.

At the bottom of the hill just before the curve, the road forked. Eubanks Country Store sat in the middle of the intersection, dividing the road. The right fork in the road went toward the small town of Wagener and eventually on to Columbia. Through the woods on the right side of the road was Scott's Lake, a small fishing spot with an adjacent wooden structure that served as a popular live music venue on the weekends.

As Ray passed through the intersection and approached the curve, he made no attempt to negotiate the turn. As a result, the speeding car

"Wadiak Curve" on Highway 302, formerly Highway 215, approximately seven miles outside of downtown Aiken, S.C.

crossed over the left lane and onto the opposite shoulder of the road. The vehicle sped unimpeded along the shoulder for approximately 425 feet. Finally, Ray jerked the steering wheel back to the right, toward the paved road, sending the vehicle into a sideways spin. The car began to lift up on two wheels. Then, it toppled over and went into a violent roll. Clauson awoke from a deep sleep when his head slammed against the Buick's roof.

Two workers inside Eubanks Country Store were startled by the sound of metal crushing against asphalt. As the car somersaulted, screams could be heard from its passengers.

Steve Wadiak was ejected out of his passenger window and landed 57 feet from where the car stopped rolling. His body lay motionless on the pavement. A small pool of blood accumulated near his head.

The car had flipped over five or six times and traveled 183 feet before resting upright on the left side of Highway 215. Steam poured out of the radiator of the badly damaged vehicle, and a hissing sound emanated from the engine.

The two employees of the store ran outside and up the hill toward the accident scene. They could hear the moans of injured passengers piercing through the solitude of a quiet Sunday morning. One of them ran back to the store and called the police.

The six passengers were transported to the hospital in downtown Aiken. Upon arrival, Wadiak and the three female passengers were quickly triaged and shipped to University Hospital in Augusta, a facility better equipped to handle the severity of their injuries. Clauson was placed in an ambulance and sent to Providence Hospital in Columbia. The driver of the car, Joel Ray, was treated and released, having suffered no serious injuries.

Shortly after arriving at University Hospital in Augusta on the morning of March 9, 1952, Steve Wadiak was pronounced dead as a result of the severe head and neck injuries he sustained in the accident. Wadiak died two months and one day past his 26th birthday.

South Carolina Highway Patrolman J.L. Gregory McTeer received a call at his home at approximately 7:25 a.m. and was summoned to the scene of the accident. When Corporal McTeer arrived, Wadiak and all the members of the traveling party had already been taken to the hospital in downtown Aiken. McTeer made some notes at the accident site and looked around for evidence of alcohol in the car. He found none.

McTeer went to Aiken County Hospital to question the driver and his passengers. The passengers had little or no memory of the events leading up to the accident. The driver, Ray, acknowledged that he had lost control of the car around the curve, and he estimated his speed to have been between 70 and 80 miles an hour as he headed into the curve.

Later that afternoon, McTeer met Captain Tee Hutto from the South Carolina Highway Department at the accident scene to conduct a more detailed investigation. The officers made exact measurements of the tire tracks along the shoulder of the road and found no evidence of skid marks on the road or on the shoulder.

The patrolmen studied the car—which was all but demolished in the wreck— paying careful attention to the condition of the four tires. They noted that the tread on the back tires was adequate, but the right front tire was an older tire that the officers did not consider safe. During the accident, this tire had been blown out, and it had an L-shaped cut in it. The officers concluded that the tire was most likely ripped apart when the car began to roll over.

Joel Clinton Ray's 1950 Buick, the car that was carrying Steve Wadiak on the morning of his death on March 9, 1952, was eventually towed back to Columbia and parked in front of Bob Newman's Garage at 1516 Heidt St.

(Photo courtesy of USC Archives)

Lois Hull, who was seated beside Wadiak, suffered a broken hip. Dugger had a broken leg, and Rhoden sustained a fractured left leg and arm. Clauson was badly bruised and spent five days at Providence Hospital recovering from the accident. On Sunday morning, news began to travel across the state about the tragedy.

Ray was charged with reckless driving and released on a $50 bond. Because of the death of Wadiak, he was informed that a coroner's inquest would be held.

Several years after the accident, the curve along Highway 215 was redesigned as a result of the number of accidents occurring along that particularly dangerous stretch of road. The curve became known among locals as "Wadiak Curve." Eubanks County Store has changed ownership, but it remains operational today. Occasionally, an older visitor will stop in and inquire about the Wadiak crash site.

Sixty years later, those who were close to Wadiak can recall with exacting detail where they were when they heard about their friend's tragic death.

"I had stopped at a service station and was on my way to Augusta," Moose Kahle remembered. "The attendant asked me if I had heard about Steve Wadiak dying. I told him, 'Don't you dare kid me about something like that.'"

"I was walking into Mass at St. Joseph's on Assembly Street, and the priest told me about Steve. I was in shock when I heard it," Pat Vella recalled.

"I remember getting the phone call about Steve's death," Vince Gargano said. "I literally dropped the phone. I couldn't even speak."

"I had been at church, and when I got home, I got a call from Coach Enright telling me to get back to Columbia as quickly as I could. My father drove me back to Columbia immediately," John LaTorre recalled.

"Steve was supposed to have dinner with our family in Charleston on that day."

Rex Enright was one of the first to be notified about the death of his former player. He had the responsibility of calling Steve's family in Chicago to inform them of the death of their loved one. He told them the authorities were requesting that an immediate family member make the trip to South Carolina to make positive identification of the body. Steve's brothers, Walter and Joe, hurried to make plans for their sorrowful 1,000-mile journey south.

The phone call was the first of many challenging duties Enright would assume in the wake of Steve's tragic death. Alone in his Raleigh hotel room on that Sunday morning, Enright began to hand write a final tribute to the boy he had loved so deeply. As he wrote the following words, he had to stop several times to wipe away tears. He expressed his heartfelt thoughts in paying tribute to the player he loved like a son. He shared these thoughts formally with the media:

> *The news of Steve's death was a staggering blow to me and the entire Carolina coaching staff. He was one of the finest boys I have ever coached. He typified a true All-American. His loyalty to his school, his teammates and his coaches always came above any personal glory. He never alibied, always gave his best. Steve was modest in victory and he took defeat gracefully. Losing Steve was just like losing a member of the family. He was tops in every respect, both as an athlete and as a man. The University of South Carolina lost a real friend. The entire world has lost a real leader and a wholesome influence during a troublesome period.*

26
Grief

After hearing the tragic news of their younger brother's accident, Walter and Joe Wadiak caught the first available flight to Columbia. Upon arrival, they were driven from the airport straight to the morgue at University Hospital in Augusta, Ga., to make positive identification of their deceased brother.

Meanwhile, family members and loved ones in Chicago prayed and hoped that the reports of the accident were somehow a terrible mistake. Walter and Joe, overwhelmed by sadness, identified their little brother. Steve's body was then transported to the Paschal-Regal Funeral Home on Main Street in Columbia.

Rex Enright arrived back in Columbia from Raleigh on Sunday afternoon, March 10. He stopped by his office on campus to make a series of phone calls in preparation for the memorial services for his fallen player. As he reached for his telephone, he froze as he caught a glance of a letter sitting on the corner of his desk.

The letter was from the National Football League, and it notified Coach Enright that Steve Wadiak had been selected to play in that year's College All-Star game in Chicago, scheduled for August 15. The annual contest pitted the very best college football players against the reigning NFL Champions. It was to be played at Chicago's Soldier Field in front of a sold-out crowd that usually exceeded 90,000 fans. It would have been Steve's triumphant return to his hometown—an opportunity to play in front of his family and friends in the stadium where he had dreamed of playing as a young boy.

Enright had recently received the letter and had planned to share the good news in person with Steve upon his return from the Southern Conference Basketball Tournament. As Enright stared at the letter, he was overcome by grief and sadness for a life that had ended too soon.

Later that afternoon, Enright met with the staff of the funeral home to coordinate the arrangements for one of two funeral services that would honor the fallen hero. Steve had two families—one in South Carolina and one in Chicago—so, two memorial services were scheduled. After the service in Columbia, Steve's body would be transported by train to Chicago for burial.

Coach Enright thoughtfully selected Steve's pallbearers from among the members of the 1951 Gamecock football squad. John "Lip" LaTorre, Bayard Pickett, Chuck Prezioso, Larry Smith, Harry Stewart, and Bob "Moose" Kahle would carry the casket of their beloved teammate and friend.

On Monday morning, sadness blanketed the USC campus. Students were still dazed by the shocking news of Steve's death. Wadiak's heroic accomplishments on the football field, along with his likeable personality, made nearly every student on campus feel a personal connection to him.

Floyd Spence, USC Student Body President and Wadiak's close friend, spoke on behalf of the entire student body when he said, "He was admired by old and young, teammate and opponent, man and woman, and athlete and non-athlete. He was admired because of his humbleness, courage, friendliness, and ability to get along with everyone on and off the football field. He was everybody's friend."

Memorial services began in Columbia with a visitation and reciting of the Rosary on Monday evening. Nearly 2,000 visitors stopped by, and many waited several hours in a long line that flowed out the doors of the mortuary and onto Main Street to pay their respects. An editorial in "The Gamecock" recalled the scene at visitation:

> *There we saw men and women, white and Negro, paying tribute to Steve. We saw bruising tackles and guards with tears in their eyes. We saw little boys who practically worshipped him as though he were a god.*

Steve's funeral service was scheduled for 10 a.m. the next day at St. Peter's Roman Catholic Church on Assembly Street, where Steve had frequently attended Mass. The service included a solemn requiem Mass officiated by Father Frederick Suggs. Steve had met Father Suggs during his first semester at Carolina in 1948 when Suggs was serving as chaplain for the Newman Club, the on-campus Catholic student organization. Like so many others, Father Suggs felt a personal loss in the wake of Steve's death.

An overflow crowd of students, teammates, and friends filled the sanctuary of St. Peter's. Students were excused from their Tuesday morning classes so they could attend the funeral, and spring football practices were suspended for the entire week. The mourners squeezed into every inch of the long wooden pews of the church, and late arrivals stood in the side aisles beneath the stained glass windows that lined both sides of the church.

The distinct smell of burning incense filled the building. Steve's casket lay in front of the marble altar, covered with a spray of dark red carnations and garnet ribbons. Wadiak's football number, 37, was woven in white carnations in the middle of the spray.

The requiem Mass was conducted in Latin. Father Suggs was sympathetic to an audience that included a large contingent of non-Catholics. He told the non-Catholics not to be intimidated by the foreign language of the Mass and that they could simply offer their prayers for

Steve and his family in their own words; God would surely understand them.

"The State's" account of the funeral noted, "Young co-eds sniffled, and the eyes of husky footballers became unashamedly wet as the service proceeded."

After the service ended, Steve's girlfriend, Nancy Fulmer, stood outside the church and wept as she was surrounded by a group of USC co-eds attempting to console her. She had lost the love of her life.

The casket was loaded into a hearse and taken to the train depot on Gervais Street, where it was put on a locomotive headed for Chicago. It was at this same train station four years earlier that Wadiak first arrived in Columbia. Coach Enright, along with the six players who served as pallbearers, carried the casket onto the train and accompanied the body to Illinois.

The day after the funeral, "The State's" sports editor, Jake Penland, paid his final respects to Wadiak in his column. He addressed some rumors that were floating around town in the aftermath of Steve's death.

> *The gossips would lead you to believe that Steve Wadiak was identified with something shady here and something shady there. The people who really knew him well tell you that he was identified with the Lord, with clean sportsmanship, with a good and wholesome feeling toward mankind. The only "hearsay" this writer is willing to take stock in came in the form of a letter yesterday from a Columbian who wrote: "I have heard many people say that Steve Wadiak had the cleanest morals of any football player they knew. A football player on the Carolina squad said that Steve kept himself in the best condition of any man on the team and had the greatest desire to win of any man on the squad."*

In Chicago, friends and family gathered in the Wadiaks' home on University Avenue to bring support, comfort, and food to the grieving family. The Burnside neighborhood rallied around their hurting neighbors. One neighborhood resident who owned a restaurant offered his establishment to host a gathering after the funeral service. Another neighbor volunteered a fleet of his company's limousines to use for the funeral procession. The Wadiaks' loss was felt by the entire Burnside community.

Several Chicago media outlets, including "The Chicago Tribune," attempted to reach the Wadiak family for comment on the tragedy. They declined to be interviewed, as they were still numbed by the reality of the tragedy and could not gather the strength or the words to discuss the horrible reality of what had happened.

While in Columbia, one of Steve's brothers was asked by university officials if the family would consider having Steve buried in Columbia. Steve's mother, however, insisted that his body be returned to his hometown of Chicago for burial.

The family had contacted two funeral homes in Chicago that refused to accept the transfer of Steve's body from South Carolina. The directors explained that transferring a body across state lines required an extensive amount of paperwork and logistics. Finally, a Burnside neighborhood funeral home agreed to accept the out-of-state transfer. Steve's final memorial service would be held at the Skeeles Colonial Chapel at 71st and Cottage Grove Avenue on Chicago's South Side.

The final remembrance for Steve consisted of a formal Ukrainian Orthodox Mass preceded by a two-day wake and visitation. For the better part of the next two days, a steady stream of visitors stopped at the chapel to view Steve's body and offer a prayer of remembrance.

The chapel was filled with the aroma of an abundance of fresh flower arrangements that surrounded Steve's open casket. Walter and Joe requested that their brother be buried in a sports shirt and slacks, as opposed to a suit and tie, because they said, "That was more like Steve." His garnet football jersey from USC was placed beside him in the casket. A bouquet of flowers featuring the garnet and white colors of the school was placed across the top of the casket.

The wake culminated with the service on Friday, March 15. The chapel was filled to capacity, with people overflowing into the street on a bright, sunny, and unseasonably warm day. The large attendance created a traffic jam at the intersection of Cottage Avenue and 71st Street, and police were summoned to help motorists navigate around the crowded chapel.

It seemed as though the entire Burnside neighborhood had come to honor a man whom so many of them remembered as an engaging little boy they affectionately referred to as "Pinchy." Grade school and high school classmates wept as they remembered sitting beside Steve in class. Steve's closest neighborhood friends recalled their carefree days playing sports on the prairie, going to movies, or just hanging out on a warm summer evening.

Steve's family had lost its youngest member, the one who had brought to the household a zest for life. He had been away from them for the past four years, and they clung to many secondhand accounts of the fame he had achieved in South Carolina. From his humble beginnings, Steve appeared headed toward a successful career in professional football. He was a source of family pride, and although the family had been separated from him by 1,000 miles, their love for him and attachment to him had not diminished. As they sat together in the front pew of the chapel, they wept throughout much of the lengthy orthodox Mass.

At the conclusion of the service, Steve's pallbearers carried the casket through the front door of the chapel as the family followed in procession. While the pallbearers waited momentarily for the hearse door to be opened, Steve's mother, Anna, stepped away from the family procession and moved toward the coffin. In one desperate movement, she stretched her arms out wide and threw herself across the top of the casket. She wept uncontrollably as she clung tightly to the metal container that held the remains of her youngest child. Her precious son would not have the long and fruitful life she had dreamed of. He was dead at the age of 26, and she could not let him go.

A large contingent of cars followed the hearse on the nine-mile drive to Mt. Hope Cemetery where Steve was laid to rest. His final resting place is now alongside his mother, Anna, and his brother, Joseph, who died tragically in an industrial accident in 1976. Anna Wadiak, who died at the age of 91, outlived four of her five children.

The grave marker for Stephan Wadiak at Mt. Hope Cemetery in Chicago

Steve's parents, Anna and Nick Wadiak, received dozens of cards, letters, and telegrams from people they had never met, expressing sympathy and support after the death of their son. The entire Duke University football team sent a signed letter expressing their sympathy and paying tribute to Wadiak's ability and sportsmanship. State politicians sent letters of condolence. School children had their parents find the Chicago address for the Wadiaks and wrote touching letters of sympathy to the grieving family.

Clemson University's newspaper, "The Tiger," paid tribute to the fallen star who for four years had been a nemesis to their football team, stating, "Wadiak was not only a great football player, but he was also a credit to the game, and it is tragic that his bright future was cut short in such a manner."

A Western Union telegram dated March 10, 1952, arrived at the Wadiak home. The telegram was from Fred Benners, a teammate of Wadiak's in the Blue-Gray game. Benners had been voted the Most Valuable Player of the Blue-Gray game and had met Steve for the first time during the week of practice leading up to the game. Steve had earned Benners's respect and friendship in the short time they were together.

After Steve's death, his good friend Peggy Shealy gave Anna Wadiak a treasured scrapbook that she had meticulously maintained during her friendship with Steve. The scrapbook contained dozens of newspaper clippings, pictures, and letters related to Anna's departed son, and it filled in many of the missing details from Steve's four years away from his family.

A few days after Steve's funeral, a hand-written letter arrived at the Wadiak home on University Avenue in Chicago. The letter wasn't from anyone famous. It came from a fellow student at the university—not an athlete, not the student body president—just a regular student who considered Steve Wadiak his friend. The sentiment contained in the letter captured the essence of the brief but heroic life of Steve Wadiak.

March 15, 1952
Dear Mr. and Mrs. Wadiak:

Steve and I roomed in rooms across from one another last summer, when I first started school at the University of South Carolina. Steve and I became very good friends. I felt as if he were my brother. He was very kind to me, as he was to everyone, and he did many things for me. I shall ever thank God for having had his friendship.

Steve was almost worshiped by all who knew him. He was what all men wanted to be. He was an example for all of us who knew him to follow. I would have done anything for Steve (and he would do anything for his friends). Now all I can do is pray God will grant eternal rest to his soul.

Is there anything I can do for you? If there is please let me know. I shall ever be at your service.

I hope God shall grant you His choicest blessings.

I remain,
Sincerely,
John Jas Anthony Henebery
Box 1822
The University of South Carolina
Columbia, SC

Steve Wadiak
January 8, 1926 - March 9, 1952

(Photo courtesy of Jeanette Wadiak Korlin)

Epilogue

On March 25, 1952, a coroner's jury trial was held at the Aiken (S.C.) County Courthouse in connection with the accident that resulted in the death of Steve Wadiak. Approximately 30 spectators showed up at the courtroom and heard testimony from Joel Ray, who was driving the car the morning Wadiak was killed, as well as two highway patrolmen who investigated the accident.

Ray stated at the hearing, "It was an unavoidable accident. I would not have had it happen for anything." After deliberating for 30 minutes, a six-man jury agreed with Ray's statement that the accident was unavoidable and absolved Ray of any blame for the fatal crash.

Ten days after Steve Wadiak's funeral, a mysterious envelope arrived at the USC football office. The outside of the plain white letter-sized envelope contained no return address. Inside were a handful of personal family pictures along with a tattered copy of Steve Wadiak's will dated July 25, 1951. A hand-written note was attached to the contents and it stated simply, "I found these papers on the ground."

The note was unsigned, and it was assumed that the envelope's contents were found near the site of the accident. Steve's wallet, a commemorative gift obtained at the Blue-Gray All-Star game, was never located at the crash site. Upon receiving the will, USC Head Coach Rex Enright called an attorney friend he knew would help facilitate the probate of Wadiak's estate.

On April 21, a hearing was held in Richland County Probate Court to validate the will. Steve's will stated that his girlfriend, Nancy Fulmer, was to serve as executrix of his estate. However, Nancy was only 20 years old at the time, and to serve in this capacity, an individual was required to be 21. The judge appointed Rex Enright to replace Fulmer as the executor.

The assets of the deceased Wadiak were listed as $3,305 in cash and a 1950 Pontiac valued at $1,800. After paying for his funeral expenses and an outstanding hospital bill from University Hospital in Augusta, the remaining assets of Wadiak were distributed as follows: Cash in the amount of $917.91 was given to Nancy Fulmer, and Steve's 1950 Pontiac was bequeathed to Steve's close friend, John LaTorre.

LaTorre drove the Pontiac until 1960, when he said he traded it in for a Ford Gran Torino. When LaTorre's son was born in 1954, he was given the name Stephen Randolph LaTorre in honor of his close friend. Another of Steve's teammates, defensive tackle Don Earley, named his first child Stephen out of a deep respect for his deceased teammate and friend.

Coach Enright made sure Gamecock football fans would always remember the player he considered his favorite of all time. He led the effort to have Wadiak's jersey, No. 37, permanently retired. Shortly after Steve's death, Enright placed Steve's worn jersey along with a bronzed pair of Steve's football cleats in a glass trophy case and displayed them on campus in the lobby of the Maxcy dormitory. The case was later moved to the new Russell House Student Center before eventually landing at Williams-Brice Stadium, where it remains today. Wadiak concluded his Gamecock career with 2,878 rushing yards, which ranks him fourth among USC backs. His 96-yard touchdown run from scrimmage against George Washington in 1950 remains a USC record. In 1967, he was inducted into the first class of the USC Athletic Hall of Fame.

A large banner commemorating Steve's retired number and accomplishments as a Gamecock hangs atop the pedestrian ramp in

Rex Enright stands beside the display of Steve Wadiak's retired jersey, bronzed shoes, and trophies.

(Photo courtesy of USC Archives)

the northwest corner of Williams-Brice Stadium in Columbia. Outside the weight room underneath the south stands are framed jerseys of four Gamecock football players whose numbers have been retired. Wadiak's No. 37 hangs in the company of 1980 Heisman Trophy winner George Rogers's No. 38 and the No. 2 of Sterling Sharpe, USC's all-time leading receiver.

A few years ago, an effort was made to have a street beside Williams-Brice Stadium named "Wadiak Way." The effort lost momentum after some changes in the school's athletic administration. In 1966, the most valuable player of the Gamecock football team began receiving an award

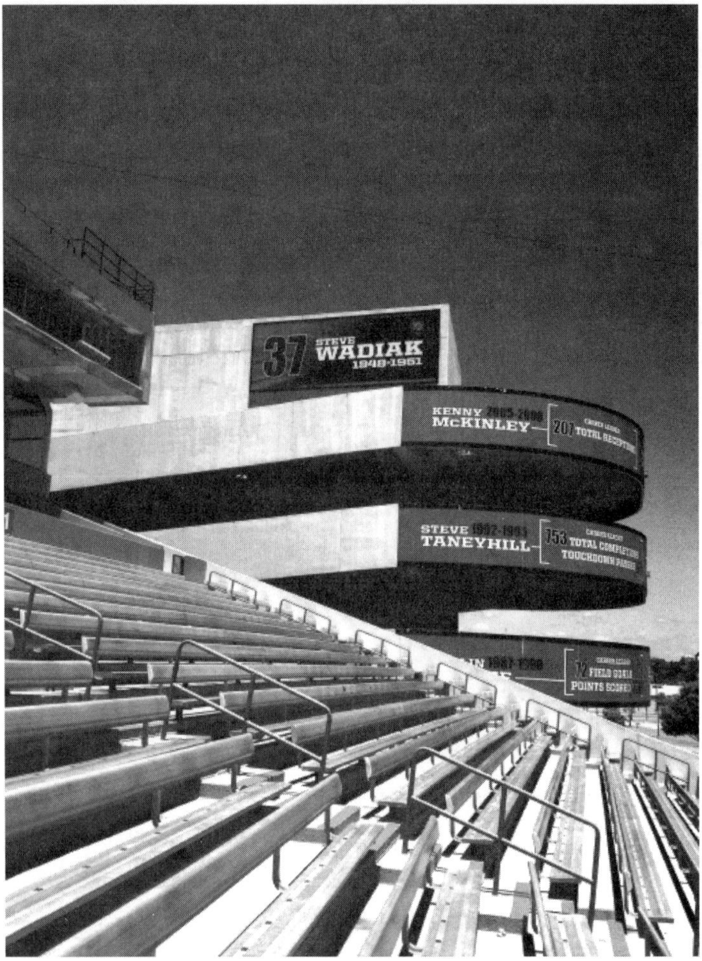

This banner commemorates the retired No. 37 of Steve Wadiak at Williams-Brice Stadium.

named in honor of Steve Wadiak. Recipients of the Steve Wadiak MVP award include George Rogers, Gamecock radio announcers Todd Ellis and Tommy Suggs (both former USC Quarterbacks), and standout running back Duce Staley, who went on to a successful NFL career. In 2004, the award was discontinued at the time of a change in the head football coaching position.

A jingle promoting a Columbia sporting goods store makes reference to Wadiak and can still be heard on local radio.

In November of 2008, Ron Morris of "The State" wrote an in-depth feature story on Wadiak entitled "The Heartbreak Kid." In this award-winning piece, Morris brought to life the legend of the great Steve Wadiak for fans who knew Wadiak's name but knew very little about his life or accomplishments.

Before home football games at Williams-Brice Stadium, former USC lettermen gather in the Letterman's Lounge underneath the west stands and share a meal and memories of their days at USC. Frequent visitors to the lounge include a handful of Wadiak's teammates and friends. Each year, the number of those lettermen who knew Wadiak grows smaller and smaller, and along with them go the firsthand memories of "The Cadillac."

Author's Note:

One of the great blessings of researching and writing this book was getting to speak with those who knew Steve Wadiak during his life. The mention of the name *Wadiak* ignited a spark in their aging voices. They laughed as they told me stories of Steve's subtle humor and spoke reverently as they remembered him as the consummate teammate and friend. They went out of their way to tell me about his character. It was as if they all spoke with a single voice when they said, over and over, that Steve Wadiak was simply a "genuine nice guy."

I sent many letters to former teammates explaining that I was attempting to write the life story of their late friend. Sadly, I discovered that many of his teammates had passed away, or their memories had betrayed them in their later years. The most touching response I received during my research was from the wife of one of Steve's former USC teammates. I will use a portion of her letter to bring this project to a close, as I believe her simple message aptly summarizes what I hope all will remember about the man they called "Th' Cadillac":

> *Dear Mike:*
>
> *I'm writing for my husband who was a teammate and friend of Steve Wadiak. He has dementia now, and he will be unable to grant you an interview. I showed him Steve's picture that you sent me and his only remark was "great football player and great guy."*

Appendix
Leadership Lessons From "The Cadillac"

It is unlikely that Steve Wadiak ever read a book on leadership, and yet as I researched his life and talked with many who knew him, it was clear to me that in many ways, he was a powerful and effective leader. I draw attention to the following seven values that were demonstrated in his life and are reflected in the stories contained in this book, in hopes that they will inspire us all on our respective journeys.

Purpose—He remained committed to a deep sense of purpose for his life as an athlete. As such, he refused to engage in behaviors that might detract from his performance or the responsibility of his calling.

Example—Wadiak led by example, giving 100 percent effort at all times.

Humility—He never forgot his humble beginnings. Fame and notoriety appeared to deepen his sense of gratitude and humility.

Discipline—From a young age, he demonstrated great physical and mental discipline in the pursuit of his goals.

Loyalty—He remained loyal to those who had cared for him and refused to speak negatively about his friends or teammates.

Teamwork—He never saw himself as bigger than the team, always deflecting personal glory toward his teammates. He endured physical pain and hardship for the sake of team.

Compassion—He showed a genuine sense of caring for the underdogs, outcasts, and the "least of those" around him.

Acknowledgments

Only those who have written a book can fully understand the physical and emotional demands of putting pen to paper. Certainly, it requires discipline and determination, but more than anything else, it takes encouragement. This book would have never been a reality without so many who encouraged me along the way.

To my wife, Cindy: This really was all your idea. You are my inspiration. Without your initial prompting, I would have never written the first sentence. Thank you for your love, support, and friendship, as well as your honest feedback on the earliest drafts.

To my sons, Matt, Phillip, and Nick: Your lives bring me a joy that only a dad can fully understand. I hope you will tell your children lots of stories someday, including the story of the "great Steve Wadiak."

To my dad: I sat at your feet listening to stories of Steve Wadiak. While in college, I tried to convince you that George Rogers was better than Wadiak, but you wouldn't buy it. I think you were partial to your friend. After researching his life, I understand why you felt such a deep connection to the man you were blessed to know. I am grateful that you accepted Rex Enright's offer to play football at USC in 1941. It opened the door for the life that my brothers and I have been able to live. I am forever grateful for all the sacrifices you made for our family, and I am honored to be your son.

To Jeanette Wadiak Korlin, her daughter Donna Cohen and granddaughter Leigh Cohen: In July of 2012, I stepped out of a meeting at a hotel in Gettysburg, Pennsylvania, to answer a call on my cell phone. Donna was calling to let me know that her mother and Steve's sister, Jeanette, had agreed to give me permission to write the story of her beloved brother. I had never written a book before and yet, for some unknown reason, Mrs. Korlin trusted me with her brother's story. Without her trust and her incredible memory, this book would not have been possible.

Mrs. Korlin: You are, without a doubt, one of the most inspirational people I have ever met. Your tireless energy, your love of family, and your faith inspired me throughout this project. It was through you that I truly got to know your brother, Steve.

Donna Cohen: Your help, your encouragement, and your prayers were a blessing to me. I know that your Uncle Steve passed away before you were able to get to know him, but I hope in some way that this project has helped you to understand the special person that he was.

Leigh Cohen: Thank you for taking the time to meet with me at your grandmother's home on that August day in 2012 and for going through all of the pictures and memories of your great uncle. Also, thank you for using your gifts on the design of the book's cover.

To my brother Tony: You are without a doubt the smartest guy I know. Thanks for your careful proofing and for your support. To my brother Paul: You were the best college roommate a guy could ask for and are the biggest Gamecock fan I know.

To Bob Stalnaker: You kept telling me to write a book. Well, now you can get off my case. Seriously, thanks for your encouragement and friendship throughout the years.

To Ray Blackston: Without you, there would be no book. Thanks for your friendship, guidance, mentoring, and editing throughout the entire process. And also, thanks for trying to teach me how to hit a knockdown sand wedge with the precision and skill that you so aptly demonstrate.

To Ron Morris: Your initial cooperation and sharing of your research from your 2008 award-winning story on Wadiak was a great catalyst for my moving forward with this project. Thanks for your edits, encouragement, and friendship over the past two years.

To J.J. Puryear: Thanks for lending your incredible skills and gifts to this project.

To Don Barton: You are truly a treasure to the Gamecock nation. Your memory is unbelievable, and your willingness to share your knowledge of Gamecock history with me was beyond gracious. Thanks for inviting me into your home and into your vast collection of Gamecock memories.

To the family of Pat Vella: One of my deepest regrets was that I was not able to complete the book in time for Pat to see it, however, I am so thankful for the time I spent with him and the fact that he got to read the chapters that address his special relationship with Steve. I am trusting that he and his friend Steve are reading the book together now.

To John "Lip" LaTorre: My visits with you in Mt. Pleasant will be lasting memories for me. It is easy for me to see why Steve liked you so much. Thanks for rescuing my wife and me on that rainy day in Charleston, and I am deeply grateful for your willingness to share so many wonderful memories of your friend.

To Peggy Shealy Burbage: You had a very special friendship with Steve, and I am very grateful for your cooperation, which allowed me to gain unique insight into Steve's life.

To Bob "Moose" Kahle, Vince Gargano, Chuck Prezioso, William "Hootie" Johnson, Hugh Merck, Jimmy Cooper, June Korn, Bill Rutledge, Don Earley, Red Wilson, Johnny Reeves, Alice Enright, Cy Szakacsi, Wally Podlecki, and Ronnie Trotter: I deeply appreciate your taking the time to talk with me about your friend.

To Clemson's Fred Cone: Thanks for sharing your life with me that day at the Lake Keowee. When I met you, I felt like I was looking at what Steve Wadiak would look like today—fit, solid, and a man who had lived a great football life—a man who even in his 80s looked like he could run over you if you handed him a football. You deserve your own book.

To Woody Dyer: Without your help, I would have never met Fred Cone. Thanks for being willing to help out a friend who happens to be a Gamecock.

To John Daye: Thanks to your extensive film collection, I was actually able to see Steve Wadiak play football. Thanks for sharing your treasures with me and with Steve's family.

To Colonel Cole Kingseed: Thanks for taking the time to read the draft manuscript and for your friendship which has enriched my understanding of what it means to be a leader of character, competence, and courage.

To Elizabeth West and the entire staff at the South Carolina Library: Thank you for preserving the history of the University of South Carolina.

To Brian Hand and the staff of "Spurs and Feathers": Thanks for all your help in getting the word out about this book and for all that you do for Gamecock sports.

To Amanda Capps: Thanks for lending your gifts and expertise as a copy editor to bring consistency and accuracy to the final manuscript.

To Jim Hamlet: Thanks for your advice and counsel on the details of writing and publishing a book.

To libraries across the country that preserve old newspapers: Without you, books like this would be impossible to write.

To the University of South Carolina: You gave my father a football scholarship in 1941 and changed the trajectory of our entire family. You gave me far more than an education. *Forever to thee!*

Finally, in memoriam, I want to thank Steve Wadiak, whose life story was worth telling. I hope I have told his story in a manner worthy of the life he lived.

Sources

Books

Barton, Don: *The Carolina-Clemson Game, 1896-1966,* The State Printing Company

Barton, Don: *They Wore Garnet & Black, Inside Carolina's Quest for Gridiron Glory,* Spur Publishers

Bolton, Clyde: *Unforgettable Days in Southern Football,* Strode Publishers

Brondfield, Jerry: *Rockne, Notre Dame Idol, Coaching Genius, Celebrity—A Legend Revisited,* Random House

Daye, John and Hamer, Fitz P.: *Glory on the Gridiron, A History of College Football in South Carolina,* History Press

Dent, Jim: *Monster of the Midway,* Thomas Dunne Books

Freiling, Thomas: *Walking with Lincoln,* Revell, Baker Publishing Company

Guido, George: *Alle-Kiski Sports History—A Century of Sports in Western PA's A-K Valley Region,* Word Association Publishers

Haney, Travis and Williams, Larry: *Classic Clashes of the Carolina-Clemson Football Rivalry: A State of Disunion,* The History Press

Hunter, Jim: *The Gamecocks South Carolina Football,* Strode Publishers, Inc.

Price, Tom: *Tales from the Gamecocks' Roost,* Sports Publishing LLC

Newspapers, Magazines, Internet

The Aiken Standard

The Atlanta Journal-Constitution

The Calumet Index

The Chicago Tribune

The Chicago Sun Times

The Columbia Record

The Daily Calumet

The Gamecock

The Garnet and Black Yearbook

The Greenville News

The Florence Morning News

The Mobile Press

The Mobile Register

The Montgomery Advertiser

The Saturday Evening Post

Sport Magazine, December 1954

The State

The Washington Post

The Washington Star

The Washington Daily News

The Washington Times Herald

Other

Hare, Benjamin: "Football at Military Training Centers During World War II," North Central College Undergraduate Archives, https://library.noctrl.edu/archives/undergradpublications/football_at_miltary_training_centers_during_wwII.pdf

The University of South Carolina Archives

The University of South Carolina Football Media Guide

About the Author

Mike Chibbaro is a 1981 graduate of the University of South Carolina. He has been an avid USC Gamecock fan since the day he crawled out of his crib. While attending USC, he served as the sports editor of "The Gamecock," USC's student newspaper. In 2012, he retired from a 31-year business career in order to devote more of his time to ministry, leadership development, and writing. Mike and his wife, Cindy, have three sons and live in Greenville, South Carolina.

Mike can be contacted at mike@thirtysevenpublishing.com.

Author photo courtesy of Bill Littell